American National Security Policy

American National Security Policy

Authorities, Institutions, and Cases

John T. Fishel

ROWMAN & LITTLEFIELD
Lanham • Boulder • New York • London

Published by Rowman & Littlefield
A wholly owned subsidiary of The Rowman & Littlefield Publishing Group, Inc.
4501 Forbes Boulevard, Suite 200, Lanham, Maryland 20706
www.rowman.com

Unit A, Whitacre Mews, 26–34 Stannary Street, London SE11 4AB

British Library Cataloguing in Publication Information Available

Library of Congress Cataloging-in-Publication Data Available

ISBN: 978-1-4422-4837-3 (cloth)
ISBN: 978-1-4422-4838-0 (paper)
ISBN: 978-1-4422-4839-7 (ebook)

∞™ The paper used in this publication meets the minimum requirements of American
National Standard for Information Sciences—Permanence of Paper for Printed Library
Materials, ANSI/NISO Z39.48–1992.

Printed in the United States of America

Contents

Foreword

The American academic community and public have long needed Professor John T. Fishel's book *American National Security Policy: Authorities, Institutions, and Cases.* Textbooks on international relations abound, and several of them have been sufficiently comprehensive, respected, and popular with professors that they have merited several updated and revised new editions. Most successful international relations texts address national security policy, and, in doing so, describe and discuss fairly well the "authorities, institutions, theory, and cases," subjects that are included in Fishel's subtitle, but most do not address all of these topics in the same book. Professor Fishel describes and deals with each of these areas superbly in this book. His additional unique contribution that makes this text so valuable is his realistic description of "process," another area included, but neglected or inadequately described in other texts with which I am acquainted. This subject might be defined as the official standardized methodology and actions for developing and implementing policy, and is absolutely essential for a comprehensive understanding of foreign affairs and national security.

Existing texts, with a few exceptions, also do not, in my opinion, deal adequately with the role and influence of the human actors (i.e., of practitioners) involved in "process." Professor Fishel's book is exceptional in describing the human element and in demonstrating how frequently human decisions and actions significantly affect and change policy implementation. Individuals' actions in interpreting authorities, making institutions function, and applying theory are fairly well understood, but the actual work of the practitioner in the conduct of foreign policy and implementation of national security policy and plans is poorly comprehended among the public and within academia. This vital subject is clearly described within this book in the area that Professor Fishel calls "process."

Trends in political "science" during the last half century had continued steadily to move the discipline away from the work of the practitioners of diplomacy and the implementation of foreign and national security policy. Political science gives expanding attention to quantitative analyses, theory, and grand studies, while regional/area studies, cultures, and languages get greater attention in anthropology and language departments. Political science in the study of international relations and national security seemingly pays less attention to history, diplomatic history, cultural studies, economics, negotiations, management, and leadership—all needed in the conduct of foreign policy and national security policy. It is important to know what has happened in the past in order not to repeat the mistakes made previously, and also to forecast, analyze, and take action to influence the future. This book brings professors and students into contact with, and, hopefully, provides them, greater understanding of the messy world and the "fog of wars" in which diplomacy's role in assuring U.S. national security is actually practiced.

Professor Fishel's organization of his new book is very logical and follows a time-proved formula for effectively providing information. He very briefly tells students what he is going to tell them; then, in Chapters 1 through 13 tells them what he wants them to know; and, in his concluding Chapter 14, he tells them, and comments upon, what he has told them. Fishel begins by addressing the theories of liberalism and realism as the mind-set of the practitioners followed by an impersonal overview of U.S. founding documents, the Constitution, the division of powers, legislation, institutions, history, and procedures that all shape the formal planning process and implementation in the field of national security. This is followed by a carefully chosen set of specific case studies that contribute to better understanding of the implementation within the established processes. In these selected cases, all of which include deployment of U.S. armed forces, he discusses what happens when events fall outside of the plans, and how the characteristics and reactions of the individual practitioners contribute to policy, plans, and actions in real, on-the-ground situations.[1] The text concludes by tying everything together. Dr. Fishel uses specific examples from the case studies in discussing how the plans were executed, the impact of the unforeseen, and thus unplanned-for, events, various interagency responses, and how these factors influenced actions and the outcomes of each case.

Dr. Fishel's description of the various institutions involved in U.S. national security in policy making, planning, and the execution of plans is accurate and balanced. With his focus primarily on the making of national security policy, and especially on its implementation, he gives greatest attention to the Department of Defense and the armed forces, primarily in his description of the defense planning systems in Chapter 5, and throughout the case studies in Chapters 6 through 13. The relatively greater size of the wealth and power of the Department of Defense and of the armed forces in comparison with all other U.S. government departments and agencies is evident in Chapter 3. The description of process in Chapter 5 is, in my opinion, enhanced and made more realistic by practitioner LTC Fishel's extensive employment of acronyms. Nearly all practitioners in both civilian and military organizations are initially somewhat bewildered and confused by this deeply ingrained practice, but soon become fluent in the word-saving and time-saving new language.

The use of case studies in teaching the conduct of national security planning and practice is very effective, and Professor Fishel uses this methodology extremely well by presenting recent and important cases. At the same time, these effective tools for learning can also convey a false sense that the successful conduct of diplomacy and national security policy is constricted to the management and resolution of threats to U.S. interests or the achievement of changes that advance U.S. national interests within a single crisis in a world of distinct and separate crises. Each single crisis is resolved, or only partially resolved, or ends unsatisfactorily or even disastrously. The reality, however, as Dr. Fishel describes it, is that diplomacy and the implementation of national security policy is without beginning or end, is connected with previous crises and events, and lays the ground for future crises and events. Each case is also affected to some degree by outside and parallel events and crises occurring simultaneously in other areas of the world.

As an example of this, in 1981 I was the ambassador in Peru, a country in severe crisis caused primarily by a vicious, dirty, and bloody insurgency led by the fanatical, Maoist-inspired Shining Path guerrillas; and second, by the Soviet Union's greatly growing collaboration and influence in Peru during the then-prevailing Cold War. Secretary of State George Schultz expressed to me his great concerns and told me that my job was to hold things together until Washington was in a position to give the country greater priority. He said that the United States was currently engrossed in seven major crisis areas around the world, and within the U.S. government there were not currently the resources or time for top-level officers to give sufficient attention to manage yet another major crisis. He commented that countries' governments vary in capacity for the number of crises with which they can simultaneously cope, and that the U.S. government was currently at its limit. He promised to turn attention and resources to Peru as soon as pressure diminished somewhat in other critical hot spots. Few people at that time included a fact like this in their analysis of the then-existing Peruvian situation. It shows, I think, that the conduct of foreign relations and ensuring U.S. national security is best understood as ongoing, unending, and affected by laterally competing events, rather than merely a series of selected single problem cases that must be solved.

My awareness that "process" (the making and implementation of national security policy) is often messy and untidy, and is frequently altered by unforeseen changes, was ingrained in me as a practitioner. When I became a diplomat-in-residence (DIR) for two years' teaching at the University of Oklahoma,[2] I immediately realized that my greatest contribution and challenge as a seasoned practitioner was to translate my 29 years of experience in the Foreign Service, and 3½ years in the U.S. Marine Corps, into lessons about the conduct of foreign and national security policy in a manner that, to the extent possible, related to the real world and also to academic courses on those subjects. My goal was to provide students an authentic picture of and lessons from the real world. Three decades later, I think this is still greatly needed, and John Fishel's book is the best effort that I have seen to help achieve this goal.

Professor Fishel has published a much-needed textbook that helps university professors and students alike to understand and prepare themselves better for the difficult work of the real world. His academic credentials and experience in terms of graduate degrees, teaching experience in reputable state and private universities, and in U.S. armed forces' premier graduate study institutions are superb. He is respected within the world of academics also for his research and publications. Equally impressive is his experience as a practicing U.S. Army officer involved directly in producing and implementing major national security plans and operations.

Dr. Fishel began his active-duty military career in 1969 by first attending the Engineer Officer Basic Course and then serving in the Pentagon Intelligence Support Branch, which produced and delivered the daily "Black Book" of the highest classified reports to the army chief of staff, the secretary of the army, and all senior military and civilian staff of the army. He learned in that assignment what subjects matter most to senior military and civilian officials, and how national security looks from the top down.

Professor Fishel graduated from Dartmouth College and then earned his doctorate from the University of Indiana in political science. John is not only a well-respected and much-admired classroom professor, a prolific author of lauded books, book chapters, and journal articles, but he is also a retired lieutenant colonel of the U.S. Army, having served in assignments key to U.S. policy, planning, and military actions for protecting and advancing U.S. interests. In 1985, he taught the army's Foreign Area Officer course at Fort Bragg, North Carolina, and then traveled extensively as an active-duty officer throughout Latin America studying a region plagued at that time with active insurgencies and civil wars. As a lieutenant colonel, John began in 1986 what turned into five years of a series of tours in the U.S. Southern Command involving him in civic action in Peru, Honduras, and Bolivia. He made major security assessments of Peru, Bolivia, and especially of El Salvador, where

I first had the privilege of working with him. Fishel subsequently developed the post-conflict civil-military operations plan in 1989 for Operation Just Cause in Panama! During and after his assignment serving in the Southern Command in the Small Wars Operations Research Directorate, Professor Fishel worked with Dr. Max Manwaring to research and produce a new paradigm for addressing low-intensity conflicts or conflicts other than major wars. This significant work is best studied in his and Manwaring's book *Uncomfortable Wars Revisited.*

The writing of *American National Security Policy* grew out of an upper-division and graduate course that Professor Fishel has taught for almost a decade, and has become one of the most popular and talked-about courses on campus. It is a "must-take" course among Reserve Officer Training Corps cadets and midshipmen of the navy, army, air force, and marines. A high percentage of students interested in working in foreign affairs as civilians, or who merely study international relations, also flock to the course. The value of this book as the primary text for an upper-division course has already been established. This book is also excellent for assignment as one of several texts (and other readings) at the graduate level.

In my opinion, the students who study national security policy using this book will be better prepared to serve the country around the globe. I would also recommend it to other Americans interested in foreign policy and international security. The book will give both groups an encompassing view of national security and introduce them to the complexity of protecting and advancing U.S. national interest.

By: Ambassador (ret.) Edwin G. Corr

NOTES

1. I note that there are many other cases for study that are important to U.S. national security in which resolution of challenges to its survival and vital and important interests did not require that U.S. combat forces be committed. Success in these cases is enormously less costly in dollars and lives.

2. This DIR assignment was followed by my resignation from the Department of State and five more years of teaching as a full professor in political science, and this by research, writing, and administrative duties at the university for another 12 years.

Acknowledgments

Many people have contributed to this book, in many different ways. First and foremost, I want to acknowledge my undergraduate students in National Security Policy at the University of Oklahoma, my graduate students in the same course, my graduate students in the online version in the College of Liberal Studies where it is called National Security Leadership, and my graduate students in National Security Leadership in the College of International Studies on campus and in Advanced Programs at RAF Lakenheath. I have learned much from all of you.

I particularly want to thank two of my graduate students, Maura Cremin and Shelby Ranger, who have reviewed the entire manuscript and made wonderfully constructive comments and suggestions. Maura is well on her way to a PhD in political science from the University of Chicago, and Shelby will graduate from OU in Spring 2017 with her BA and MA in international studies. I also want to thank Shelby for compiling the bibliography out of my endnotes. This is academic "scutwork," without which no book can be completed, and I am truly grateful for her efforts here. I wish to thank Allison E. Mee and Grant K. Schatzman, who, as volunteer research assistants, found and reproduced the U.S. government organization charts used in this book.

A very special thanks to my daughter, Karina C. Fishel, who re-created the diagram called "The Rolling Donuts" in Chapter 5, out of my chicken tracks. Karina is a multitalented young woman who will graduate from high school this academic year and is concurrently enrolled in Japanese at OU.

I want to thank my editor at Rowman & Littlefield, Marie-Claire Antoine, and her entire team. It has been a pleasure working with you.

Thanks, too, to my friends and coauthors of numerous other books and articles, Max G. Manwaring and Ambassador Edwin G. Corr. Thanks to Ed, as well, for his superb foreword to this book. Thanks to Gabriel Marcella, my friend from SOUTHCOM and the Army War College, whose early review was instrumental, as was that of my colleague from the Center for Hemispheric Defense Studies, Mary Grizzard. Thanks also to my military colleagues, superiors, and subordinates who all taught me aspects of what is represented in these pages.

Finally, I owe a total debt of gratitude to my stiffest critic, who tempers her criticism with complete love, my colleague, my wife, Kimbra L. Fishel, who beat me up unmercifully to make this a better book.

Needless to say, all errors and omissions are mine alone.

Preface

This book grew out of a course I have been teaching at the University of Oklahoma for most of the last decade. It began as American National Security Policy for upper-division undergraduates. Fairly soon after I started teaching it, I began reserving five places for graduate students with additional requirements. This is where we were in my home college, the College of International Studies, when the OU College of Liberal Studies asked me to offer the course, under the title "National Security Leadership" to graduate students in the Masters of Administrative Leadership, online. So, now I had two versions of the course. Then, last year, my home college asked me to teach a separate, graduate version for both U.S. regular Masters of International Studies students, and for its mostly military students in Advanced Programs that is a combination of online and face-to-face education. In all, I developed four related versions of the course.

The course also derives from my experience as an officer in the U.S. Army. My first tour of active duty was in the Pentagon as an intelligence analyst in the army's current intelligence shop. We produced daily analytical reports using all sources, including the most highly classified, for the secretary of the army, the chief of staff of the army, and the rest of the army staff. I began in that office in 1969 and served full time until 1971. Then I continued my service there as a reserve officer until 1978. By my last tour, I had done every job in the office except command it. On my final tour, I was the editor of the daily intelligence brief and the weekly brief for the chairman of the Joint Chiefs of Staff. During that same period, I began an association with the Army Command and General Staff College at Fort Leavenworth, which lasted until 1998 both as a military officer and as a civilian professor. In that association, I found myself engaged in research and teaching about national strategy, arms control, the Grenada operation, a variety of peace operations, and counterinsurgency. In my varied career as a reserve officer, I qualified as a foreign area officer and as a psychological operations officer. In addition, I worked as a civil affairs officer in the U.S. Southern Command. In 1986, I went back on active duty full time in Southern Command, where I served as the chief of Research and Assessments in the Small Wars Operations Research Directorate; the chief of the Policy & Strategy Division of the Policy, Plans, and Strategy Directorate; the executive officer of the Combined El Salvador Armed Forces Assessment Team; and the deputy chief of the U.S. Forces Liaison Group (to the Panama National Police). These jobs gave me a view of policy from the point of view of the practitioner at the Geographic Combatant Command level, the American embassy abroad, and the national level as seen from the military school house.

I also brought my extensive academic research experience to developing the course that has always had a focus on issues I dealt with as a practitioner. Finally, in all my courses, I finish them with a capstone simulation exercise that is either entirely free play or semi-free play, which allows the students to experience in real time the difficulty of making decisions with less than adequate information.

This book draws on all those experiences and all the iterations of my courses on national security policy. It replicates the way I teach the course, focusing, first on the international relations theories that guide policy makers. Second, it addresses the laws, rules, and regulations under which those policy makers operate. Then it explores the tools they actually have, the government departments and agencies that have the capabilities the policy makers want and need, and sometimes do not have. The last part of this second section considers the procedures and processes by which the policy makers make and coordinate national security policy, or are, at least, supposed to. Chapters 6 through 13 then consider a number of cases over the past three decades that illustrate how the system works in practice. The final chapter attempts to distill lessons from the cases that expand our understanding of how national security policy is made beyond what practitioners and scholars are taught. In short, I hope with this book to make a contribution to the understanding of the next generation of scholars, citizens, and, especially, practitioners of how American national security policy is really made and implemented.

Part I

A TOUCH OF THEORY

Chapter 1

A Practitioner's Guide to Realism

THE AMERICAN NATIONAL SECURITY PRACTITIONER

American national security practitioners are, most often, career members of the federal government. They are foreign service officers who hold positions from country desk officer to ambassador and assistant secretary of state. They are also fairly senior civil servants in the State Department filling positions in such bureaus as Intelligence and Research. Practitioners also include military officers upward from the rank of major and lieutenant commander, who hold policy-related positions on staffs as well as senior commanders of forces. In addition, there are the career civil servants within the Department of Defense and Department of Homeland Security. Another included group of career employees are those working in the intelligence community, especially the CIA and the Office of the Director of National Intelligence.

Outside of the career bureaucracy, national security practitioners are found in the ranks of the political appointees of various administrations. Many of these are academics who hold government appointive office from time to time. The most famous of these was Henry Kissinger, who held the offices of national security advisor and secretary of state. These same posts were held by Condoleezza Rice in the administration of George W. Bush. Another source of practitioners is the legal profession where former national security advisors Sandy Berger (Clinton administration) and Stephen Hadley (George W. Bush—second term) were drawn. Moreover, both active (Colin Powell) and retired (Brent Scowcroft and James Jones) military officers have served as the president's national security advisor.

Regardless of from where they come, all of these practitioners share a general intellectual and philosophical outlook. They are all, in practice, international relations (IR) realists tempered by varying degrees of liberalism. They may differ in policy preference, but those differences are more a matter of nuance than gross divergences.

THE LIBERAL TRADITION IN AMERICA

The American political tradition is liberal in many senses of the word. As Louis Hartz argued, there is no conservative political tradition.[1] American liberalism derived from John Locke, Thomas Jefferson, Alexander Hamilton, and Adam Smith. It opposed classic conservatism and was optimistic rather than pessimistic in its view of human nature. In international affairs, it was epitomized by free trade, support for republicanism, and freedom of the seas. A seminal example was the Monroe Doctrine of 1823, which supported all three goals and, in an ironic gesture, thumbed its nose at Great Britain, in the person of Foreign Secretary George Canning, who had proposed it to Secretary of State John Quincy Adams as a joint venture, but Britain would enforce Monroe's proclamation, nonetheless.

Modern American international liberalism derives from a strong support for international law and the several international courts at The Hague, culminating in the Permanent Court of International Justice and its successor, the International Court of Justice. It also supported international organizations, especially the vision of President Woodrow Wilson of a League of Nations. Despite the failure of the League, President Franklin Roosevelt resurrected the idea as the United Nations. In addition, modern American international liberalism follows Wilson's imperative to establish democracies. His characterization of the reason for American participation in World War I "to make the world safe for democracy" was a clear statement of that goal. Less lofty was his comment on the reason for the American seizure of the Mexican city of Vera Cruz in 1914, "to teach the Mexicans to elect good men."

Nevertheless, this aspect of liberalism has become known as Democratic Peace Theory. It is interesting because it is empirical, rather than normative, theory although it has normative implications (like those in Wilson's statements). Democratic Peace Theory derives from the fact that since 1815 democratic states have rarely gone to war with each other. And since 1945, they never have.[2] The reason for this fact, according to liberal theorists of the Democratic Peace, is democracy itself.[3] Robert Jervis demonstrates that these theorists do not fully make their case, but he notes that "this claim is 'as close to anything we have to an empirical law in international politics.' "[4]

Other examples of American IR liberalism are found in programs ranging from President Truman's Marshall Plan aid to Europe in 1947–1948, his Point 4 foreign assistance plan, John F. Kennedy's Peace Corps and Alliance for Progress, and President George W. Bush's President's Emergency Program for AIDS Relief, the Millennium Challenge Corporation, and Freedom

Agenda. All of these approaches tapped into U.S. liberal idealism as critical to its foreign policy. It is, nonetheless, worth noting that none of the examples of liberalism mentioned in this section—except for the League of Nations—are totally incompatible with the realist tradition.

THE REALIST TRADITION

Realism is an ancient way of looking at the world, tracing its origins to Thucydides' *History of the Peloponnesian War*, written in late fifth century B.C. Realist theory resurfaces in the Renaissance with the writing of Niccolo Machiavelli. In the nineteenth century, it was the policy of British statesmen like Lord Palmerston to whom is attributed, "England has no permanent friends or enemies, she only has permanent interests." George Washington's farewell admonition not to become involved in "entangling alliances" is an early example of American realism. In 1823, British foreign secretary, George Canning, proposed to American secretary of state, John Quincy Adams, a joint declaration to the European powers to keep their hands off the newly independent Latin American states. This resulted in Adams's reply by way of President James Monroe's unilateral declaration of the Monroe Doctrine (enforced by the Royal Navy[!] because it was in Britain's interest). It should be noted that the Monroe Doctrine is both an example of American liberalism and an example of realism; it corresponded to America's republican ideals, and it was in the interest of the United States to keep the Europeans out of its hemisphere.

After World War II, realism came to dominate American foreign policy-making and American academic writing on international relations with the publication in 1948 of Hans Morgenthau's *Politics among Nations*. Morgenthau's text, subtitled *The Struggle for Power and Peace*, would go through six editions and be the dominant text until 1985.[5] For 40 years, American foreign policy practitioners and IR scholars were nurtured on Morgenthau either directly or derivatively in works by other realist scholars, including Frederick Hartman, Kenneth Waltz, and Robert Gilpin.[6]

REALISM AND THE RATIONAL ACTOR MODEL

One critical assumption of realism is, as Hans Morgenthau said, "We assume that statesmen think and act in terms of interest defined as power."[7] He defines power as

> compris[ing] anything that establishes and maintains the control of man over man. Thus power covers all social relationships which serve that end, from

physical violence to the most subtle psychological ties by which one mind con-
trols another. Power covers the domination of man by man, both when it is disci-
plined by moral ends and controlled by constitutional safeguards, as in Western
democracies, and when it is that untamed and barbaric force which finds its laws
in nothing but its own strength and its sole justification in its aggrandizement.[8]

We may, therefore, simply say that power is the ability of A to get B to do
what A wants—whether A is an individual, organization, or state, and B is
likewise.

Considering that power is the "coin of the realm" in IR, it helps to look at
ways of seeing it. Morgenthau is quite catholic in his view of power, which
deviates from the general view in political science that for power to exist it
must be resisted. But he also addresses power in terms of largely static elements. Joseph Nye recently made a splash with his concept of a dichotomy
between "hard" (military and economic) power and "soft" (diplomacy, information, and everything else) power.[9] The problem with dichotomizing is that
it creates something totally artificial. How do diplomacy, economic aid, and
military threat work with a psychological campaign to achieve goals? In fact,
all these elements of power work in tandem.

A better way of viewing power is by seeing it in terms of sources of power
and instruments of power. This approach separates the multiple elements of
power into sources, like population, territory, educational system, governing
system, industrial base, and natural resources, and instruments, of which there
are four major ones: the political, psychological, military, and economic.
These instruments can be organized, disaggregated, and reorganized by leaders to achieve their goals.[10]

In addition to seeing policy as driven by interests, especially the maxi-
mization of power, realism makes a number of key assumptions about how
foreign and security policy is made. These assumptions are especially well
articulated by Graham T. Allison in his seminal article, "Conceptual Models
and the Cuban Missile Crisis," and subsequent book, *Essence of Decision.*[11]
The first of these assumptions is that the key actor is the state, seen as a
single, unitary player. Even though we know that the state is made up of
organizations and individuals, we can treat it as if it were a single individual.
Thus, classical IR writing and journalism speaks of actors like Britain, London, Whitehall, or Thatcher (to cite just one example) for a discussion of
policy made by civil servants, parliamentarians, ministers of government,
and the prime minister (collectively, Her Majesty's Government). Any of
these terms can be used interchangeably. Nevertheless, we know them to be
simplifications of reality but use them anyway because a more complex presentation of the policy process, in general, does not add that much explana-
tory power.[12]

The second assumption of realism is that the actor follows a rational decision process in seeking to maximize his or her interest. In this assumption realism and liberalism are identical. Both derive from Adam Smith's theory as expressed in his 1776 *An Inquiry into the Wealth of Nations*. This argument for economic liberalism is also the foundation for the approach in the discipline of political science known as rational choice theory that has been advanced as a major explanation of political behavior.[13] As rational choice, statesmen first identify the goals and objectives they wish to achieve. Then, they consider the available options (or options that could become available to them). Then the statesmen evaluate the options in terms of their costs and benefits and, finally, choose a course of action from among the options considered.[14] Once again, it is worth pointing out that whatever term is being used—statesmen, president, prime minister, Washington, or London—we are seeing the state as a single rational actor.

This approach has the advantage of both simplifying the task of the analyst and being very effective at both explaining and predicting state behavior. It simplifies by its assumption that states behave rationally, which allows the analyst to look for certain patterns of behavior. The first question asked by the analyst is, what interests is a state pursuing?[15] This would be followed by an examination of the specific goals and objectives of policy, alternative approaches to achieve those goals, evaluation in terms of costs and benefits, and choice. Issues would have to do with why a state would pursue a particular objective rather than another, or why it chose a course of action with higher, rather than lower, costs. In any case, making these assumptions about state behavior has served well in the past and appears likely to do the same for the foreseeable future. One qualification, however, is necessary. While this approach gives a very good picture of the overall policy process, it often leaves out detail, which is where the devil hides.[16]

THE EDUCATION OF THE PRACTITIONER

Until about 1990 all students of IR in the United States studied under the realism paradigm. In 1962, the introductory IR course at Dartmouth College (a sophomore-level course) used Morgenthau's *Politics among Nations* (3rd edition) as its principal textbook. One of its major competitors, as noted previously, was by Frederick Hartman of the Naval War College. Both are examples of the realist paradigm. Beginning in the 1980s the realist paradigm began to break down. One of the more successful textbooks, now in its 12th edition plus updates, is *World Politics: Trend and Transformation* by Charles W. Kegley, Jr., and Shannon L. Blanton. (In the first six editions Eugene Wittkopf was Kegley's coauthor.) Unlike books written under the realist paradigm, this text is eclectic in its point of view, addressing the major theories of realism, idealism, and constructivism while touching on variants such as Marxism, feminism, and "critical" theory. Of the 18 chapters in the book, only 5 are clearly realist in their perspective.[17] What this has meant is that undergraduate students of IR—and graduate students as well[18]—have a wider view of IR theory than their predecessors but one that is both less in depth and not so firmly grounded in a specific theory, that is, realism. This issue is compounded by the fact that a recent survey of IR professors in the university indicates that 22% view themselves as constructivists, 21% as liberals, and 16% as realists. A mere 2% see themselves as Marxists, while 39% were not identified by theoretical perspective.[19]

Another factor related to the teaching of IR theory at the university level is the rather common failure to distinguish clearly between empirical and normative theory. While this was also true during the period of the dominance of realism, it becomes more significant in an era without an academic paradigm. Morgenthau, however, was not guilty of this failing; in his formulation realism was empirical, used for explaining and predicting reality. If there were policy implications in the theory—and there were—then they were drawn out separately for use in specific situations. Idealist theories[20] (liberalism, Marxism, Islamism), by contrast, focus on what ought to be (the normative) and only secondarily on what is (the empirical). Thus, even modern texts, like Kegley's and Blanton's, devote a significant number of pages to realism in its empirical guise.

Unlike his predecessors, the modern practitioner comes into the arena with a view of theory that, as the cliché says, is a mile wide and an inch deep. The corrective for this is found in the professional education of U.S. government practitioners, especially in the military staff and war colleges. A minor digression is appropriate at this point. The army, navy, marines, and air force all have year-long staff courses for their middle-grade officers—junior majors and lieutenant commanders. Likewise, the services have year-long courses (war colleges) at the senior (colonel and navy captain) level. At the senior level, the National Defense University runs two colleges—the National War College and the Dwight D. Eisenhower School for National Security and Resource Strategy (formerly known as the Industrial College of the Armed Forces)—for senior officers of all services and senior national security civilians. All of these schools grant master's degrees and, with the exception of the Army Command and General Staff College (intermediate level), have some civilian students in attendance, all of whom are national security practitioners. One purpose of all of these schools is to prepare officers and civilians to participate in the making of national security policy. To accomplish this, they teach the making of strategy in the curriculum. And this education on strategy focuses essentially on the realist paradigm.

The realist paradigm, as elaborated in the strategy curricula of all of these schools, begins with the concept of "national purpose"—"the enduring beliefs, ethics, and values" of American society.[21] It is particularly interesting that the realist paradigm for the teaching of strategy to practitioners begins with a concept that is most often associated with the theory of liberalism. While there are ways of formally reconciling the two theoretical approaches, it is not necessary as the practitioners can operate easily within these boundaries. Examples of American national purpose/values come from the Declaration of Independence and the Constitution, and they assume the existence of a higher natural law. They include "life" and "liberty" from both documents, the "pursuit of happiness" from the Declaration, and "property" from the Constitution. Freedom, both political and economic, is central to America's national purpose.

Once the practitioner has analyzed and restated the national purpose, the focus shifts to national interests. Interests are seen in descending order as survival, vital, and important. Survival interests are just what the name implies—that which is necessary for the state to survive with its beliefs and values intact. Vital interests are usually defined as those which are worth going to war to defend, while important interests are those on which the state is willing to expend resources but not go to war over. Survival interests tend to be fairly obvious. During the Cold War, the American survival interest was to be able to prevent a Soviet first nuclear strike on the United States. At present, Israel defines as a survival interest preventing Iran (a hostile and apparently irrational state) from acquiring any nuclear weapons because that would threaten Israel's survival. By contrast, the United States has defined keeping Iran from acquiring nuclear weapons as a vital interest. (An American administration could, of course, redefine that interest as merely an important one, as the Obama administration, apparently, has done.)

Once interests are identified and ordered, the practitioner looks to the grand strategy or strategic vision of the state. This is where statesmen define what their desired end-state should look like. For example, the strategic vision of the United States in Israel and the Palestinian territories is two states with secure boundaries, living in peace with each other. How that strategic vision is achieved is the subject of national policy.

For example, the strategic vision of the United States during the Cold War was to contain communism until such time as the internal contradictions of the Soviet Union caused the system to collapse.[22] George Kennan's article (note 18) is an updated version of his official analysis to the State Department sent from Moscow in 1946, known as the "Long Telegram." This analysis provided the strategic vision that produced the policies of the Truman Doctrine, the Marshall Plan, and John F. Kennedy's Alliance for Progress. These policies were stated in speeches by President Truman, Secretary of State

George Marshall's 1948 commencement address at Harvard University, and John F. Kennedy's inaugural address on January 20, 1961, where he said, "We will pay any price, bear any burden, support any friend, oppose any foe, to assure the survival and success of liberty."

Policy, however, has little meaning if it is not supported by a specific strategy constructed in an ends, ways, and means format. The ends of strategy are its specific objectives, as in the Marshall Plan, to rebuild Western Europe. These objectives are to be achieved through specific courses of action (strategic methods), such as the Marshall Plan administrative organizations that every recipient state was required to establish to work with the U.S. government's Marshall Plan administrator. Finally, the means (resources) to achieve the objectives must be provided. In the case of the Marshall Plan, the resources were in the form of appropriations by the U.S. Congress.

Lastly, the practitioners must regularly evaluate their policies and strategies to see if they are achieving their intended goals. If so, then the statesmen should press on. If not, then they should revise their methods, resources, and, if necessary, their objectives. In the example given previously of the U.S. interest in preventing Iran from acquiring nuclear weapons, if its policies and strategies are not having the desired effect, then it has the choice of increasing resources, revising courses of action, modifying objectives, or modifying its view of the type of interest represented.

HOW THE PRACTITIONER SEES THE WORLD

Realism, particularly that brand of realism called neo-realism, posits a world of sovereign independent states, a world where there is nothing greater than the state, where anarchy reigns. This view of an anarchic world, while extreme, remains generally accurate, although it must be modified with respect to a large number of details. First, the international financial institutions (IFIs), such as the World Bank, the International Monetary Fund (IMF), and the World Trade Organization (WTO), all put some quite severe constraints on their members. The result is that in the economic realm, the world is far less anarchic than it is in other venues. Many other international governmental organizations (IGOs) limit the freedom of action of their members but not nearly as much as do the IFIs.

The central IGO, in what scholars used to call the "high politics" of IR, is the United Nations (UN), especially the UN Security Council (UNSC). Although the UN is the literal "child" of the League of Nations, the paragon of Woodrow Wilson's American liberal idealism, it is not entirely an organization founded on liberalism. The UNSC, unlike its predecessor, the League's Council, rests clearly on a key feature of the realist architecture, the balance of power. Thus, the five permanent members of the UNSC—the United States, the United Kingdom, Russia, France, and China—are the Great Powers of the modern world. They each wield a practical veto of actions against them that is simply ratified in their permanent member status. As a result, with their consensus, plus the votes of four additional members, the UNSC can act and "anything" is possible. Without their agreement, little can be done by the international community as a whole. The UNSC, therefore, replicates and provides a means for controlling the anarchic international system.

TENSIONS REGARDING AMERICA'S "SPECIAL PROVIDENCE"

Historian Walter Russell Mead took the title of his well-received 2001 book on American foreign policy, *Special Providence*, from a quote attributed to the great chancellor of Imperial Germany, Count Otto von Bismarck: "God has a special providence for fools, drunks, and the United States of America."[23] Given the timing of his statement, and however ironically it was meant, it is interesting that the "Iron Chancellor" recognized, in the late nineteenth century, what has become known as American exceptionalism. Unlike the citizens and leaders of other nations, Americans have generally believed that their country is unique and uniquely good. While Mead argues that there are four major strains of U.S. foreign policy—Hamiltonian, Jeffersonian, Wilsonian, and Jacksonian[24]—each emphasizing a different aspect but ones that cross the lines of IR liberalism and realism—all four see America as a special place with a special destiny.

Mead argues that the four strains represent different traditions with the Hamiltonian seeing security in economic terms and the Wilsonian addressing exporting American political ideals to the rest of the world—democracy (in the American form, rule of law under international courts, etc.). The Jeffersonian tends to emphasize American political ideals but for Americans, as an example to be emulated, not to be imposed on others. Finally, the Jacksonian is populist, defensive, and offensive at the same time. Mead is careful to point out that most American statesmen are not merely followers of one of these strains but rather of several either at the same time or sequentially depending on the circumstances.[25] As an example, it is clear that the George W. Bush administration came into office largely committed to a Hamiltonian and Jeffersonian policy. September 11, 2001, changed that to one that was first Jacksonian and then Wilsonian, retaining as many of its Hamiltonian objectives as possible while relegating them to a lower priority.

Regardless of the particular set of policies, they were all predominantly realist with overtones of the several strands of liberalism. A relatively recent example of some of the tensions of how to interpret and apply America's "special providence" (exceptionalism) comes from a meeting of the National Security Council principals fairly early in the Bush administration over how to deal with the rogue president of Liberia, Charles Taylor. In her memoir, then national security advisor, Condoleezza Rice, tells how the subject of a minor U.S. military intervention in this troubled African country with significant American ties was approached by the key players. "Sitting in the Situation Room, it was easy to read the body language of the Vice President [Dick Cheney] and Don [Rumsfeld], who saw no earthly reason for U.S. involvement in the affair."[26] This was in contrast to Rice, herself, and secretary of state, retired general Colin Powell. What was demonstrated here was the inherent tension between the foreign policy liberalism of Rice and Powell and the narrower realism of Cheney and Rumsfeld. Or, to put it in Mead's terms, there was the Wilsonian impulse of Rice and Powell contrasted with the Jacksonian bent of the other two. Once again, all four of these statesmen were realists, although they were each influenced by separate strands of the American foreign policy tradition, as was the president, George W. Bush, who decided the issue in favor of Rice and Powell.

THE CONSTANTLY SHIFTING BALANCE

The lesson of this vignette from Secretary Rice's memoir is not that she and Colin Powell were right and the others wrong, nor that liberalism trumps realism, but rather that realism provides a major basis for analysis while liberalism influences the way some/many American players respond in specific situations. Nevertheless, the players in the vignette all asked the key question for the realist, "what is the interest of the United States?" For Rumsfeld and Cheney, American interests were defined in narrow and specific terms— terms that only had to do with American security. For Powell, Rice, and the president, the terms of American interest were broader and harkened back to America's national purpose—its values, beliefs, and ethics. For the name, Charles Taylor, is not African, it is American and comes from an American slave-owning family in the 1820s. In the eyes of Bush, Rice, and Powell, they had an ethical obligation (interest) in dealing with Charles Taylor and the threat he posed to the people of Liberia.

For the American practitioner as a realist, the issues are the practical ones of how to analyze the environment, the players, our interests (in light of our values), the interests of the other players, and devising policies and strategies that will enable us to achieve our objectives. In the end, realism does not point toward any specific policies. It does, however, provide a set of tools to understand the situations that confront us. Realism is, indeed, the best tool set for analyzing international threats and opportunities. Yet, it must be expanded by the appropriate alternative theories within the realist tradition as well as outside it. American liberalism is perhaps the most dominant of the alternative traditions, and it usually is not incompatible with realism.

NOTES

1. Louis Hartz, *The Liberal Tradition in America.* New York: 1991, Harvest/HBJ.

2. See Bruce Russett, *Grasping the Democratic Peace.* Princeton, NJ: 1993, Princeton University Press.

3. See Robert Jervis, *American Foreign Policy in a New Era.* New York and London: 2005, Routledge. 18–22.

4. Ibid., 18.

5. Hans J. Morgenthau, Revised by Kenneth W. Thompson, *Politics among Nations: The Struggle for Power and Peace* (Sixth Edition). New York: 1985, McGraw-Hill Publishing Company.

6. See, for example, Frederick H. Hartman, *The Relations of Nations* (Sixth Edition). New York: 1983, Macmillan. Kenneth N. Waltz, *Man, the State, and War.* New York: 2001, Columbia University Press. Robert Gilpin, *War and Change in International Politics.* New York: 1981, Cambridge University Press.

7. Morgenthau, 5.

8. Ibid., 11.

9. See Joseph S. Nye, Jr., *Soft Power.* Cambridge, MA: 2004, Public Affairs.

10. U.S. staff and war colleges characterize the instruments of power by the acronym DIME, which stands for diplomatic, informational, military, and economic. I prefer the formulation in the text. For a view as to how to organize the instruments of power, see John T. Fishel and Max G. Manwaring, *Uncomfortable Wars Revisited.* Norman, OK: 2006, Oxford University Press, Chapter 14.

11. Graham T. Allison, "Conceptual Models and the Cuban Missile Crisis," in the *American Political Science Review*, Volume 63, Issue 3 (September, 1969), 689–718.

12. Allison's article and the subsequent book address this issue in detail but show that the realist model, unmodified, explains the bulk of events. Adding additional models sharpens the picture, clarifying nuance, but they don't change it in the main.

13. Allison discusses the general relationship with economic theory in his footnote 37 on page 694.

14. Ibid.

15. While classical realism always answers that power is the key interest, power can be broken down into components such as survival, aggrandizement, economic well-being, and wealth, the classic elements of power.

16. This is the point of Allison's work in the article, and both the first and second editions of his book (the second edition written more than 30 years after the first).

17. See, Charles W. Kegley, Jr., and Shannon L. Blanton, *World Politics: Trend and Transformation* (12th Edition). Boston: 2010, Wadsworth.

18. See the curriculum, for example, of American Military University/American Public University's graduate program in IR, especially their introductory MA-level courses IRLS 500 and 502.

19. *Foreign Policy*, "The Ivory Tower," www.foreignpolicy.com/articles/2012/01/03/the_ivory_tower.

20. I define idealist theories and idealism as theory that is simply drawn from ideas about the best government for all.

21. This section is taken from Chapter 7 of *Teaching Strategy: Challenge and Response*, edited by Gabriel Marcella, specifically, Harry R. Yarger, "How Do Students Learn Strategy? Thoughts on the U.S. Army War College Pedagogy of Strategy," Carlisle, PA: SSI, 179–202. Especially 187, 2010.

22. Mr. X (George Kennan), "The Sources of Soviet Conduct," in *Foreign Affairs*, July 1947, 556–582.

23. Walter Russell Mead, *Special Providence: American Foreign Policy and How It Changed the World.* New York: 2001, Knopf.

24. Ibid.

25. Ibid., 87–88.

26. Condoleezza Rice, *No Higher Honor: A Memoir of My Years in Washington.* New York: 2011, Crown. 231.

Part II

THE PRACTITIONERS' TEXTBOOK

Chapter 2

Legal Authorities

In Chapter 1 we considered the way in which American national security practitioners look at the world. We concluded that they use a realist paradigm, tempered by American liberal values, to view a world that is largely anarchic, made up of sovereign states and other independent (and sometimes interdependent) actors. America's national security practitioners analyze that world using a methodology of rational choice—although much of the time rationality is of a limited variety for all actors, not just American ones.

In this chapter, we will consider other constraints and enablers of national security policymaking, including the legal authorities, the laws and regulations that govern what we can and must do, or not do. The oath of office of every officer of the federal government enjoins us to "preserve, protect, and defend the Constitution of the United States." Thus, it is that Constitution where the legal authorities for national security policy begin.

THE CONSTITUTION

The Preamble states, "We the People of the United States, in order to form a more perfect Union, establish Justice, insure domestic Tranquility, provide for the common defence, promote the general Welfare, and secure the Blessings of Liberty for ourselves and our Posterity, do ordain and establish this Constitution of the United States of America." Almost in its entirety, the Preamble speaks to America's national security and to the need for policies to achieve it. Specifically, justice, defense, and liberty are security goals. However, the methods to achieve those goals are the subject of specific parts of Articles I and II of the Constitution.

Article I, Section 8 speaks to the powers of Congress. It charges Congress to "provide for the common Defence," "regulate Commerce with foreign Nations," "To define and punish Piracies and Felonies committed on the high seas, and Offenses against the Law of Nations," and "To Declare War . . . raise and support Armies . . . provide and maintain a Navy . . . make Rules for the Government and Regulation of the land and naval Forces . . . to provide for the calling forth of the Militia . . . provide for the organizing, arming, and disciplining the Militia." In other words, the Constitution gives Congress numerous powers involved in the national security of the country. However, those powers overlap with the powers granted to the president in Article II.

Article II states, "The President shall be Commander in chief of the Army and Navy of the United States, and of the Militia of the several States when called into the actual Service of the United States." "He shall have Power, by and with the Advice and Consent of the Senate to make Treaties . . . shall appoint Ambassadors, other public Ministers and Consuls." Although there is the obvious overlap between the roles and authorities of the president and Congress, the main point of contention is between what the president can do as commander in chief and Congress can do with respect to its roles in declaring war and making rules for the governing of the forces. Does this include telling the president when he can deploy or how he can employ the military forces of the United States? Congress tends to argue that it does while presidents contend that it does not.

The Federalist Papers discuss, to some extent, the role of the executive and of Congress in the conduct of foreign and defense policy. Of particular interest are Federalist 41, and 69–74. These articles by Alexander Hamilton and James Madison are generally designed to present a limited view of Executive Power; however, some (specifically Federalist 70) suggest a more expansive role. Hamilton returned to the expansive theme writing as Pacificus in debate with Madison (Helvidius) over President George Washington's Neutrality Proclamation. Constitutional scholar Harvey C. Mansfield notes the general silence of the Constitution on this issue and recalls Edward Corwin's (another renowned scholar) remark that it "is an invitation to struggle for the privilege of directing American foreign policy."[1]

THE NATIONAL SECURITY ACT OF 1947

While the Constitution sets the stage and the parameters within which national security policy in the United States is made, it was the National Security Act of 1947 that created the specific institutions of the national security policy community. The Act grew out of the experiences of World War II and its immediate aftermath. First, the war, although not unexpected, came as a surprise both in its manner and its enemy. One aim of the Act was to prevent such a surprise attack from ever happening again. Second, the war saw the growth of land-based airpower beyond the institutional capacity of the army to develop effective air strategy and tactics. Third, experience with the wartime combined chiefs of staff (American and British) demonstrated the need for something like it for the American military services alone, coupled with the role personally played by army chief of staff, George C. Marshall. And, fourth, the fact that President Truman, as vice president under Franklin Roosevelt, was in the dark on so many security issues pointed to the need for a mechanism to coordinate American national security policy at the highest level.

The congressional drafters of the National Security Act took on each of these issues. Taken in the order from easiest to most difficult, the Act first created a separate air force out of the army air forces, ratifying what, for practical purposes, was already in existence. Even though there was opposition to an independent air force within the army, the fact that U.S. allies had independent air forces and had them for a long time was compelling. Closely related was the need for a separate military department comparable to the Departments of War and Navy, thus creating the Department of the Air Force. Separating the air force also suggested that the War Department be renamed and so it became the Department of the Army.

Only slightly more difficult was the creation of a national-level intelligence agency. During World War II, the Office of Strategic Services (OSS) was, in fact, just such an agency. Created by and led by BG William J. Donovan (a Wall Street lawyer, and friendly Republican competitor of President Roosevelt), the OSS combined intelligence collection, analysis, and covert operations under one roof. While Donovan had patterned the OSS on his British counterpart, the Secret Intelligence Service, also known as MI-6, he did not follow the British lead of having the covert action capability housed in a separate organization.[2]

At the end of the war, President Truman had disbanded the OSS, giving some of its capabilities to Military Intelligence and some to the State Department. Finally, a rump capacity had been left as an independent entity that grew into the Central Intelligence Group. Experience in the immediate postwar period showed that this dispersed intelligence capability was less than effective, which gave rise to fears that it would be unable to discern another "Pearl Harbor." State was especially weak while the military intelligence entities tended to be much too tactically focused. As a result, Congress resurrected the notion that Donovan had for a postwar intelligence agency based on his OSS. The result was the Central Intelligence Agency (CIA), whose director would both direct the agency and coordinate the collection and analysis of all national-level intelligence. Nevertheless, the Director of

Central Intelligence (DCI) was given the responsibility for coordination but not the authority. As a result, successive DCIs built their agencies into the most powerful institution within the far-flung intelligence community (that would ultimately encompass some 17 agencies). One clause in the National Security Act—that the CIA "will perform such other functions and duties related to intelligence affecting the national security as the President may direct"—covers its entire covert action mission.[3]

The creation of a third military department (air force) implied some unification of the armed forces, and this was more or less achieved by the National Military Establishment under the "leadership" of a secretary of defense. This hybrid lasted a mere two years, and in a 1949 amendment, the Department of Defense (DOD) was created with the military departments clearly subordinated. The National Security Act also established the institution of the Joint Chiefs of Staff (JCS) (made up of the chiefs of the army, navy, and air force under a chairman) to collectively provide military advice to the secretary and the president. Note that the chairman was an equal member, not the leader of the group, and the commandant of the Marine Corps was not included. The result was a cumbersome mechanism where advice was limited to the lowest agreed-on common denominator. To assist this group, a small Joint Staff was created. Its limited size was due to congressional fears of the infamous militarism of the German General Staff from the Franco-Prussian War through World War II. For the U.S. military, then, an assignment to the Joint Staff was not "career enhancing."

The final component of the system created by the National Security Act was the National Security Council (NSC). Consisting of the president, vice president, secretary of state, and secretary of defense, with the JCS and the DCI as statutory advisors, and an executive secretary to coordinate the paperwork, the NSC was designed to assist the president in making decisions regarding national security and make certain that the vice president—unlike Harry Truman in 1945—was engaged in the decision-making process.[4] Of course, telling the president how to conduct his office infringes on his constitutional power, and the history of the NSC shows that presidents have used it, or failed to use it, in a wide variety of ways. A particularly egregious example of a presidential use of the NSC that subverted its basic intent was President Lyndon Johnson's Tuesday Lunch, which substituted for NSC meetings and specifically excluded Vice President Hubert Humphrey.

THE WAR POWERS RESOLUTION (1973)

One of the most controversial pieces of legislation that seeks to set limits on presidential war powers is the War Powers Resolution of 1973.[5] The resolution was passed over the veto of President Nixon in reaction to both the Vietnam War and a presidency weakened by the Watergate scandal. Nevertheless, every president since Nixon—except for Barack Obama—has argued vigorously that the act is unconstitutional. Several sections of the resolution are, in fact, constitutionally questionable at the very least. These include the requirement that the president get congressional approval in all instances where he introduces troops to a situation where combat is a likelihood, the requirement that he withdraw troops within a set time limit unless he has specific congressional authorization, and that he must withdraw troops at any time if Congress directs him to do so by joint resolution.[6] The last provision constitutes a legislative veto that is particularly dubious as a result of the Supreme Court decision in *INS v. Chadha* in 1983, where the Court declared the legislative veto unconstitutional.[7] Nevertheless, all presidents since Richard Nixon—again, except for Barack Obama—have been careful to notify Congress of their decision to put troops potentially in harm's way "consistent with" but not "in accordance with" the War Powers Act.

THE GOLDWATER-NICHOLS ACT AND THE COHEN-NUNN AMENDMENT (1986)

The Goldwater-Nichols Act (DOD Reorganization Act—DODRA) of 1986 was the culmination of 40 years of tinkering with the organization of the Defense Department. As noted, in 1949 the National Security Act was amended to create the department from the National Military Establishment. The DOD Reorganization Act of 1958 was the most significant change prior to the Goldwater-Nichols Act (GNA) by giving the chairman of the JCS (CJCS) a vote for the first time and establishing that he was in the warfighting chain of communication, although not the chain of command. Twenty years later, the commandant of the Marine Corps was made a full member of the JCS.[8]

The GNA and its companion legislation, the Cohen-Nunn Amendment to the 1986 Defense Appropriations Act, were driven by two significant perceived failures of U.S. military operations. The first was the 1980 disastrous attempt to rescue the diplomats held hostage by Iran since November 1979. This special operations mission was marked by the failure of interservice coordination and command and control. Similar failures were noted in the conventional Grenada operation of 1983. These events prompted the CJCS, General David Jones, USAF, to propose changes in the law to increase jointness. He was supported by Senators Barry Goldwater, William Cohen, and Sam Nunn as well as Representative William Nichols. The key drafter of the subsequent legislation (both bills) was James Locher, a staffer for Senator Nunn.[9]

The GNA focused on effective joint operations—jointness. It made the CJCS the principal military advisor to the president and secretary of defense. It created the position of vice chairman. It removed the service chiefs from the operational chain of command that now ran from the president to the secretary of defense to the commanders of the unified commands. Orders usually went through the CJCS, who was in the chain of communication but not the chain of command. The GNA also gave the CJCS oversight of service budgets as well as responsibility for developing the National Military Strategy (an unclassified document) and its classified "annex," the Joint Planning Document. The GNA also requires the president to produce his National Security Strategy as an unclassified report to Congress on an annual basis (the last honored in the breach by Presidents George W. Bush, who only produced two, and Barack Obama, who also produced only two).[10] Lastly, the GNA both enlarged and strengthened the role of the Joint Staff making an assignment there highly desirable to any officer hoping to advance to the rank of general or admiral. This was coupled with Joint Professional Military Education requirements and the creation of a corps of Joint Staff Officers qualified as such by specific education and a series of recognized joint assignments.

The Cohen-Nunn Amendment established the United States Special Operations Command (USSOCOM) at MacDill Air Force Base in Tampa, Florida, with responsibility for all service special operations forces. This includes Army Special Forces, the Ranger Regiment, the 160th Special Operations Aviation Regiment, certain army special mission units like Delta (SFOD-D), air force special operators, Navy SEALs including the special mission unit known as SEAL Team Six or DEVGRU, along with Army Civil Affairs and Psychological Operations.[11] In addition, the operational Command and Control Headquarters, the Joint Special Operations Command, came under USSOCOM. Because USSOCOM has budgetary authority for special operations unique equipment and training—a service-like responsibility—the Office of the Assistant Secretary of Defense for Special Operations and Low Intensity Conflict (ASD-SO/LIC) was established to provide civilian oversight for SOCOM.[12] (In 2006, the Marine Corps Special Operations Command was established and made a part of USSOCOM.[13])

THE HOMELAND SECURITY ACT (2002)

The Homeland Security Act (HSA) of 2002, the largest reorganization of the federal government since the National Security Act of 1947, was passed in the wake of the terrorist attacks of September 11, 2001, and was designed to bring some order to the many government agencies that have some responsibility for internal security.[14] Although it grew out of the Office of Homeland

Security established by President George W. Bush only 11 days after the attacks, the administration initially opposed its creation. However, once the legislation was introduced, the president supported it. The HSA created the Department of Homeland Security out of 22 separate government agencies. Some of these were the former Immigration and Naturalization Service, U.S. Customs, the U.S. Secret Service, the Border Patrol, and the U.S. Coast Guard.

The mission of the department is to prevent terrorist attacks within the United States, reduce the vulnerability of the United States to terrorism, and minimize damage and assist in the recovery from acts of terrorism that occur within the United States.[15] Thus, although one of the agencies rolled into the department, the Federal Emergency Management Agency, is mainly concerned with recovery from natural disasters, it was included due to its recovery from acts of terrorism function. Likewise, the U.S. Coast Guard has multiple functions, of which countering terrorism is only one.

As interesting as the agencies included are those that are not. Among these are the FBI and the Bureau of Alcohol, Tobacco, and Firearms (which is responsible for dealing with guns and explosives). Moreover, no intelligence agencies (except Coast Guard Intelligence) are part of the department, although a small intelligence analysis office has been created.

While the creation of the DOD involved more people than the DHS's, it created only one new military service and amalgamated three services and their departments under one new departmental roof. Moreover, each of the services shared a similar military culture. By contrast, the DHS took 22 different organizations, most of which have very different organizational cultures and attempted to integrate them into a single department. It should be noted that it took 40 years for the DOD to even get the legislation right and another decade (post GNA) to make it work. How long it will take the DHS is anybody's guess.

THE INTELLIGENCE REFORM AND TERROR PREVENTION ACT (2004)

Although the Intelligence Reform and Terror Prevention Act (IRTPA) incorporates and subsumes a number of other laws and updates of those laws,[16] the heart of the law is in its restructuring of the now 17-member Intelligence Community (IC). The centerpiece is the creation of an independent Director of National Intelligence (DNI) charged with developing and overseeing the budget of the National Intelligence Program.[17] This budgetary authority is significant because it gives the DNI the power to influence how funds are spent in a number of Cabinet departments, especially the DOD, with respect

to intelligence activities. This authority extends under the law to the independent CIA and the quasi-independent FBI.

A second major authority for the DNI lies in the area of appointments:

> The DNI shall recommend to the President nominees for Principal Deputy DNI
> and for the CIA Director. The DNI has the right to concur in the appointment
> or the recommendation for nomination of the heads of NSA, NRO, and NGA;
> the Assistant Secretary of State for INR; the Directors of the Offices of Intel-
> ligence and Counterintelligence at DOE; the Assistant Secretary for Intelligence
> and Analysis at the Department of the Treasury; the Executive Assistant Director
> for Intelligence of the FBI; and the Assistant Secretary of Homeland Security for
> Information Analysis. The DNI must be consulted for appointments or recom-
> mendations for the Director of DIA and the Deputy Assistant Commandant of
> the Coast Guard for Intelligence.[18]

Again, this authority grants significant power to the DNI in that he rec-
ommends to the president who will be the director of the CIA and must
concur with the appointments of the directors of intelligence agencies
within the DOD, State, and other departments. Under President Bush, this
all worked pretty much as intended following a relatively brief period of
personnel instability. With the appointments of retired admiral Mike McConnell as DNI and GEN Michael Hayden, USAF, as director of the CIA,
the leadership relationship within the IC seemed to be relatively effective.
However, as Hayden put it in a 2010 article, "Even in the best of times, the
DNI-DCIA relationship is a challenging one."[19] But despite the fact that
they "had known each other for years . . . [they] still found that this relationship took a lot of effort."[20] In addition, there remained questions about
how much authority the DNI actually had over DOD intelligence, especially
with Donald Rumsfeld as secretary of defense. That said, McConnell and
Hayden were both (1) intelligence professionals and (2) military officers,
whose shared cultures worked toward the resolution of potential issues. The
arrival of Barack Obama to the presidency changed the equation. Obama
perceived that he was seen as inexperienced in national security affairs.
As a result, his personnel choices reflected that perception beginning with
his choice of Senate Foreign Relations Committee chairman, Joe Biden, as
his vice president. Then, he asked Secretary of Defense Robert Gates to
stay on and named his rival for the nomination, Senator Hillary Rodham
Clinton (former First Lady), as his secretary of state. As national security
advisor, he appointed USMC GEN Jim Jones, the former commandant of
the Corps and former Supreme Allied Commander in Europe (dual hatted
as commander of U.S. European Command). Those appointments left the
two key intelligence leadership positions, DNI and director, CIA (DCIA).
For the former, he chose Admiral Dennis Blair, previously commander,

U.S. Pacific Command (a key intelligence consumer). As DCIA, however, he appointed Leon Panetta, an old Washington hand who had been White House chief of staff under President Bill Clinton. The power mismatch was obvious.

The issue actually came to a head over a minor controversy; DNI Blair sought to name the senior intelligence officers at U.S. embassies overseas, a position that had always been that of the CIA station chief. Blair wanted the option to name someone other than the station chief, the defense attaché, for example, if that person was better qualified in his opinion. Panetta resisted and President Obama sided with him. Blair resigned shortly thereafter. He was replaced by retired USAF Lt. Gen. James Clapper, former director of the Defense Intelligence Agency, an intelligence professional but in no way a powerful political player in his own right. Panetta was clearly king of the intelligence castle. When Panetta took over as secretary of defense, he was replaced as DCIA by General (retired) David Petraeus, who clearly outranked Clapper. Again, power remained with the DCIA. When Petraeus resigned as a result of a personal scandal, his replacement was John Brennan, President Obama's counterterrorism advisor and a former long-term senior CIA officer.

The result of all of these political maneuvers has been to largely nullify the structural reform of the IC intended by the IRTPA. The director of the CIA remains the most powerful player in the IC, with the DNI merely coordinating among more or less equal players.

Although other legislation provides certain specific authorities for the conduct of national security policy, those discussed here are the principal ones. Together, they set the legal and constitutional parameters within which the various departments and agencies work. Those departments and agencies are the subject of Chapter 3.

NOTES

1. Quoted in Harvey C. Mansfield, Jr., *Taming the Prince: The Ambivalence of Modern Executive Power*. Baltimore, MD: 1993, The Johns Hopkins University Press. 277–278.

2. British practice had created the Special Operations Executive for that purpose. Donovan considered it inefficient and gathered the capability under the OSS.

3. National Security Act, 1947 Section 104d (4).

4. National Security Act, 1947, Section 101.

5. 50 USC Sections 1541–1548.

6. See ibid. and Library of Congress, Law Library, "War Powers," http://loc.gov/law/help/war-powers.php.

7. Ibid.

8. Armed Forces Staff College, *Joint Staff Officers Guide*, 1997, Chapter 2.

9. James R. Locher III, *Victory on the Potomac*, College Station: 2002. Texas A&M Press.

10. Finally published in 2015.

11. In recent years, the marines have created special operations forces that fall under USSOCOM, while reserve Psyop and Civil Affairs now fall under the Army Reserve Command. In addition, Psyop has been renamed Military Information Support Operations. It has recently reverted to Psyop.

12. ASD-SO/LIC is the only assistant secretary of defense established by law—all others are by administrative action.

13. Dick Couch, *Always Faithful, Always Forward*. New York: 2014, Berkley. 29.

14. See www.dhs.gov.

15. Homeland Security Act, 2002, Title I.

16. Foreign Intelligence Surveillance Act and the USA PATRIOT Act, among others.

17. U.S. Senate, "Summary of Intelligence Reform and Terror Prevention Act," Washington, DC: December 6, 2004 (http://www.fas.org/irp/congress/2004_rpt/s2845-summ.pdf), 1.

18. Ibid., 4.

19. Michael Hayden, "The State of the Craft: Is Intelligence Reform Working?" *World Affairs Journal*. September–October 2010, http.//www.worldaffairsjournal.org/article/state-craft-intelligence-reform-working.

20. Ibid.

Chapter 3

National Security Organizations

The Constitution and legislation passed by Congress and signed by the president create the authorities under which the American national security process is conducted. However, it takes organizations—made up of human beings—political appointments, civil servants, and uniformed personnel—to build policies and carry out the process. This chapter focuses on the roles, functions, missions, and structures of the principal organizations of that process.

THE NATIONAL SECURITY COUNCIL (NSC)

We begin with the National Security Council, generally known by its abbreviation as the NSC. The NSC was created by the National Security Act of 1947 and was made up of four statutory members and two statutory advisors. The members, by law, are the president, the vice president, the secretary of state, and the secretary of defense. The statutory advisors are the Director of National Intelligence (DNI) and the chairman of the Joint Chiefs of Staff (CJCS). An executive secretary and a small staff are also authorized by the law.[1] The purpose of the NSC is to advise the president on issues of national security policy. Of course, Congress telling the president whose advice he must listen to steps on his prerogative as a co-equal branch of government. So, in practice, the NSC is made up of the people the president wants and it is used—or not used—as he wishes. Over time, it has become a useful tool for most presidents.

In addition to the statutory members and advisors the NSC usually has a number of other players named by each president. Most important is the national security advisor (technically, the assistant to the president for national security affairs, known as the NSA). The NSA serves at the president's discretion, is a member of his staff, and is not subject to confirmation by the Senate. The NSA organizes the NSC staff, runs meetings, develops position papers, and sees that NSC products are drafted, debated, and staffed. The NSA's West Wing office in the White House is usually in proximity to the president's Oval Office. Most NSAs have been very close to the presidents they have served.

The NSC staff includes the deputy NSA, senior directors, and directors, most of whom are career members of the agencies of the federal government seconded to work at the NSC. These include serving military officers, Foreign Service officers (from the Department of State), CIA officers, and FBI agents, among others. A few come from outside the permanent government such as Dr. Peter Feaver from the Duke University's Political Science Department who served on the NSC staff under President George W. Bush.

Although each president since Harry Truman has organized and used—or not used—his NSC as he saw fit, the current organization took shape during the presidency of George H. W. Bush and his NSA, Brent Scowcroft.[2] He organized the NSC around a series of committees. At the apex of the system is the NSC itself, presided over by the president as described in the legislation. Below the NSC is the Principals Committee (PC), which is the NSC minus the president and vice president. The PC is chaired by the NSA and includes, as full voting members, the statutory advisors to the NSC—the CJCS and the DNI—well as those others that the president has determined he wants as members of his NSC. Below the PC is the Deputies Committee (DC) chaired by the Deputy NSA and made up of the deputies of the members of the PC. Deputies can substitute for principals in the PC if a principal is unable to attend. Similarly, a more junior member of a department like the undersecretary of defense for policy, the undersecretary of state for political affairs, or the J-3 of the Joint Staff (a lieutenant general or vice admiral) may substitute for a Deputy in the DC. Both the PC and DC have functioned under these names since 1989.

Below the DC are a number of interagency committees or working groups. The names and numbers have varied from presidency to presidency with both Presidents Bush calling them Policy Coordinating Committees (PCC), while President Clinton called them Interagency Working Groups (IWG) and President Obama has labeled them Interagency Policy Committees (IPC). Regardless of name, they have been organized both functionally and regionally. A functional example is terrorism, while a regional example is Europe. Functional committees/working groups are chaired by senior directors on the NSC staff, while regional ones are chaired by the appropriate regional assistant secretary of state. Representation at this level is more fluid than at the higher levels, with representatives of various agencies ranging from the assistant secretary level to civil servants of the GS-15 rank and military representatives ranging from general/flag officers to colonels/captains (USN).[3] In general, the subordinate committees/groups are made up of senior professionals from the relevant departments and agencies of the governmental national security community.

DEPARTMENT OF STATE

The senior department of the federal government is the Department of State. It is headed by the secretary, who is the president's principal advisor on foreign affairs. The secretary of state heads a department that is made up of multiple bureaus in Washington and nearly 200 embassies along with many more consulates and diplomatic posts abroad. The professionals in the Department of State are mainly Foreign Service officers (FSOs) (commissioned officers in federal service) as well as a large number of civil service personnel in many of the Washington DC bureaus. For example, a number of senior positions in the Department of State's Bureau of Intelligence and Research are held by civil servants and not FSOs.

Several interesting anomalies exist in American embassies and diplomatic posts. Among these are that a large number of the personnel assigned to a post are not employees of the State Department but rather of departments like Commerce, Justice, and Defense as well as agencies like the CIA. Even stranger is the fact that the head of all American embassies, the ambassador, does not work for the Department of State but rather is the personal representative of the president of the United States. Although most recent American ambassadors are career FSOs, they are required to resign from the Foreign Service to accept an ambassadorial appointment. (They are reinstated when they return to a non-ambassadorial appointment with pay, allowances, and time served as if they had never left.)[4]

Since the presidency of John F. Kennedy the fact that an American ambassador is the personal representative of the president and is in charge of all official U.S. government personnel in the country to which he is accredited has been codified in the ambassador's letter of appointment. This includes all civilian and military personnel and does not exclude members of the CIA station. There are only two exceptions to this command relationship. The first are those CIA personnel in country under nonofficial cover (e.g., posing as business people or third-country nationals). The other exception is when a major U.S. military operation is ongoing in the country and then it is not entirely clear as to who is in charge—the ambassador or the military commander or both for their own operations.[5] We will return to this situation in later chapters as we consider the issues raised in the case studies.

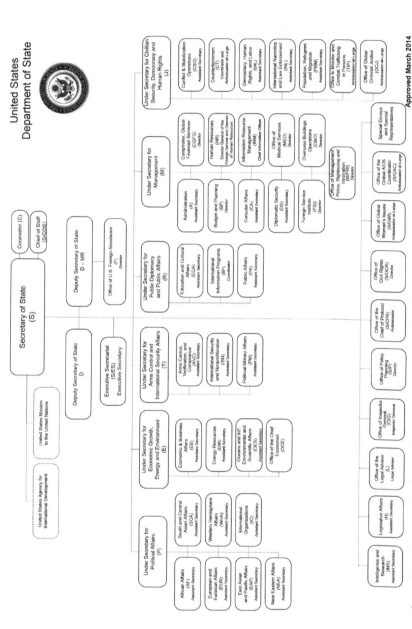

United States Department of State. http://www.state.gov/r/pa/ei/rls/dos/99494.htm

Figure 3.1   Department of State.

USAID

The U.S. Agency for International Development (USAID), while subordinate to the secretary of state, is not actually part of the Department of State. The USAID mission in a host country is subordinate to the ambassador, and its director is a member of the ambassador's Country Team (the senior member of each agency represented in the embassy as well as key State Department personnel in the embassy). USAID's purpose in those countries where it is assigned is to administer American foreign assistance appropriated under the Foreign Assistance Act (of 1961 as amended) and other legislation for which USAID has been given responsibility. Over the last 50 years USAID has gone from directly administering most aid to supervising contracts mainly with nonprofit NGOs (such as World Vision).

PEACE CORPS

The Peace Corps is not usually considered a part of the national security structure especially because it was insulated by law from any relationship with the Intelligence Community. Moreover, the Peace Corps' relationship with the ambassador and his Country Team is, at best, arm's length. That said, the Peace Corps provides critical national security capabilities as a people-to-people development agency. Its relationship to national security, while indirect, is very real and can be seen in its impact on local people's views of America and Americans. It can also be seen in some of the tangible benefits of its development work. For example, in the 1960s in Peru, a Peace Corps project brought locally written newspapers to many villages and towns in the northern part of the country.[6]

DEPARTMENT OF DEFENSE

The Department of Defense (DOD) is the largest single department in terms of personnel in the U.S. government with 3,017,414 military and civilian employees as of July 2010. While the numbers vary over time and with mission and budgetary requirements, the DOD tends to hover around three million. Of these 1.4 million are active duty, 465,000 in the National Guard, 380,000 in the selected reserve, and 752,000 are civilians.[7] These personnel are organized into three military departments (the departments of the army, navy, and air force) and four services (army, navy, marines, and air force). The navy department and its secretary own both the navy and the marines. Each military department is headed by a civilian secretary who is subordinate to the civilian secretary of defense. Each service is headed by a four-star chief, who also serves as a member of the Joint Chiefs of Staff. The army and air force are headed by chiefs of staff, while the head of the navy is the chief of naval operations and the head of the Marine Corps is the commandant.

The senior uniformed member of the military is the chairman of the Joint Chiefs of Staff (CJCS), whose deputy is the vice chairman (VCJCS) who must be from a different service than the chairman. Both are appointed by the president and confirmed by the Senate for two-year terms that can be renewed for one additional term. The service chiefs are appointed by the president and confirmed by the Senate for four-year terms. In 2012, the chief of the National Guard Bureau became a member of the JCS. Collectively, these seven generals and admirals make up the Joint Chiefs of Staff. Any or all of them can be removed by the secretary of defense during their term of office. Although the Goldwater-Nichols Act makes the CJCS the principal military advisor to the president and the secretary of defense, the other members of the Joint Chiefs continue to be advisors and all may be called to testify before Congress. While the chiefs are expected to testify to the administration policy, they are required by law to respond with their honest, personal opinion, if requested, even if it contradicts administration policy.[8]

As can be seen from Figure 3.2, the DOD is more than the three military departments, four services, and the Office of the Secretary of Defense. It includes a large number of defense agencies, including four national-level intelligence agencies—the Defense Intelligence Agency (DIA), National Geospatial-Intelligence Agency (NGA), the National Reconnaissance Office (NRO), and the National Security Agency (NSA), all reporting to the undersecretary of defense for intelligence. DOD also houses a number of assistant secretaries, one of which was created by law (Cohen-Nunn Amendment), the office of the Assistant Secretary of Defense for Special Operations and Low Intensity Conflict, which provides similar civilian oversight to Special Operations forces as the military departments do for the services.

The various offices of the under secretaries, assistant secretaries, and their deputies form what is generally called the Office of the Secretary of Defense (OSD). The OSD is basically the civilian side of the DOD, but it is neither entirely civilian nor entirely career civil service. Although most employees are career civilian civil servants, a significant number are political appointees and some of these are in middle-grade civil service positions.[9] Most of the political appointees are people who have made their careers in the defense sector rising to ever higher offices depending on the political fortunes of their party.[10] When their party is out of office, they often work in academia or in Washington think tanks preparing for the return of their party to office.[11]

In addition to political appointments to the OSD a number of posts are filled by both military officers and civilian FSOs (detailed from the Department of State). For example, the office of the deputy assistant secretary of

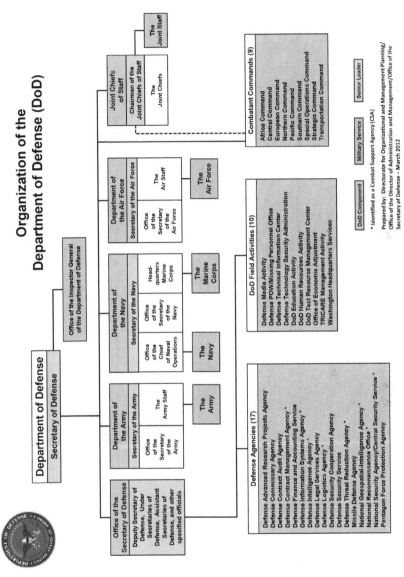

Figure 3.2 Department of Defense. http://odam.defense.gov/Portals/43/Documents/Functions/Organizational %20Portfolios/Organizations%20and%20Functions%20Guidebook/DoD_Organization_March_2012.pdf

Organization of the
Department of Defense (DoD)

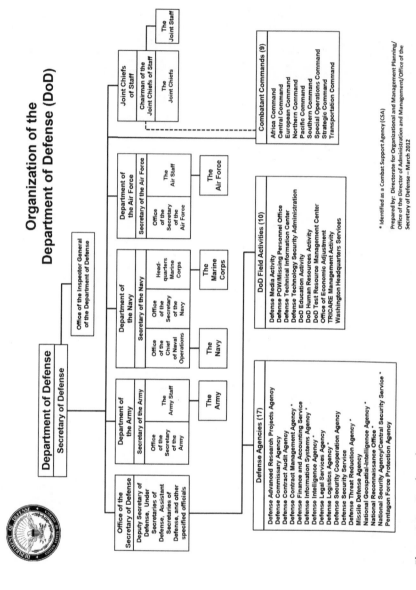

Department of Defense

Secretary of Defense

Office of the Inspector General of the Department of Defense

Office of the Secretary of Defense

Deputy Secretary of Defense, Under Secretaries of Defense, Assistant Secretaries of Defense, and other specified officials

Department of the Army

Secretary of the Army

Office of the Secretary of the Army

The Army Staff

The Army

Department of the Navy

Secretary of the Navy

Office of the Secretary of the Navy

Office of the Chief of Naval Operations

Headquarters Marine Corps

The Navy

The Marine Corps

Department of the Air Force

Secretary of the Air Force

Office of the Secretary of the Air Force

The Air Staff

The Air Force

Joint Chiefs of Staff

Chairman of the Joint Chiefs of Staff

The Joint Chiefs

The Joint Staff

Combatant Commands (9)

Africa Command
Central Command
European Command
Northern Command
Pacific Command
Southern Command
Special Operations Command
Strategic Command
Transportation Command

Defense Agencies (17)

Defense Advanced Research Projects Agency
Defense Commissary Agency
Defense Contract Audit Agency
Defense Contract Management Agency *
Defense Finance and Accounting Service
Defense Information Systems Agency *
Defense Intelligence Agency *
Defense Legal Services Agency
Defense Logistics Agency *
Defense Security Cooperation Agency
Defense Security Service
Defense Threat Reduction Agency *
Missile Defense Agency
National Geospatial-Intelligence Agency *
National Reconnaissance Office *
National Security Agency/Central Security Service *
Pentagon Force Protection Agency

DoD Field Activities (10)

Defense Media Activity
Defense POW/Missing Personnel Office
Defense Technical Information Center
Defense Technology Security Administration
DoD Education Activity
DoD Human Resources Activity
DoD Test Resource Management Center
Office of Economic Adjustment
TRICARE Management Activity
Washington Headquarters Services

* Identified as a Combat Support Agency (CSA)

Prepared by: Directorate for Organizational and Management Planning/
Office of the Director of Administration and Management/Office of the
Secretary of Defense – March 2012

Figure 3.2   Continued

defense for Western Hemisphere Affairs has a large number of its personnel drawn from the ranks of military Foreign Area Officers. The ASD-SO/LIC during the Clinton administration was Ambassador Allen Holmes, a career FSO. And, during the G. H.W. Bush administration, the DASD for policy and missions in the office of the ASD-SO/LIC was marine BG Charles Wilhelm, who would go on to command the U.S. Southern Command as a four-star general.[12] Likewise, the Joint Staff, which is the military counterpart of the OSD, is made up mainly of uniformed military personnel. However, some civilians are assigned to it. For example, Dr. Kori Schake, a well-known civilian defense expert, served on the Joint Staff under CJCS Colin Powell in the George H. W. Bush administration.[13]

There are two interwoven chains of command in the DOD: an operational chain and an administrative chain. The former runs from the president to the secretary of defense and then directly to the commanders of the nine combatant commands. The normal chain of communication, however, runs from the secretary through the CJCS, to the combatant commander, which makes the CJCS an important player despite being outside the chain of command. The administrative chain (which addresses issues of raising, maintaining, equipping, and training the forces) runs from the president to the secretary of defense to the secretaries of the military departments to the service chiefs. The CJCS, although not in this chain at all, still plays an important role, as will be discussed in Chapter 5, "Defense Planning Systems."

As shown here, the DOD is a highly complex organization with a very large manpower and equipment footprint. Its organization is also highly complex with a mix of career civilians and military along with civilian political appointees all intertwined. It is worth pointing out, however, that unlike the State Department, where a significant number of Ambassadors are purely political,[14] the majority of the DOD political appointees are people who are the defense experts of their respective political parties and have served in appointed positions within the DOD on more than one occasion.

DEPARTMENT OF HOMELAND SECURITY[15]

The Department of Homeland Security (DHS) (see Figure 3.3) was created in 2002 by the Homeland Security Act, which merged 22 separate and disparate government agencies. These agencies are found in six line operating divisions with a new seventh organization, the Transportation Security Administration (TSA). The other line agencies are Customs and Border Protection (CBP), which includes the Border Patrol, U.S. Citizenship and Immigration Services, the U.S. Coast Guard, the Federal Emergency Management Agency (FEMA), Immigration and Customs Enforcement (ICE), and the U.S. Secret Service.

U.S. DEPARTMENT OF HOMELAND SECURITY

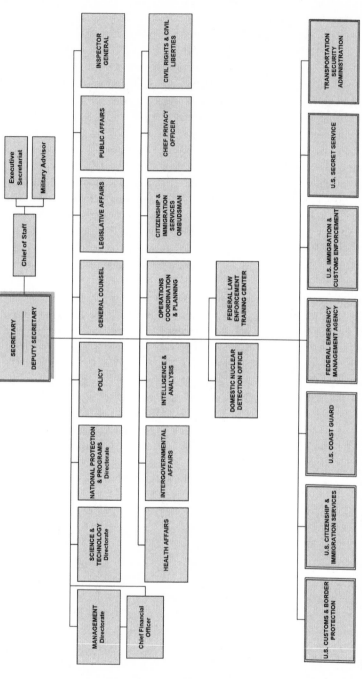

Figure 3.3 Department of Homeland Security. http://www.dhs.gov/xlibrary/assets/dhs-orgchart.pdf

There are a number of apparent anomalies within this organization. Among them we find the following:

1. The Secret Service was created in the Treasury Department to control counterfeiting, one of its two responsibilities. It later acquired presidential and other VIP protection responsibilities. Yet, control of counterfeiting falls more within the purview of Treasury than of the DHS.
2. It is not clear why the Border Patrol—an enforcement agency—is found in CBP and not in ICE.
3. Nor is it clear why the old Immigration and Naturalization Service was separated into Enforcement and Services and the latter combined with Customs Enforcement.
4. Similarly, why is Customs divided between CBP and ICE?

It is worthwhile to recall that when the secretary of defense was created in 1947 it took two years to turn the National Military Establishment into the DOD, 40 years to make the legislation fully workable, and another decade to get the bugs out. The apparent anomalies within the DHS will likely work themselves out over time. For the present, it is worth commenting on several aspects of the organization.

First, advising the secretary through the chief of staff is a military advisor. Although one might think that the military advisor would come from one of the services of the DOD, in fact, the military advisor is a coast guard rear admiral who comes from the fifth U.S. military service, which is a line component of the DHS.

Second, the DHS has an Intelligence Analysis division as one of its staff directorates reporting to the secretary. This is an analytical capability only. Such collection capabilities are found within the law enforcement elements of the line agencies and the Coast Guard. The latter, like its sister military services, has an intelligence branch that is part of the Intelligence Community.

As noted, the U.S. Coast Guard is the nation's fifth military service. Founded in 1790 as the Revenue Cutter Service (in the Treasury Department), it grew by accretion adding, among others, the Lifeboat Service. The Coast Guard has had a peripatetic home life moving from Treasury to the Department of Transportation, to the DHS with wartime sojourns in the Department of the Navy. (In time of declared war, the Coast Guard becomes a part of the navy.) However, the Coast Guard is not only a military service, it is also a federal law enforcement agency with powers of arrest. This is in contrast to the army and air force, which are prohibited by law from law enforcement and the navy and marines, which are constrained by regulation.[16] One of the remarkable success stories of interagency coordination in the last two decades is that of Joint Interagency Task Force—South (JIATF-South). This organization, based in Key West, Florida, is subordinate to the Commander of USSOUTHCOM (a DOD command) but is commanded by a U.S. Coast Guard rear admiral as its director. JIATF-South comprises U.S. Navy ships, Coast Guard cutters and aircraft, Drug Enforcement Administration (DEA) agents, ICE agents, and army special mission personnel, along with any other service or agency needed.[17] Its mission is the interdiction of drugs and other contraband coming into the United States by sea from Latin America and the Caribbean.

DEPARTMENT OF JUSTICE

The U.S. Department of Justice (DOJ) plays a major role in both domestic law enforcement and national security matters. The chart reproduced here (see Figure 3.4) is interactive on the DOJ website, where brief explanations of each of its components can be found. The principal parts of the DOJ focused on national security issues are the National Security Division, and the four DOJ law enforcement agencies—FBI, DEA, ATF, and the U.S. Marshals Service. Because of its prominence and central role, the FBI will be treated separately later.

The National Security Division was created out of the Criminal Division after the terrorist attacks of September 11, 2001. It coordinates both intelligence and operations that affect national security within the DOJ.

The Drug Enforcement Administration (DEA) is the principal law enforcement agency concerned with the control and interdiction of illicit drugs. The DEA operates both within the United States and overseas based out of American embassies, where the DEA representative is called the narcotics attaché. During the 1980s, for example, the DEA maintained a regional office for Latin America in Panama. From there it mounted a major cocaine interdiction operation in Bolivia called Operation Blast Furnace in cooperation with Bolivian Mobile Rural Police and the U.S. Southern Command's 193rd Infantry Brigade. The DEA also operates a major drug intelligence center called EPIC in El Paso, Texas.

The Bureau of Alcohol, Tobacco, Firearms, and Explosives (ATF) is responsible for law enforcement in those areas. As a national security law enforcement agency its focus is on the illegal possession, transport, and use of firearms and explosives. It also enforces laws relating to the legal possession, transport, and use of those items. In recent years, the ATF has come under significant criticism from Congress for its involvement in schemes to stop illegal arms trafficking to Mexican drug cartels involving allowing weapons to "walk." The particular case was known as Operation Fast and Furious. In 2013 Congress finally confirmed a director of the ATF for the first time in

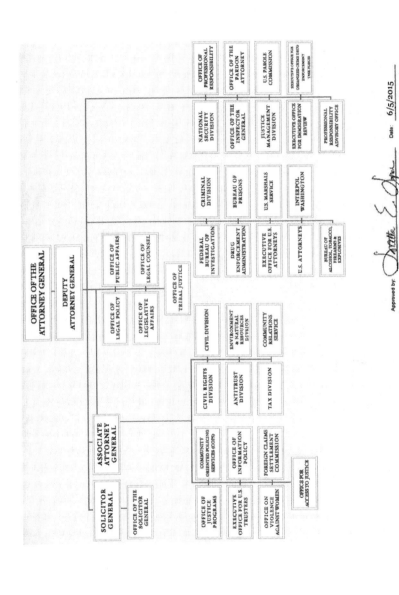

Figure 3.4   Department of Justice. http://www.justice.gov/agencies/chart

several years. However, prior to 2006, the director was not subject to Senate confirmation.

The U.S. Marshals Service is a federal law enforcement agency that can enforce any and all federal laws. However, it is primarily responsible for the security of the federal courts and the transport of federal prisoners to and from prison or anyplace such as to or from a foreign jurisdiction.

FBI

The Federal Bureau of Investigation (FBI) is the premier U.S. law enforcement agency. Located within the Department of Justice, its director, who serves a ten-year term of office nominated by the president and confirmed by the Senate, is subordinate to the attorney general, a member of the president's Cabinet. The FBI is both a law enforcement agency and an intelligence agency. Thus, its director also reports to the Director of National Intelligence. Its current organization is shown in Figure 3.5.

Established in 1908, the FBI came to prominence under its longtime Director, J. Edgar Hoover. In the 1930s the bureau focused on bank-robbing gangsters. During World War II it got into the intelligence business and was in charge of all counterintelligence inside the United States. It was also responsible for offensive (foreign) intelligence in the Western Hemisphere, with a focus on Latin America. During the Cold War the FBI targeted Soviet espionage within the United States, while beginning in the 1960s it began to emphasize civil rights investigations.

Prior to September 11, 2001, as identified by the 9/11 Commission, the FBI had erected an impenetrable wall between its intelligence operations and its criminal investigations. Subsequent to the terror attacks of that date the FBI reorganized, created the National Security Division, and began sharing information between its intelligence and criminal investigations sides.

The FBI, outside of its Washington DC headquarters, is organized in regional Field Offices, each headed by a Special Agent in Charge (SAC). The FBI also provides a legal attaché (legat) at many, if not most, American embassies outside the United States. The legat office provides liaison with host nation police and, to a lesser extent, intelligence services.

The FBI ranks its current priorities as follows:

National Security Priorities

1. Terrorism
2. Counterintelligence
3. Cyber crime

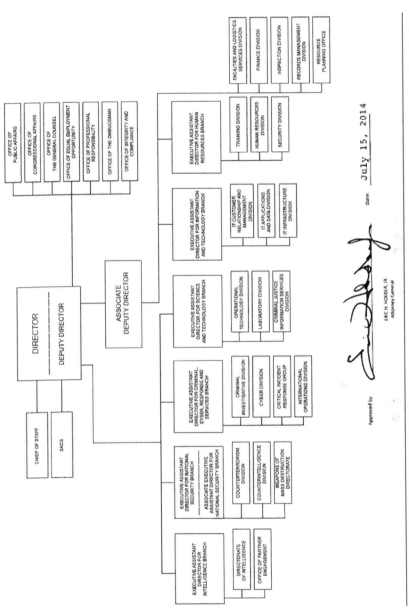

Figure 3.5 Federal Bureau of Investigation. http://www.fbi.gov/contact-us/fbi-headquarters/org_chart/organizational_chart

Criminal Priorities

4. Public corruption
5. Civil rights
6. Organized crime
7. White-collar crime
8. Violent crime and major thefts[18]

What is interesting about this prioritization is that it ranks the FBI's intelligence function above its law enforcement function. This also makes for confusion between the two roles. That confusion is precisely what the pre-9/11 wall of separation had been established to avoid. Thus the question is open whether the bureau has gone too far in the other direction.[19]

DEPARTMENT OF TREASURY

Treasury is the second-oldest department of the U.S. government, having been established in the administration of George Washington (see Figure 3.6). Its first secretary was Alexander Hamilton, and it was always one of the most important of departments. Prior to the attacks of September 11, 2001, Treasury had a limited role in international matters. After the attacks, it added an entire office—Terrorism and Financial Intelligence—to deal with those threats.

Treasury has always focused on the administration of international economic sanctions. This is normally handled by the Office of International Affairs. During the Panama crisis of 1987–1990 Treasury administered a very strong set of unilateral sanctions. Currently, Treasury administers and coordinates American participation in U.N. sanctions against Iran as well as unilateral U.S. sanctions. Most of these have been removed or relaxed by the 2015 nuclear agreement with Iran.

OFFICE OF THE DIRECTOR OF NATIONAL INTELLIGENCE (DNI)

The Director of National Intelligence was created in 2004 by the Intelligence Reform and Terrorism Prevention Act. The DNI took from the old DCI the management of the 16-member Intelligence Community (IC). As part of the Office of the DNI (ODNI) (see Figure 3.7), a number of centers were established to address cross-community functional areas.

The functional areas, as is most of ODNI, are staffed with personnel detailed from the agencies within the IC. The first, and oldest of these

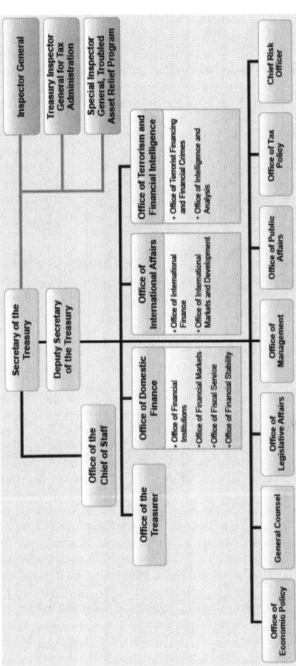

Figure 3.6 Department of Treasury. http://www.treasury.gov/about/organizational-structure/PublishingImages/organizational-chart.jpg

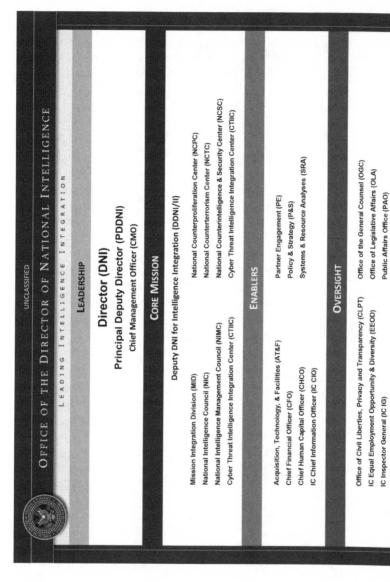

Figure 3.7 Office of the Director of National Intelligence. http://www.dni.gov/files/documents/ODNI%20 Org%20Chart.pdf

agencies, is the National Intelligence Council (NIC), which is staffed by the senior intelligence analysts of the IC, known as National Intelligence Officers (NIOs). The NIC is responsible for producing National Intelligence Estimates on a regular basis and special estimates as needed.

The National Counterterrorism Center was established as a result of the September 11, 2001, attacks and serves to provide early warning for potential acts of terrorism. The National Counterproliferation Center focuses on addressing the proliferation of nuclear, biological, chemical, and radiological weapons. Like most of the centers it is staffed by personnel detailed from other agencies of the IC as well as from the DOD and the Department of Energy.

The Office of the Counterintelligence Executive is, as its name suggests, focused on coordinating counterintelligence activities across the IC. Its current head is a senior FBI agent.

CENTRAL INTELLIGENCE AGENCY

The Central Intelligence Agency (CIA) was created by the National Security Act of 1947. Although the names of some of its organizations have changed over the years, the basic organization remains the same. The CIA is organized into a number of directorates and divisions (see Figure 3.8). The Directorate of Intelligence and Analysis provides the agency's analytical capability. Its best known, unclassified product is *The World Factbook*, available to all on the internet. What was once known as the Directorate of Plans, then Operations, is now the National Clandestine Service. It is responsible for covert intelligence collection and, by virtue of a single sentence in the National Security Act, covert political action. A relatively small element within the National Clandestine Service is the Special Activities Division, which provides the agency's paramilitary capability. The last directorate of major interest is Science and Technology, which provides the agency with its "James Bond"-type gadgetry.

CONCLUSION

This chapter has, very briefly, addressed the major organizations that make up the U.S. national security policy community. Almost all are directly represented on the NSC either by statute or by invitation from the president. All represent capabilities that can be used by the president to achieve his foreign policy and national security goals. They are all enabled and constrained by the legislation that created them, and they are all limited by the capabilities

OFFICE OF THE DIRECTOR

DIRECTOR

DEPUTY DIRECTOR

EXECUTIVE DIRECTOR

DEPUTY EXECUTIVE DIRECTOR

ENTERPRISE FUNCTIONS

ASSISTANT TO THE DIRECTOR FOR FOREIGN INTELLIGENCE RELATIONS

ASSOCIATE DIRECTOR FOR MILITARY AFFAIRS

CHIEF FINANCIAL OFFICER

CORPORATE POLICY STAFF

CRITICAL MISSION ASSURANCE PROGRAM

DIRECTOR'S EXECUTIVE SUPPORT STAFF

EXECUTIVE SECRETARIAT

MEASURES OF EFFECTIVENESS OFFICE

OFFICE OF CONGRESSIONAL AFFAIRS

OFFICE OF THE GENERAL COUNSEL

OFFICE OF THE INSPECTOR GENERAL

OFFICE OF PUBLIC AFFAIRS

PROCUREMENT EXECUTIVE

STRATEGY AND CORPORATE GOVERNANCE

TALENT CENTER OF EXCELLENCE

CENTER FOR THE STUDY OF INTELLIGENCE

DIVERSITY AND INCLUSION OFFICE

ENGAGEMENT AND INNOVATION STAFF

LEARNING ENTERPRISE OFFICE

TALENT DEVELOPMENT OFFICE

TALENT MANAGEMENT OFFICE

DIRECTORATES

ANALYSIS

OFFICE OF ADVANCED ANALYTICS

OFFICE OF ANALYTIC PRODUCTION AND DISSEMINATION

OFFICE OF RESOURCES AND SUPPORT

OFFICE OF STRATEGIC PROGRAMS

DIGITAL INNOVATION

AGENCY DATA OFFICE

CENTER FOR CYBER INTELLIGENCE

INFORMATION TECHNOLOGY ENTERPRISE

OPEN SOURCE ENTERPRISE

TALENT OFFICE

OPERATIONS

HUMAN RESOURCES STAFF

INTELLIGENCE AND FOREIGN AFFAIRS

OPERATIONS AND RESOURCE MANAGEMENT STAFF

POLICY COORDINATION STAFF

SUPPORT RESOURCE STAFF

SCIENCE & TECHNOLOGY

OFFICE OF GLOBAL ACCESS

OFFICE OF INTEGRATED MISSIONS

OFFICE OF MISSION RESOURCES

OFFICE OF SPACE RECONNAISSANCE

OFFICE OF SPECIAL ACTIVITIES

OFFICE OF TECHNICAL COLLECTION

OFFICE OF TECHNICAL INTELLIGENCE OFFICER DEVELOPMENT

OFFICE OF TECHNICAL READINESS

OFFICE OF TECHNICAL SERVICE

SUPPORT

CENTER FOR TALENT MANAGEMENT

OFFICE OF CORPORATE BUSINESSES

OFFICE OF FACILITIES AND MISSION DELIVERY

OFFICE OF GLOBAL SERVICES

OFFICE OF INNOVATION AND INTEGRATION

OFFICE OF MEDICAL SERVICES

OFFICE OF PERSONNEL RESOURCES

OFFICE OF SECURITY

RESOURCE MANAGEMENT GROUP

MISSION CENTERS

AFRICA

COUNTERINTELLIGENCE

COUNTERTERRORISM

EAST ASIA AND PACIFIC

EUROPE AND EURASIA

GLOBAL ISSUES

NEAR EAST

SOUTH AND CENTRAL ASIA

WEAPONS AND COUNTERPROLIFERATION

WESTERN HEMISPHERE

Last updated on 09 October 2015

Figure 3.8 Central Intelligence Agency. https://www.cia.gov/about-cia/leadership/ciaorgchart.jpg/image.jpg

inherent in their bureaucratic structure. One further limitation is, of course, the degree to which they are resourced by Congress. A recent example is found in the cuts made by Congress to the programs the State Department planned for the stabilization of Iraq after the withdrawal of all American troops. Budget cutbacks made numerous programs planned by the State Department simply unworkable.[20]

NOTES

1. In 1947 the act named the director of Central Intelligence and the collective body of the Joint Chiefs of Staff (JCS) as statutory advisors. The CJCS became the sole military advisor to the NSC with the passage of the Goldwater-Nichols Act in 1986, while the DNI replaced the DCI in 2006 with the passage of the IRTPA.

2. Lt. General Brent Scowcroft, USAF, had served as deputy NSA under Henry Kissinger and then as NSA during the Richard Nixon and Gerald Ford presidencies before President Bush tapped him to reprise the role.

3. General/flag officers have from one to four stars, while colonels/captains are in the pay grade of O-6.

4. This discussion of ambassadorial appointments draws from a series of lectures given by Ambassador David Passage to the U.S. Army Command and General Staff College during the 1990s. It should also be noted that under President Obama the average number of ambassadors who come from the Foreign Service has been reduced to only a little over 60%.

5. This odd situation could be easily rectified if the president would simply designate one of the two to be in charge. However, I know of no situation where any president of the United States has explicitly said to the military commander and the ambassador that one is in charge and the other works for the person designated.

6. Field Notes 1967. While doing my doctoral research I collaborated with the Regional Peace Corps representative and a number of volunteers to get support for the establishment of a newspaper in the village where I was working.

7. www.globalsecurity.org/military/agency/end-strength.htm. Data as of July 2010. Accessed July 22, 2013.

8. This happened in congressional testimony during the Clinton administration and was televised at the time. I watched this testimony on video tape at the Center for Hemispheric Defense Studies in Washington, DC.

9. I worked with a young man who entered the DOD as a GS-13 Schedule C political appointment. He left the Pentagon as a GS-15 regular civil service appointee.

10. See James Mann, *Rise of the Vulcans*. New York: 2004, Penguin.

11. During the Clinton administration, I did a project for the principal deputy assistant secretary of defense for strategy, Michelle Flournoy. During the George W. Bush administration, Ms. Flournoy worked in the Institute for National Strategic Studies at the National Defense University, the Washington think tank, CSIS, and was a cofounder of the Center for a New American Security before returning to government with President Obama as undersecretary of defense for policy.

12. I first met General Wilhelm when he was DASD and saw him many times when he regularly visited the Center for Hemispheric Defense Studies when he commanded SOUTHCOM.

13. Personal communication from Kimbra Fishel, a student of Dr. Schake at the University of Maryland.

14. See the July 2013 nomination of Ms. Caroline Kennedy to be ambassador to Japan.

15. See www.dhs.gov.

16. The 1878 Posse Comitatus Act prohibited the army from enforcing federal law within the states of the United States. Its passage was part of the settlement ending Reconstruction after the Civil War. That it did not apply to the navy and marine corps is due to the fact that neither was engaged in the occupation of the former states of the Confederacy. Posse Comitatus applies to the USAF because that service was created out of the U.S. Army. It was applied to the navy and marine corps by regulation at a later date.

17. See John T. Fishel, "The Interagency Arena at the Operational Level: The Cases Now Known as Stability Operations," Chapter 10, in Gabriel A. Marcella (ed.), *Affairs of State: The Interagency and National Security*. Carlisle, PA: 2008, Strategic Studies Institute. 409–446.

18. www.fbi.gov/about-us/investigate/What (accessed September 17, 2013). FBI. gov is also the major source for this entire section.

19. That question was recently raised in a report by the American Civil Liberties Union; see https://www.aclu.org/national-security/aclu-report-documents-fbi abuse-911 (accessed October 31, 2016).

20. Jeff Gerth and Joby Warrick, "Promises Unfulfilled: How a State Department Plan to Stabilize Iraq Broke Apart." *The Washington Post*. August 16, 2016.

Chapter 4

The National Security Council Process

As stated in Chapter 3, the National Security Council (NSC) was established by the National Security Act of 1947, something President Harry Truman was none too happy about. Over time, however, he found it sufficiently useful that he did not try to get rid of it. How the NSC evolved over time, how it is expected to operate compared to how it does operate, and what products it produces is the subject of this chapter.

BACKGROUND AND THE EARLY NSC

The NSC was a product of the World War II experience and especially the impact of the death of Franklin Delano Roosevelt. FDR may have been an innovator in many ways, but in how he dealt with his vice presidents he was extremely traditional. His VP for his first two terms, John Nance, Garner was quoted as saying that the vice presidency "wasn't worth a bucket of warm piss."[1] FDR's other two VPs, Henry Wallace and Harry S. Truman, were likewise kept in the dark. This was true despite a world war and, during the abbreviated fourth term, FDR's rapidly deteriorating health.

On April 12, 1945, when FDR died in Warm Springs, Georgia, the newly installed president Truman was not aware of the existence of the Manhattan Project to build a nuclear bomb. He had never been briefed. Just over three months later, a nuclear device was successfully exploded over the New Mexico desert. This, of course, was simply the most egregious omission of Truman's tenure as vice president; there were many more, including the outcomes of the Yalta Conference with Churchill and Stalin about the shape of postwar Europe. Yet, almost inexplicably, Congress established the NSC with the president, secretary of state, the newly created secretary of defense, and the service secretaries as statutory members. Advisors, according to the National Security Act, were the newly created director of Central Intelligence and the collective Joint Chiefs of Staff. Finally, the law gave the body a small staff under an executive secretary. The vice president was notably omitted. Perhaps, that was due to the fact that there was no vice president at the time since Truman had succeeded to the presidency on the death of FDR. In any case, by 1949 President Truman had decided that the NSC was useful to him and he rectified that when he asked Congress to update the National Security Act by removing the service secretaries from the NSC, adding the vice president, and creating the Department of Defense.[2]

THE EVOLUTION OF THE TRUMAN NSC AND THE DEVELOPMENT OF NSC-68

The concept of the NSC had, however, not appeared out of thin air. As Joseph M. Jones recounts in his superb memoir, "the Secretaries of State, War, and Navy had established the habit of meeting informally at a fixed time each week to discuss problems."[3] On some occasions, they were joined by the military service chiefs.[4] Thus, there were definitely precedents for what became the NSC prior to the passage of the National Security Act. Moreover, these precedents functioned during the crises of 1946 and 1947 with respect to Turkey, Greece, and Western Europe resulting in the Truman Doctrine and the Marshall Plan.[5]

The deepening Cold War prompted the Truman administration to consider developing a long-term strategy for dealing with the Soviet Union. This resulted in a number of NSC papers, the most important of which was NSC-68 issued in 1950.[6] NSC-68 developed out of a series of documents that began with George Kennan's famous "Long Telegram" from Moscow in 1946 where he was serving as U.S. chargé d'affaires. In it, Kennan outlined the nature of the Soviet threat and the notion of a policy of containment. This he later elaborated in his "Mr. X" article in *Foreign Affairs* in 1947. Kennan went on to be the first chief of the State Department Policy Planning Staff Undersecretary of State GEN George C. Marshall. Kennan was replaced by his deputy, friend, and rival, Paul H. Nitze.

The foreign and defense policy intellectual heart of the Truman administration in the late 1940s was in the State Department and, especially, its Policy Planning Staff. Thus, it is not surprising that when President Truman called for a new, long-range, national strategy he turned to that organization to draft it. Paul Nitze became the principal author of NSC-68 under Secretary of State Dean Acheson. What Nitze and his team drafted was a classic and relatively complete national security strategy (NSS).

After discussing the nature of the Soviet threat and the differences between the U.S. democratic system and the "Soviet design," NSC-68 laid out the ends or goals of the American strategy, the ways or methods, and the means or resources needed to carry it out.[7] Most of the arguments about the strategy focused on resources. Those resources were mainly a major buildup of American military forces. According to Nitze, "The report contained no budget figures, although we made no attempt to disguise our belief that our recommendations would be costly. The lack of figures came at the direction of Acheson, who decided that the Government should first decide the policy it ought to follow and then deal separately with implementation."[8]

NSC-68 was delivered to the president on April 7, 1950. President Truman did not accept NSC-68 as drafted calling for much greater specificity on costs. This was provided in NSC-68/1 of September 21, 1950.[9] Three other iterations of the strategy followed on September 30, and December 8 and 16, all refining the resources. Although much of the opposition to NSC-68 due to its costs dissipated with North Korean attack on South Korea on June 25, 1950, resourcing had remained an issue because it was crucial to the success of the strategy. It is worth noting here that NSC-68 was classified TOP SECRET and remained classified until 1975; nevertheless, much of it was made known by presidential proclamation and various articles over the years. NSC-68 is the first of a long line of strategic products of the NSC system, products that have taken many different names over the years.

THE EISENHOWER NSC

On January 20, 1953, Dwight David Eisenhower was inaugurated as president of the United States. General of the army, Eisenhower was one of only a handful of American military officers ever to attain the rank of five stars. As the architect of the World War II victory in Europe and the first Supreme Allied Commander in Europe under the new NATO alliance, "Ike" was a consummate believer in staff work. As his mentor GEN Marshall had done when he took over the State Department and created the Policy Planning Staff, Ike sought to vitalize the NSC to serve him as his military staffs had done in the past. One of the president's first actions was to create the position of Special Assistant to the President for National Security Affairs (SAPNSA) to act as the chief of staff. Ike named Robert Cutler, a banker who had served Secretary of War Henry Stimson during World War II, to the post.[10]

Eisenhower established two major committees of the NSC, "the NSC Planning Board, which prepared studies, policy recommendations, and basic drafts for NSC coordination, and the Operations Coordinating Board, which was the coordinating and integrating arm for all aspects of the implementation of national security policy."[11] Like the Truman NSC, the Eisenhower NSC produced a series of what were called NSC papers. Some were studies while others directed action. Ike also changed his SAPNSA three times with Cutler replaced by Dillon Anderson after two years, then returning for an additional six months after a year and a half absence. Cutler was then replaced by Gordon Gray, who served for the remainder of Ike's term.

President Eisenhower began the establishment of the modern NSC by viewing it as a military staff, creating its committee structure, and establishing the position of the National Security Advisor (NSA). While each of these structures, roles, and procedures would evolve over time, all subsequent NSCs would derive from these developments in the early 1950s. Most important was the shift from the locus of power and creativity during the Truman administration in the State Department and its Policy Planning Staff, to the NSC and its committees.

THE NSC UNDER JFK AND LBJ

John F. Kennedy assumed the presidency determined to control the foreign and national security process in his own way. He, and his team, believed the NSC system that Eisenhower bequeathed was both too large and too cumbersome to be useful. Thus, the staff size was reduced dramatically from 71 to 48.[12] Formal NSC staff committees were abolished and replaced by ad hoc working groups. The most well known of these was the ExComm (Executive Committee of the NSC) established during the Cuban Missile Crisis and most often chaired by President Kennedy's brother, Robert, the attorney general of the United States. One key outsider on the ExComm was former secretary of state Dean Acheson. Another important change was the introduction of outside experts to the NSC staff.[13] Kennedy also increased the importance of the NSA, in part by combining the roles of the Eisenhower SAPNSA and the staff director as well as with his choice of Harvard dean, McGeorge Bundy, for the job.[14] Bundy used the position to reorient the NSC staff to provide independent advice to the president through the APNSA. (The "S" for Special was dropped.) This resulted in changing the voluminous NSC papers previously issued to the newly created National Security Action Memoranda (NSAM), which were both briefer and, as the name implies, more action oriented.[15]

When Lyndon Johnson succeeded to the presidency on JFK's assassination, he generally maintained the Kennedy NSC system. Soon, however, he made changes that added formal structure creating a Senior Interdepartmental Group (SIG) and a number of subordinate Interdepartmental Regional Groups (IRGs) each chaired by the appropriate assistant secretary of state.[16]

Despite this new formal structure, President Johnson did not make much use of it and rarely held formal NSC meetings. Rather, he held a regular Tuesday Lunch with his NSA (initially Bundy and later, Walt W. Rostow, another academic who had previously served as Bundy's deputy), secretaries of state and defense, the director of Central Intelligence, and the chairman of the Joint Chiefs of Staff (CJCS). Conspicuously absent from this rump NSC was the vice president, a statutory member of the NSC.

AN EVALUATION OF THE EARLY YEARS OF THE NSC

Clearly, the first four presidents to use the NSC established by the National Security Act chose to use them very differently. For Truman, the NSC was dominated by his State Department led by two very strong secretaries of state, George Marshall and Dean Acheson both of who were supported in the critical Policy Planning Staff by extraordinary diplomats and public servants, George Kennan (father of the Containment policy) and Paul Nitze (drafter of NSC-68). President Eisenhower built the NSC staff and established the position of NSA but the role of the NSC was that of a military staff, the coordination of the activities of the line departments and organizations. While Kennedy dismantled the formal structures of the Eisenhower NSC and halved the size of the staff, he greatly expanded the role of the APNSA and made the NSC staff an advisory body independent of the cabinet departments. The staff served the interests of the president.

THE OPERATIONAL NSC UNDER KISSINGER

The biggest change in the role of the NSC came during the presidency of Richard Nixon and continued through that of Gerald Ford, his successor. The key player in both presidencies was the NSA, Henry Kissinger, who served for a time as both NSA and secretary of state. Even after he gave up the NSA post, Kissinger dominated national security decision making, although now he was conducting it from the State Department. Still, Kissinger acted as he had while merely the NSA.

A key part of the role of the NSC was that it functioned to serve the needs of President Nixon. Nixon, like Kennedy, intended to dominate foreign and defense policy, but as a more formal and much less gregarious individual, Nixon wanted the NSC to present him with a number of real options or choices of policy. This clearly suited Kissinger's style since he was the one who would present the written options to the president. Nixon would then choose, marking an X in the appropriate box on the decision paper, often after discussing the options with Kissinger. The products of the Kissinger-led NSC system were called National Security Decision Memoranda (NSDM) in contrast to the Kennedy–Johnson NSAM, reflecting Nixon's focus on the decision as opposed to Kennedy's on action.[17]

Kissinger constructed Nixon's NSC with himself at the very center. The NSC proper consisted of the statutory members plus the CJCS and the NSA (Kissinger), with the DCI attending when intelligence matters were the focus.[18] Staff support works (essentially NSC studies) were the product of six interdepartmental committees, similar to LBJ's IRGs.[19] The heart of the NSC was a set of committees, each chaired by Kissinger:

- Washington Special Action Group: headed by Kissinger and designed to handle contingency planning and crises.
- NSC Intelligence Committee: chaired by Kissinger and responsible for providing guidance for national intelligence needs and continuing evaluations of intelligence products.
- Defense Program Review Committee: chaired by Kissinger and designed to achieve greater integration of defense and domestic considerations in the allocation of natural resources. This committee was intended to allow the president, through the NSC, to gain greater control over the defense budget and its implications and policy requirements. As a result of opposition by Defense Secretary Melvin Laird, its role was, however, significantly circumscribed.
- Senior Policy Review Group: chaired by Kissinger, this group directed and reviewed policy studies and also served as a top-level deliberative body.[20]

This structure not only made Kissinger the center of almost all national security decision making but it also put him in the position to influence President Nixon on most, if not all, critical foreign and defense policy decisions and actions. There is no indication that any of this changed at all when Kissinger became secretary of state at the same time as he was NSA. When he left the NSA post under President Ford, he still retained most of his primacy due to the perception of his successes during the Nixon administration and the fact that his successor was his former deputy, USAF Lt. Gen. Brent Scowcroft.

Not only did Kissinger take center stage in the making of national security and foreign policy during the Nixon–Ford years but his NSC was clearly an operational arm of the government. Kissinger undertook numerous difficult, and often secret, negotiations with or without the support of the State Department, making use of his NSC staffers for expertise and backup. Among these were the opening to China and his shuttle diplomacy during and in the aftermath of the 1973 Yom Kippur War between Israel and the Arab states.

THE CARTER INTERLUDE

When Jimmy Carter took office in 1977 he and his new NSA, Zbigniew Brzezinski, were reacting to Henry Kissinger's domination of the foreign policy and national security process. Carter took great pains to distinguish his NSC from his predecessor's, starting with giving its principal document a new name. Henceforth, the NSDM (formerly NSAM and before that NSC papers) would be called a Presidential Directive (PD). Second, Carter and Brzezinski reduced the number of NSC committees from seven to two, the Policy Review Committee (PRC) and the Special Coordinating Committee (SCC).[21] They also reduced the size of the staff and returned to a more ad hoc structure for staff committees.

The focus of the PRC was, as the name suggests, on reviewing policies that were the primary responsibility of a particular department. Thus, the PRC was chaired by a senior member from the principal agency involved, most often the State Department or the DOD. When matters dealt this intelligence the DCI chaired the PRC.[22] One critical document that spelled out the responsibilities of, and participants in, the two committees was Executive Order (EO) 12036, significant parts of which addressed intelligence matters.[23] The SCC focused on issues that cut across departments and, under EO 12036, addressed all covert intelligence operations.

While President Carter's intent was to push more responsibilities to the departments, over time this became less and less possible. In part, it was due to the development of significant conflict between Secretary of State Cyrus Vance and NSA Brzezinski. Another part was simply due to the need for control over national security policy from the president and his staff without the parochial concerns of the cabinet departments. Although there had been conflict between the NSA and the State Department before, particularly in the Nixon administration, where Nixon had tended to resolve issues in favor of Kissinger, Carter vacillated between Brzezinski and Vance, leaving a lack of clarity over policy.[24] Ultimately, Vance resigned over his disagreement with Carter's decision to authorize a rescue mission for the Iranian hostages, a mission championed by Brzezinski.

OPERATIONAL AGAIN UNDER REAGAN: DISASTER AND RECOVERY

The Reagan administration took office in January 1981 with a distinct view of how it wanted to operate national security policy, a view that was, apparently, quite different from that of its predecessor. President Reagan made this manifest when he changed the name of the PD to the National

Security Decision Directive (NSDD, pronounced Niz-did).[25] And, in an unrecognized gesture to President Carter's original intent, Reagan sought to return power to the cabinet departments. This was to be accomplished partly by making the new NSA, Richard Allen, subordinate to presidential counselor, Edwin Meese. It was further achieved by creating three Senior Interagency Groups (SIG) for foreign policy, defense, and intelligence, respectively, chaired by the deputy secretaries of state and defense, and the director of Central Intelligence (DCI). Subordinate regional and functional groups were chaired by senior officers from the appropriate cabinet department. Finally, the vice president was nominally in charge of crisis management.[26]

Contributing to the notion of devolving power to the cabinet departments was the fact of two strong personalities at the State Department and the DOD. The new secretary of state, Alexander Haig, an army general, who had served as Kissinger's deputy NSA and as Richard Nixon's final chief of staff, saw himself as "the vicar" of foreign policy, while secretary of defense, Casper Weinberger, was a close personal friend and long-term ally of the president. This made for significant conflict between the State Department and the DOD, which was not resolved when Haig resigned and was replaced by George Schultz. Needless to say, the downgrading of the NSA did not work well at all, and Allen resigned by the end of the year to be replaced by another Reagan friend and ally, William Clark, who moved over from the position of deputy secretary of state. A little over a year later, Clark became secretary of the interior and was replaced as NSA by his deputy, Robert McFarlane.[27]

As deputy NSA McFarlane had simultaneously served as special envoy to the Middle East and was deeply involved in the Lebanon peacekeeping operation of 1983 that ended with the bombing of the U.S. Marine barracks in Beirut that killed 241 marines. On his return to Washington, McFarlane was made NSA, where he initiated the "arms for hostages" deals that became known as Iran–Contra affair, run by the NSC staff. McFarlane stated that he had recommended that the weapons transfers to Iran end just prior to his resignation in early December 1985.[28]

Vice Admiral John Poindexter, McFarlane's deputy who succeeded him as NSA, however, continued the program that was run by an NSC staff director, marine Lt. Col. Oliver North. The program ended in scandal when a private cargo aircraft went down over Nicaragua with arms for the contras and a crew member was captured. His activities were traced back to North and the NSC. Thus, under Reagan, the NSC staff became operational again but not at the high policy level it had been under Kissinger. Whether this was an intentional development by two operationally oriented NSAs, a reaction to congressional opposition to the administration's support for the Nicaraguan contras, just the expansion of policy by opportunistic action on North's part, or all three is somewhat immaterial. The result was an operational NSC staff at the level of implementation and not policy.

The Iran–Contra scandal came close to bringing down the Reagan presidency. It did not do so because President Reagan owned up to a major error and took steps to clean up his NSC and White House staff. He demanded the resignation of Admiral Poindexter, replacing him with Frank Carlucci. Carlucci brought army LTG Colin Powell on board as his deputy. When Carlucci replaced Casper Weinberger as secretary of defense, Powell moved up to NSA. Both Carlucci and Powell strongly opposed an operational NSC staff and were supported by the new White House chief of staff, former Tennessee senator Howard Baker (brought in to oversee the cleanup of Iran–Contra).

Carlucci, in stabilizing the NSC, established two committees that replaced the three SIGs of the first six years of the administration. The first, the Senior Review Group, consisted of the statutory NSC principals not including the president and vice president. This was chaired by the NSA. The second, chaired by the deputy NSA, was the Policy Review Group made up of the deputies or other senior second- or third-level officials of the agencies represented on the NSC.[29]

One final change in the NSC was the requirement in the 1986 Department of Defense Reorganization Act (Goldwater-Nichols Act) to make an annual report to Congress simultaneously with the presidential budget submission on the NSS of the United States. This report was to be unclassified but it was the first time Congress had required the president to develop an annual strategy. Reagan's 1987 NSS was the first formal strategy developed by the NSC since NSC-68.

The Reagan years were tumultuous for the NSC. They did serve to drive the final nail in the coffin for cabinet department dominance of the national security policy process. In addition, the disaster of an operational NSC making policy through implementation should have been a warning to all future presidents and their national security teams.

THE BUSH–SCOWCROFT REFORMS: THEORY AND PRACTICE

Vice President George H. W. Bush was elected president in November 1988, taking office on January 20, 1989. For the NSC structure, his administration was the most consequential in history.[30] President Bush brought Brent Scowcroft, who had served as NSA under Gerald Ford, back as his NSA. Scowcroft had also served as Kissinger's deputy NSA when the latter was also serving as secretary of state. So, Scowcroft was well aware of the Nixon/Kissinger system and how it had been used operationally. He was also cognizant of how an operational NSC had been abused during the Reagan years. Moreover, he had seen just how ineffective attempts to drive national security policy from the cabinet departments had been during both the Carter and Reagan administrations. President Bush was of a like mind himself.

Thus, when the new team came in, Bush and Scowcroft considered both the errors of the past and the structure of the NSC during the final Reagan years. The two committees that Frank Carlucci had established had much to recommend them, and they became the basis for the Scowcroft reforms. These began with the creation of the Principals' Committee (PC), chaired by the NSA and made up of the principals (the heads of each cabinet department) represented on the NSC. In addition, the two statutory NSC advisors, the DCI and the CJCS, were full members of the PC. The second committee was the Deputies' Committee (DC) formally made up of the number two to each of the principals, and chaired by the deputy NSA. Although the DC was supposed to consist of deputies, they were often replaced by a third-rank member of the department in question. Nevertheless, both committees were controlled by a person outside of any department and focused on making sure that the president got complete and honest advice even when there was disagreement among the members.

Below the DC were a number of Policy Coordinating Committees (PCCs), some regional and others functional.[31] Regional PCCs usually were chaired by the State Department, while functional PCCs usually were chaired by an NSC staff senior director, although occasionally the chair might come from the cabinet department or agency most closely associated with the issue.[32]

Ideally, the system was designed to surface an issue from the field to the relevant PCC, typically coming through one or more department or agency. For example, Panama issues in 1989 came from the American Embassy, U.S. Southern Command, the Panama Canal Commission, and the CIA to the appropriate PCC. An effort would be made at this level to agree on policy for dealing with the issue. If there were areas of disagreement, the issue would be raised to the DC. If there was still disagreement, it would be raised to the PC and finally to the NSC and the president for resolution. If, however, agreement had been achieved, then only a recommendation was forwarded up, ultimately, to the president.

Some issues, however, began at the top and were addressed from the PC to the DC to the appropriate PCC; the latter would manage the implementation of the policy and/or its interagency coordination. The system was designed to make sure that the efforts of the cabinet departments and agencies were fully coordinated and that the president made policy based on complete and honest advice from the line agencies and their experts, leavened by staff expertise from within the NSC staff. Note that most of the NSC staff comes from the line agencies; however, a few members are hired from the outside to serve directly. Often these are academics, one of whom, Dr. Condoleezza Rice of Stanford University, served as a director and later senior director for the USSR under Scowcroft.

The products of the Bush–Scowcroft NSC included National Security Directives (NSD) which replaced Reagan's NSDD—an effort to both simplify and put the stamp of the new president on the central national security document. Nevertheless, the name chosen also maintained continuity between the Reagan and Bush administrations. In addition, the NSC continued to produce the annual, congressionally required NSS. This document was based on input from the line departments, but its managing editor was a senior director of the NSC staff, typically a colonel or a navy captain detailed to the NSC.[33]

Although some national security decisions during the Bush presidency deviated from the formal process described previously—President Bush did rely on an informal inner circle of advisors—the process served him well to manage his national security policy. It served so well that the general structure has been maintained by each of the succeeding presidents.

THE CLINTON NSC

The newly inaugurated Clinton administration made a number of significant changes in the NSC. Like its immediate predecessors, it changed the name of its major document from the NSD to the Presidential Decision Directive (PDD) looking back to the Carter PD. Many of Clinton's national security team were veterans of Carter's and had rather negative memories. According to James Steinberg, they liked the way the Bush NSC worked, although they disagreed with the policies.[34] As a result, Clinton and his new NSA, Anthony Lake, kept the basic NSC structure of the Principals' and Deputies' Committees. However, instead of the standing PCCs, they created a number of Interagency Working Groups (IWGs). Like the PCCs they were both regional and functional, but many of the functional IWGs were created ad hoc. Later in the administration's term, a number of even more ad hoc committees called EXCOMMs were established, especially to handle crises.[35]

Other important changes included making the secretary of the Treasury a regular member of the NSC and the PC, dual appointing members of the new National Economic Council to the NSC staff, and, in the second term establishing a second deputy NSA position. Also, in the second term Tony Lake was replaced as NSA by his deputy, Sandy Berger. Lake had been on Kissinger's staff and was an academic, while Berger was a lawyer who had served as director of Policy Planning in the State Department during the Carter administration. In addition to emphasizing economics in the NSC, both Lake and Berger greatly enhanced the role of the lawyers (the office of the

General Counsel), which had not been of any great significance in previous NSCs. Yet, the success of Clinton in institutionalizing the role of the General Counsel depended, according to Rand Beers, on "a succession of lawyers who were far more prepared to get to yes than to give you straight legal advice and tell you why you couldn't do something."[36]

The Clinton NSC was mainly an example of accretion of functions and institutionalization of structure. The PC and DC began to be set in stone. Economic issues became a formal part of the NSC process. And the need for good legal advice from within the NSC staff was finally recognized on a formal level.

BUSH 43 AND THE "RETURN" OF THE SCOWCROFT MODEL

George W. Bush's NSC was designed to replicate that of George H. W. Bush. The new NSA, Condoleezza Rice, had been mentored by Brent Scowcroft under the elder Bush and deliberately sought to model her tenure and the institution of the NSC after Scowcroft's.[37] President Bush followed the now established precedent and changed the name of his primary document to the National Security Presidential Directive (NSPD). The NSC was still built around the Principals' and Deputies' Committees. The PC remained under the chair of the NSA despite an abortive attempt by the office of the vice president to have him chair the PC.[38] The DC was chaired by the deputy NSA, Stephen Hadley. Hadley would become NSA during Bush's second term when Bush named Rice secretary of state. Rice reinstituted the PCCs, which were somewhat more formal than the IWG and EXCOMMs of the previous administration. Regional PCCs were chaired by the State Department, while functional PCCs were most often chaired by the appropriate NSC senior director. Bush added the attorney general to the NSC for relevant issues.

The NSC was developing in a relatively routine manner when the terrorist attacks of September 11, 2001, suddenly ended all routine. The early deliberations involved what was often called the War Cabinet, which was a mix of statutory and non-statutory members of the NSC, but hardly all, key staffers, and important deputies. There was also some confusion as to whether the War Cabinet was the NSC, the PC, both, or something else entirely. In any case, it worked reasonably effectively to coordinate the government response.[39] Later, however, conflict developed, particularly between Secretary of State Colin Powell and Secretary of Defense Donald Rumsfeld, conflict that could not be effectively mediated by NSA Rice. The result, according to Rice, was that the day-to-day management of national security policy that had been a key feature of the DC in both the Bush 41 and Clinton administrations had to be elevated to the PC because the deputies were not sufficiently empowered to act.[40]

The September 11 attacks also caused President Bush to name a homeland security advisor, former Pennsylvania governor Tom Ridge, and create a Homeland Security Council, parallel to the NSC. Subsequently, the Homeland Security Act established the Department of Homeland Security, whose first secretary was Tom Ridge and was invited to attend NSC meetings as well as HSC meetings. In 2004, the Intelligence Reform and Terrorism Prevention Act established the position of director of National Intelligence (DNI), who replaced the director of Central Intelligence (DCI, now downgraded to director of the CIA) as the statutory intelligence advisor to the NSC.

The Bush administration made a significant change in the documentary products produced by the NSC. Under the Goldwater-Nichols Act of 1986, the president was to issue an unclassified NSS Report to Congress in conjunction with his annual budget submission. The Reagan, Bush 41, and Clinton administrations had all made serious efforts to meet the annual requirement, although the latter two had each missed a year. George W. Bush made a conscious decision to produce only one NSS during his first term (2002) and one during his second term (2006). This was on the grounds that nothing had changed sufficiently to warrant creating a new document each year. Instead, the administration issued a number of supporting strategies: A National Strategy for Counter Terrorism in 2003 and again in 2006; a National Strategy for Cyber Security in 2003, and a National Strategy for Homeland Security in 2007. This production suggests that the president and his team made a concerted effort to meet the spirit of the requirement if not the exact letter.

The final two years of George W. Bush's presidency saw the NSC return to the way it had been intended to function. Rumsfeld had been replaced as secretary of defense, in November 2006, by Robert Gates, who was far more direct in his leadership and open in his dealings with the other NSC principals. He and Rice, who had been elevated to secretary of state for the second term, had an excellent professional working relationship as they both did with Stephen Hadley, the second-term NSA (and Rice's former deputy). This comfort level among the principals allowed the DC to do the day-to-day work of managing national security policy through the PCCs and only raising issues of significant disagreement to the level of the PC.

OBAMA'S NSC AND THE ECLIPSE OF THE CABINET DEPARTMENTS

Like its immediate predecessors the Obama administration maintained the formal NSC committee structure for the PC and DC. President Obama did, however, choose to abandon the standing PCCs at the lower level, opting instead for Interagency Policy Committees (IPC) established, ad hoc, to address specific issues as they arose. Obama also followed the new precedent and changed the name of his major document to the Presidential Policy Directive (PPD). Obama also expanded on the decision of George W. Bush to avoid the letter of the requirement for an NSS report to Congress. He submitted one NSS in 2010, another in 2015, and a single National Strategy for Counter Terrorism in 2011.

In terms of personnel, the president started out strong naming as NSC principals Hillary Rodham Clinton as his secretary of state and retaining Bob Gates at Defense. The chairman of the Joint Chiefs of Staff (CJCS) as principal military advisor to the president and statutory advisor to the NSC holds a two-year appointment that is renewable for a second two-year term. President Obama inherited Admiral Mike Mullen and then reappointed him to a second term on October 1, 2009. The other statutory advisor to the NSC is the DNI, and Obama appointed Admiral Dennis Blair, former commander of U.S. Pacific Command. But he added, as a regular attending member of the NSC his director of the CIA, Leon Panetta, immediately undercutting the authority of his DNI. Finally, the president named retired marine general Jim Jones (former commandant of the marine corps and former Supreme Allied Commander Europe) as his NSA. Jones's deputy was Tom Donilon, a lawyer who had previously served as a senior political appointee (Public Affairs and Chief of Staff) in the State Department during the Clinton administration. Among the regular attendees at NSC meetings were the White House chief of staff, the U.S. representative to the UN, and the counsel to the president.[41]

One significant functional innovation of the Obama administration was to merge the Homeland Security Council and its staff with the NSC and NSC staff. For several years the merged staff was known as the National Security Staff until 2014, when the name was changed back to NSC staff. One result was a significant increase in the total number of NSC staff personnel. The homeland security advisor, while retaining direct access to the president, became a deputy NSA reporting through the NSA.

Although the original group of principals on the NSC was strong, there were indications early on that all was not well. NSA Jones never was able to put his mark on the staff and was undercut by his deputy, who had strong connections to the political officials who regularly attended NSC and PC meetings. According to David Rothkopf, "Jim Jones was never given a chance . . . being cut off by a group of former Obama campaign members."[42] Jones resigned in 2010, replaced by Donilon, who, somewhat surprisingly, often sided with Gates, Clinton, and Panetta on substantive issues. Blair, the DNI, also resigned relatively early after a role/function/power conflict with Panetta that he lost when the president sided with the DCIA. He was replaced by James Clapper, who clearly seemed to know his place. Nevertheless, through 2010 it seemed that the cabinet and agency principals tended to get more of what they wanted out of the NSC system decisions. That seemed to change after the killing of Osama bin Laden in May 2011, followed soon after by Gates's resignation and replacement by Panetta. Other changes included David Petraeus replacing Panetta at CIA, his resignation and replacement by John Brennan coming from the NSC staff, Susan Rice replacing Donilon as NSA, and then Chuck Hagel taking over at the DOD. In 2015, Hagel was forced to resign, and was replaced by former deputy secretary of defense Ash Carter.

The turnover of personnel, coupled with the president's desire to centralize decision making in the White House, empowered the NSC staff and the political functionaries there. According to former NSAs Brzezinski and Scowcroft, the NSC staff climbed to between 300 and 350 from somewhere around 40 or 50 under Brzezinski.[43] Under Rice the staff had been around 100.[44] One consequence of both the huge increase in the NSC staff was significant micromanagement of not only policy development but also policy execution. "The decision on how many U.S. troops would remain in Afghanistan in 2015 was the subject of 14 meetings of NSC deputies, four meetings involving Cabinet secretaries and other NSC 'principals,' and two NSC sessions with the president. . . . The consequence of those meetings was to pare back the military's request by just 700 troops—from 10,500 to 9,800."[45] The tendency to micromanage had plagued both Gates and Panetta earlier in the administration, but both had resisted forcefully with Gates ordering commanders to tear out direct secure telephone lines to the White House.[46] Subsequently, the micromanagement has continued and even increased.[47] The result has been to shift responsibility for policymaking and especially implementation away from the cabinet departments into the hands of political operators in the White House, most of whom serve as regular members of the NSC and the PC.

CONCLUSION

Reviewing the development of the NSC system shows that, no matter what Congress intended, it is what the president wants it to be. That said, the NSC has proven to be useful to every president since Harry Truman.

The first major shift in the system came in the transition to the Eisenhower administration, where the center of gravity moved from the State Department's Policy Planning Staff to the NSC and its staff headed by the NSA. Over time the NSC staff developed from a military staff–like coordinating mechanism to an independent source of advice and effective presidential control of national security policy. This also created a major debate over the proper role of the NSC that persisted well into the Reagan administration.

The Kennedy, Carter, and Reagan administrations all came into office determined to restore power to the cabinet departments and shift it away from centralization in the NSC staff. Kennedy's effort suffered from both a diffident secretary of state coupled with a strong NSA and the drive of the president to run his own foreign policy. Nixon and Kissinger had no intention of allowing anyone but the president and his NSA to develop and manage national security issues and centralized all decision making in NSC committees chaired by the NSA. This really did not change under President Ford despite the fact that Kissinger was now secretary of state; he continued to operate largely as "a one-man band." Under Kissinger the NSC staff inevitably grew but still remained under 100.

Carter cut the size of the NSC staff and tried to return the driving of decisions to the cabinet departments by having the department most concerned with an issue chair the NSC committee meetings. Power shifted, however, to the committees chaired by NSC staff both as a result of conflict between Secretary of State Vance and NSA Brzezinski and the need to coordinate issues across departments.

Reagan made a truly heroic effort to "return" to "cabinet government" when he downgraded the NSA. This failure became obvious early on, but the new NSA did not dominate policy making either. Reagan's next two NSAs began to conduct tactical national security operations using the NSC staff both because of conflict between the State Department and the DOD—the secretaries were barely on speaking terms even when they agreed on the issues—and because Congress had acted to constrain the administration's actions on a major foreign policy issue limiting what could be done through normal channels. An operational NSC at the tactical level was an utter disaster, resulting in a complete overhaul of the NSC system.

Begun by NSAs Carlucci and Powell, the overhaul was completed by President George H. W. Bush and his NSA, Brent Scowcroft who created the two top-tier NSC committees that have existed ever since. The PC is made up of the regular attendees at NSC meetings—generally cabinet secretaries or principals—but chaired by the NSA, who represents the national security interests of the president. The DC is made up of the number two (or number three) to each of the principals and is chaired by the deputy NSA. This structure makes certain that departmental interests are addressed but that recommendations are fully coordinated and that the president gets unfiltered advice from the departmental experts.

Lower-tiered committees have tended to be more structured in Republican administrations than in Democratic ones, while those in Democratic administrations have tended to be created to address situations as they arise. Typically, regional committees are chaired by the State Department, while functional committees are chaired by senior directors on the NSC staff.

Over time, the NSC staff has been strengthened by the addition of outside experts, often from academia but still the majority of its members are detailed from the various government departments and agencies. While they do bring their agency experience with them, they tend to see the world from the viewpoint of the White House.[48] The NSC staff has also grown over the years from between 40 and 50 during the Carter administration to around 100 during the George W. Bush years. The Obama administration saw a major expansion to between 300 and 350 that is only partly explained by merging the Homeland Security Council with the NSC. Some of the rest is explained by the addition of political White House aides as regular NSC and PC attendees (with their staffs to the NSC staff). The rest of the expansion is seemingly explained by a desire to control all aspects of national security policy from the White House and the natural tendency for bureaucracy to expand.

One final point that largely brings us back to where this concluding section began is that how the NSC system actually works depends on people. It does not depend on structure. Structure can, and often does, make it easier to accomplish the president's purpose. But it also depends on how the principals, deputies, the NSA, and staff act to get the system to do what they want it to do. When there is conflict among these players the system does not work as well unless the conflict is effectively mediated by the NSA, or the president changes the players.

NOTES

1. Patrick Cox, "John Nance Garner on the Vice Presidency—In Search of the Proverbial Bucket." www.cah.utexas.edu. The final word in the quote is disputed, most often given as "spit."

2. Amy B. Zegaart, *Flawed by Design: The Evolution of the CIA, JCS, and NSC.* Stanford, CA: 1999, Stanford University Press. 260, Note 37.

3. Joseph M. Jones, *The Fifteen Weeks.* New York: 1995, Harcourt Brace Jovanovich. 62.

4. Ibid.

5. Jones's memoir tells the story of how all this came about. As noted, he recognized that the NSC formalized what had previously been informal (and incomplete); it still had antecedents as cited earlier.

6. NSC papers are simply one of the historical names for the products of the NSC system, all of which are technically Executive Orders (EOs). The other historical names will be identified in their proper place, but it is worth noting that those involving covert action by the intelligence community have been called "Findings" since 1974. See Alan G. Whittacker et al., *The National Security Policy Process: The National Security Council and Interagency System.* (Research Report, August 15, 2011, Annual Update). Washington, DC: Industrial College of the Armed Forces, National Defense University, U.S. Department of Defense.

7. The discussion in this paragraph and the preceding one derives from S. Nelson Drew (ed.), *NSC-68: Forging the Strategy of Containment*, (with analyses by Paul H. Nitze). Washington, DC: 1994, National Defense University Press.

8. Ibid., 13.

9. Ibid., 98–110.

10. Richard A. Best, *The National Security Council: An Organizational Assessment.* Washington, DC: 2010, Congressional Research Service. 8.

11. Ibid., 8–9. Note that these organizations mimic, to some extent, the intelligence, plans, and strategy directorates of a military staff.

12. Ibid., 10.

13. Ibid., 11.

14. Zegart, 84.

15. Best, 10.

16. Ibid., 12.

17. Whittaker, Appendix A. It should also be noted that in addition to the NSDM the NSC staff produced National Security Studies Memoranda (NSSM). which were longer research documents. See Ivo H. Daalder and I. M. Destler, *The National Security Council Project: Oral History Roundtables*, "The Nixon Administration National Security Council." Washington, DC: Brookings, December 8, 1998, 35, www.brookings.edu/~/media/Projects/nsc/19981208/PDF.

18. Best, 13.

19. Ibid.

20. Ibid.

21. Ibid., 15.

22. Ibid., 16.

23. Ibid. The use of an EO here was somewhat unusual as these changes could as easily have been incorporated in a PD. Of course, in practical terms there is no difference between an EO, a PD (by whatever the current name), a memorandum, or a finding.

24. Ibid., 17.

25. The NSDD clearly harkens back to the Kissinger NSDM, which also emphasized the notion of decision. Yet, the NSDD also, oddly, paid homage to Carter's PD by accepting the term "directive."

26. Best, 17–18.

27. McFarlane was a career marine officer who retired as a lieutenant colonel. He had been an Olmsted Scholar and had earned a master's degree in international affairs in Switzerland. He had also served on Kissinger's staff in the NSC. However, unlike Kissinger or Brzezinski, McFarlane's academic credentials were not that strong; nor were they as strong as those of Brent Scowcroft. As important was the fact that McFarlane had no outside political connections or a close personal relationship with President Reagan.

28. Philip Shenon, "Ex-Official Says Bush Urged End to Iran Arms Shipments," *New York Times*, January 23, 1989.

29. Best, 19.

30. Best, 20, gives short shrift to President Bush's NSC. However, as will be seen, his institutionalization of the structure has set the organizational context for how the NSC has operated over the past 25 years.

31. Regional PCCs were, for example, Western Hemisphere among others, while an example of a functional PCC was terrorism.

32. Best, 20 (for only the final clause in the statement). Best is simply not correct about the normal pattern of PCC chairs.

33. The final NSS of the Bush presidency was produced under the direction of army colonel Geoff Jones, who had commanded the Fourth PSYOP Group in Saudi Arabia and Kuwait during Desert Shield/Desert Storm. COL Jones was a friend of the author. The NSS that he produced is the one most consistent with the ideal of a strategy since NSC-68 and remains so to this day.

34. Quoted in Daalder and Destler, "The Clinton Administration National Security Council," 11–12, PDF. James Steinberg is an academic and foreign policy expert who has served recent Democratic presidents. In the Clinton administration he served as deputy NSA, while in the Obama administration he served as deputy secretary of state.

35. Ibid., 13.

36. Quoted in ibid., 15. Rand Beers was a career State Department officer (both Foreign Service and Civil Service) who served as a senior NSC staffer for President Bush, President Clinton, and President Obama. He also served as acting secretary of the Department of Homeland Security.

37. Condoleezza Rice, *No Higher Honor*. New York: 2011, Crown Publishers. Chapter 2.

38. Ibid.

39. See Bob Woodward, *Bush at War*. New York: 2002, Simon & Schuster.

40. Rice, Chapter 2.

41. Best, 23 and PPD-1.

42. Quoted in an interview by Jeffrey Goldberg in *The Atlantic*, November 12, 2014, http://www.theatlantic.com/international/archive/2014/11/a-withering-critique-of-president-obamas-national-security-council/382477/.

43. Quoted by Nicholas Ballasy, "Brzezinski. Scowcroft: Obama Should Shrink 300-Plus National Security Staff," November 9, 2014, http://pjmedia.com/blog/brzezinski-skowcroft-obama-should-shrink-3.

44. Rice, Chapter 2.

45. *Washington Post*, November 25, 2014, "White House Seeks a Stronger Hand at Pentagon to Manage Crises," http://www.washingtonpost.com/national/white-house-seek-a-stronger.

46. Ibid.

47. Ibid. See also Rothkopf quoted in Goldberg.

48. This is comparable to the experience of military officers serving on Joint Staffs. Although each brings his or her own experience in the home service, they each tend to see the world from a joint perspective while serving as a joint staff officer.

Chapter 5

Defense Planning Systems

In Chapter 4 we reviewed the development and functioning of the National Security Council (NSC) system. This system focuses on national-level decision and policy making. Historically, and by law, it develops the national security strategy of the United States. That strategy is then carried out by the various departments and agencies of the government charged with roles in the national security process. Of those departments and agencies, only the Department of Defense (DOD) has a robust and formal approach to strategy and planning.[1] Moreover, that approach is, in fact, followed very closely in the execution and implementation of strategies and plans. This chapter addresses the three major defense planning systems:

1. The Joint Strategic Planning System (JSPS)
2. The Planning, Programming, Budgeting, and Execution (PPBE) system
3. The Joint Operations Planning and Execution System (JOPES)

These three interrelated systems drive how the military is organized, trained, equipped, deployed, and employed to carry out the policies and strategies of the United States. They also address how the DOD intends to work with other agencies of the U.S. government as well as allied military forces.

BACKGROUND

The formal birth of modern defense planning systems took place in 1961 with the arrival of Robert S. McNamara as secretary of defense in the Kennedy administration. McNamara introduced the Planning, Programming, Budgeting System (PPBS), a form of program budgeting used in the private sector (from which he came) and popular among academic economists. The planning portion of PPBS introduced what was essentially the first formal defense strategy. This was in the form of a document called the Defense Guidance that, for most of the rest of the Cold War, addressed countering the Soviet threat. Other threats were secondary. Toward the end of the Cold War the document became the Defense Planning Guidance (DPG) and, instead of being focused on a single threat, addressed multiple threats through the concept of a series of "illustrative planning scenarios."[2] Recent developments, particularly the introduction of the QDR, caused the PPBS to be renamed and reconfigured as the PPBE.

THE PLANNING, PROGRAMMING, BUDGETING, EXECUTION SYSTEM (PPBE)

Subsequent developments changed the DPG into two separate guidance documents, the DOD Fiscal Guidance and the DOD Programming Guidance.[3] Another document that is essential to the Planning Phase of PPBE is the Quadrennial Defense Review (QDR).

> The congressionally mandated Quadrennial Defense Review (QDR) directs DoD to undertake a wide-ranging review of strategy, programs, and resources. Specifically, the QDR is expected to delineate a national defense strategy consistent with the most recent National Security Strategy by defining force structure, modernization plans, and a budget plan allowing the military to successfully execute the full range of missions within that strategy. The report will include an evaluation by the Secretary of Defense and Chairman of the Joint Chiefs of Staff of the military's ability to successfully execute its missions at a low-to-moderate level of risk within the forecast budget plan.[4]

The QDR has had other effects on the PPBE, including tying the Future Years Defense Program (FYDP) to the four-year election cycle. Previously, the FYDP began with the current Fiscal Year (the budget execution year); the following Fiscal Year (FY) was the Budget Year in which the programs (program budget) were converted to the annual congressionally required line item format. The following five FYs (or so) are known as Program Years. With each new FY the previous Budget Year became the current year, the first Program Year became the Budget Year, and a new Program Year was added. From Current Year to the last Program Year the FYDP covered seven years. The advent of the QDR requires a full review of defense strategy every four years, which has the effect of limiting effective out year programming to three years—Current Year, Budget Year, and three Program Years before major changes may be required. The QDR had the additional effect of changing the structure of PPBS to PPBE by shifting the Current Year from the beginning of the process to the end and calling it the "Execution Phase."

In addition to the QDR, the Fiscal, and the Programming Guidance, three other non-PPBE documents drive the Planning Phase. They are the National Security Strategy (NSS), the National Defense Strategy (NDS), and the National Military Strategy (NMS). The NSS was discussed in Chapter 4, while the NDS and the NMS will be discussed here. Another non-PPBE process has major impact on the Planning Phase and that is the Chairman's Program Recommendations (CPR). Although it is part of another system, it is one of the factors that put the chairman of the Joint Chiefs of Staff (CJCS) at the center of all three defense planning systems as a result of the Goldwater-Nichols Act's reorganization of the DOD. To reiterate: The Planning Phase of PPBE is driven by the NSS, NDS, NMS, whenever issued, the QDR every four years, and the CPR annually. The two specific products of the Planning Phase are the DOD Fiscal Guidance and the DOD Programming Guidance.

The guidance documents drive the Programming Phase of PPBE. This is the phase where the program budgets for the 11 Major Force Programs of the DOD are developed in a series of Program Objective Memoranda, known as POMs. These POMs are developed by multiple agencies having responsibility for raising, training, equipping, and maintaining the force under Title 10 of the U.S. Code. Following is a list of the 11 Major Force Programs (MFPs):

MFP 1. Strategic Forces
MFP 2. General Purpose Forces
MFP 3. Command, Control, Communications, Intelligence and Space
MFP 4. Mobility Forces
MFP 5. Guard and Reserve Forces
MFP 6. Research and Development
MFP 7. Central Supply and Maintenance
MFP 8. Training, Medical, and Other General Personnel Activities
MFP 9. Administration and Associated Activities
MFP 10. Support of Other Nations
MFP 11. Special Operations Forces[5]

Generally, there is not a single POM developed for each program; rather, Title 10 agencies develop POMs for multiple programs. For example, the army POM addresses MFP 2, 3, 4, 6, 7, 8, 9, and 10. In a similar manner both the navy and air force POMs address MFP 1 along with other MFPs. The sole MFP addressed by the POM of a single agency is MFP 11, which is produced by U.S. Special Operations Command (USSOCOM), the only unified command with Title 10 responsibilities.

POM development is, of course, part of the FYDP. As the first Program Year becomes the Budget Year and a new Program Year is added as the last out year, the individual POMs are revised by the responsible agencies. As the POMs are finished the CJCS intervenes again with what is called the Chairman's Program Assessment (CPA). Essentially, he reviews each POM for congruency with his NMS. If he finds that, for instance, the army POM does not support his strategy he will make his position clear to the army chief of staff, but also—and more importantly—to the secretary of defense (SECDEF), who is able to order the secretary of the army to modify the army POM to fully support the NMS. Major changes in the POMs are most often seen in the wake of each new QDR, which often makes for wholesale changes in both the NDS and NMS. It should be noted here that the QDR process is led by the undersecretary of defense for policy (USDP), the number three person in the department.

In the budgeting phase, the program budgets developed in the POMs and the FYDP are converted to the line item form that Congress requires. The document in which this is done is called the Budget Estimate Submission (BES). The BES is then subject to both program and budget reviews (including the CPA), which results in a major budget issues document. These issues are resolved by a series of resource management decisions, which, while the responsibility of the deputy secretary of defense (with significant support and input from the vice chairman of the Joint Chiefs of Staff), are largely handled by the staff of the Cost Analysis and Program Evaluation (CAPE) organization within the DOD.[6] With the resolution of issues, the consolidated DOD budget is submitted to the Office of Management and Budget (OMB) and incorporated into the president's budget submitted to Congress in February of each year.

The Execution Phase begins when Congress funds the DOD either by passing an appropriations bill or a continuing resolution, either of which requires analysis and evaluation of the expenditures. Since the appropriated funds often do not match the resources in the budget, this requires some modification in the execution of DOD programs. And while the Execution Phase is ongoing, the Planning Phase is beginning again.

THE JOINT STRATEGIC PLANNING SYSTEM (JSPS)

The second system, really the center piece of the three interrelated systems, is the Joint Strategic Planning System and revolves around the role of the chairman of the Joint Chiefs of Staff (CJCS).[7] As such, it is a product of the Goldwater-Nichols Act (GNA) of 1986 and its subsequent evolution in policy. The GNA required the president to produce a national security

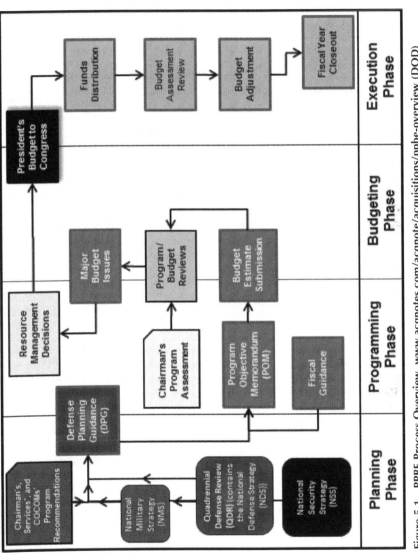

Figure 5.1   PPBE Process Overview. www.acqnotes.com/acqnote/acquisitions/ppbe-overview (DOD)

strategy (as discussed previously) and the CJCS to produce its derived military strategy counterpart, the national military strategy (NMS). Not required by Congress, but instituted by Secretary of Defense Donald Rumsfeld, is the national defense strategy (NDS), produced by the Office of the Secretary of Defense (OSD). The NMS supports directly the NDS and the NSS, and is derived from the Joint Strategy Review (process and report), national and OSD guidance including the NSS and NDS, as well as input from both the services and the combatant commanders.

The NMS focuses on the strategic environment in which military forces operate, the military objectives (ends), military courses of action (methods or ways), and military resources (means). It assesses risk, mainly by comparing courses of action, and includes annexes as required. Since the document itself is unclassified, most of the annexes provide needed detail in classified form. The NMS, as are the NSS and NDS, is directive. It tells the joint force (the military) what strategic plans to draft, what capabilities to develop, sustain, and maintain, and the kinds of joint concepts and experimentation to undertake. While we will consider strategic plans here, it is important that the NMS is the vehicle the CJCS compares service POMs to (in the PPBE system) when he reviews them. Because the NMS is unclassified it has a significant informational function focused on the general public, various OSD agencies and activities, and other government agencies.

While not exactly a part of the JSPS, the Unified Command Plan (UCP) is essential to it. The UCP is the annual document that specifies each unified command and its area of operational responsibility (AOR) for geographic commands and its functional responsibility for functional commands. It is a product of discussion, debate, and bargaining among OSD, the Joint Staff, and the unified commands themselves. Moreover, it bridges the three separate defense planning systems. Issues raised in the discussions include things like how much of the South Atlantic and South Pacific oceans should be included in the USSOUTHCOM AOR.[8] The resolution was to give SOUTHCOM more of the oceans than it previously had but less than it desired. What the UCP does is give the CJCS the baseline from which he will recommend to the SECDEF how to deploy and employ forces as well as which Geographic Combatant Commander (GCC) will be in charge of any operation (as the supported GCC).

To produce the NMS and other strategic directives, the JSPS should be seen as a process directed by the CJCS. It begins with the Comprehensive Joint Assessment (CJA), which produces a shared database among the services, unified commands, Joint Staff, and OSD that is used to analyze issues faced by all of these organizations. As a start point in the JSPS, the CJA informs the Joint Strategy Review Process (JSR). The JSR is conducted continuously by the Joint Staff, which produces a series of documents that feed into the JSR. For example, the J-1 (Personnel) produces a Health of the Force Estimate, while the J-2 produces the Joint Intelligence Estimate and the J-4 a Joint Logistics Estimate. All of these and other estimates feed into the Chairman's Risk Assessment (CRA), which is managed by the J-5. The CRA is the documentation of the advice of the CJCS to the secretary and the president on both the level and nature of military risk to U.S. national objectives that is found in the world. Based on the CRA, the chairman develops and presents his Chairman's Program Recommendation (CPR), which is a critical driving force in the development of the service and USSOCOM POMs. In other words, the CJCS is giving guidance as to how he expects the Major Force Programs to be designed over the course of the FYDP to address the risks he has identified.

The JSR also serves as a basis for revising the NMS. Although there is no specific schedule for releasing a new NMS, this will happen when there is a new NSS and/or NDS or when the chairman decides it is needed. Because the JSR is an ongoing process, it should uncover both risks and solutions to the issues raised by those risks that can be best addressed by revising the NMS. Revisions in the NMS lead, inevitably, to revisions in one of the most critical planning documents in the entire JSPS, the Joint Strategic Capabilities Plan (JSCP). Before discussing the JSCP, it is important to note that the JSR requires a JSR Report in odd-numbered years or as required.

Although there are two other guidance documents in the JSPS, the Guidance for Employment of the Force and the Guidance for Development of the Force, the JSCP is both the linchpin between JSPS and JOPES, and the driver for planning the deployment and employment of the force. Formally titled the Joint Strategic Capabilities Plan, the JSCP tells the combatant commanders what to plan for and with what resources. The JSCP is made up of the following sections:

- Introduction
- Strategic Context and Global Priorities
- Resources and Forces
- Global Defense Posture
- Campaign Plan Requirements
- General Planning Guidance
- Regional Planning Guidance
- Implementation Guidance
- Assessments
- Supplemental Instructions[9]

The JSCP functions to direct the combatant commanders to plan for specific contingencies, campaigns, and security cooperation. It also directs, in

Formal Execution: Major JSPS Components

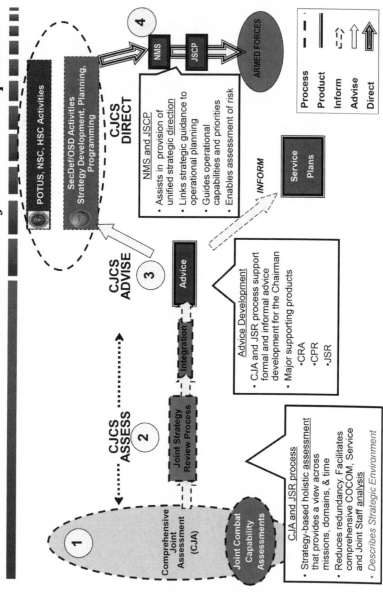

Figure 5.2 Formal Execution: Major JSPS Components. dde.carlisle.army.mil/LLL/DSC/ppt/L13_JSPS.pdf

general terms, how these plans will be implemented. To do so the JSCP does what is called apportioning forces to the combatant commanders for each specific plan. That is, each designated plan is given a list of *combat* forces that the commander can plan to use. Support forces are not included except those that are organic to the combat units. So, if an army division is apportioned, its division support command goes with it because it belongs to the division. But the nonorganic support units like a corps support command is not apportioned since it does not belong to the division. Another feature of force apportionment is that combat units are not explicitly identified for planning purposes. Thus, a plan will be apportioned an armored division, a Marine Expeditionary Force, an Air Force Wing but not a specifically identified unit. This sometimes gives an appearance of silliness as when a plan is apportioned an airborne division and the U.S. military has only one such division in its entire inventory, the 82nd Airborne Division. What then happens if the time comes and the 82nd is committed elsewhere? In the case of the armored division example given earlier another armored division is substituted. But there is no other airborne division. In that case, a provisional division could be made up of several different, smaller airborne units with the addition of a headquarters and support elements. It would, however, be a jerry-rigged affair. Alternatively, the plan could be changed so that a different type of unit could carry out the mission that would likely be less than the ideal outcome. Plans, however, are meant to be changed.[10]

The discussion so far indicates that the JSCP is top-down driven. While that is generally correct, it depends to a great extent on inputs from the combatant commanders regarding what is threatening in their AOR. Thus, the JSCP directs a commander to plan to address a particular contingency based on political and military guidance from above, intelligence from all sources in the intelligence community, and observations and developments within the AOR as reported by interagency players like American embassies, defense Attaché offices (through DIA but in direct coordination with the command J-2 as well), and security cooperation offices (also known as MiILGPs, ODCs, MLOs, etc.). All of these and other offices are stationed in American embassies in the AOR. In general, it is the JSCP that triggers the initiation of planning in the third system, JOPES.

JOINT OPERATIONS PLANNING AND EXECUTION SYSTEM (JOPES)

JOPES is the planning system used by the combatant commands, reviewed by the Joint Staff, and approved by the secretary of defense on the advice of the CJCS, to develop the plans called for by the JSCP, and any other contingency plans that may be required. It is, therefore, essentially planning at the theater (AOR) strategic and operational level. The discussion here will first lay out the normal planning sequence and then address certain possible alternative sequences.

JOPES consists of two levels of planning: Deliberate (now called Contingency) Planning and Crisis Action Planning. In normal circumstances the two are intimately related. As a defense planning system, JOPES was preceded by the Joint Operational Planning System (JOPS). The weakness of JOPS was that it left out the execution phase of planning—that is, JOPS ended with the deployment of forces. What they did once they got to theater was not included in the plans. JOPES, introduced at the end of the 1980s/beginning of the 1990s, was designed to remedy that. How forces were to be used in combat operations became a part of the plan developed by the Geographic Combatant Commander (GCC). The transition will be discussed in the first two cases in this book in Chapters 6 and 7.

As one would expect, Contingency or Deliberate Planning begins with the JSCP. There the GCC is told what contingencies he must address in planning, at what level of detail, and what generic combat forces he can plan to use. The JSCP also tells him to develop a Theater Campaign Plan for the conduct of operations in peace, conflict, and war, and a Security Cooperation Plan in support of host government allies in the AOR. All of these plans are developed concurrently, although in reality, it is necessary to prioritize the development of the several contingency plans that a GCC must make. This prioritization is both in detail and in order of planning because it takes a significant amount of time to draft a plan. This is due both to the nature of planning and the fact that the planners on the staff are relatively few in number and there is only so much that can be expected of them in a non-crisis setting. Prior to changes in JOPES in the early 1990s, a deliberate plan was calculated to take two years from initiation to completion, After the changes, deliberate plans were to be developed in a time frame that would be as long as necessary and as short as possible. In practice, deliberate planning still takes about two years.

Contingency, or deliberate, planning is initiated by the strategic guidance commonly given in the JSCP. It proceeds to the phase of Concept Development, where an overview of the operation is put together. This follows from both the JSCP and the GCC's own strategic vision given in his regional strategy, other formal guidance, and verbally to his J-5 and Plans chief. From here, the planners move to the phase of Plan Development. In this phase some significant decisions need to be made, among them the level of detailed plan that that will be produced.

There are three levels of detail in plans: the highest level of detail is a full-blown Operations Plan (OPLAN); the intermediate level is the Concept Plan (CONPLAN) with TPFDD; and the lowest level of detail is found in the CONPLAN without TPFDD. The TPFDD, the acronym for Time Phased Force Deployment Data, is the central piece that separates more detailed from less detailed plans. Where the JSCP apportioned combat forces for planning, the TPFDD lists each and every combat and supporting unit, when it will depart from home station, and when it will arrive in theater as well as where. Because the TPFDD is an electronic document it can be revised continuously.

The other details that distinguish the level of planning are the number and specific annexes that are included with the plan. An OPLAN has all the annexes, while a CONPLAN with TPFDD has many, but not all possible, annexes. A CONPLAN without TPFDD has only the minimal number of annexes necessary to have a reasonable basic plan. For example, a CONPLAN with TPFDD will have the annexes for Task Organization, Intelligence, Operations, Logistics, Personnel, and Communications. It would most likely not have a Public Affairs or Civil Affairs annex. The CONPLAN without TPFDD probably would have only the annexes for Task Organization, Intelligence, Operations, Logistics, and Communications.

Between each stage of the planning cycle, there is an in-progress review (IPR) conducted by the GCC and the Joint Staff (in the Office of the Joint Chiefs of Staff). The result of these IPRs is approval from the CJCS at each stage of the cycle. While the chairman is not usually involved personally in the IPR, it is his signature that goes on the approval and the GCC commander can always address any issues with him directly or, take it up with their mutual boss, the SECDEF.

The last stage of the contingency planning cycle is Plan Assessment. This stage includes four possibilities, refine (to include letting it stand as is), adapt that would involve significant changes, terminate when it is no longer needed, and execute when and if it becomes necessary. The JOPES process calls for each plan to be reviewed every six months[11] so as to rationally choose which one, if any, of the above outcomes.

GCCs do not operate in a vacuum. Thus, every contingency plan has supporting plans written by subordinate units. Thus, every GCC plan is typically supported by the plans of its military service components (army, navy, air force, and marines), its sub-unified commands like the theater Special Operations Command (SOC), and any Joint Task Forces that are included in the GCC plan. Similarly, the GCC is supported by other GCCs and functional combatant commands, each of which produces a supporting plan.

The underlying purpose of the Contingency Planning process in JOPES is to leave nothing to chance. The best political and military analysis, driven by the best possible intelligence produced by the 17 agencies of the U.S. Intelligence Community, along with that of our allies, is designed to leave the U.S. military prepared to address all likely contingencies. The plans produced

JOPES Process Contingency and Crisis Action Planning

Operational Activities	**Situational Awareness**				
	Planning				
	Execution				

| **Planning Functions** | Strategic Guidance | Concept Development | Plan Development | Plan Assessment (Refine, Adapt, Terminate, Execute) | Six Month Review Cycle |

IPR — Approved Mission
IPR — Approved Concept
IPR — Approved Plan

Base Plan (BPLAN)
Concept Plan (CONPLAN)
Operation Plan (OPLAN)

| **Products** | Warning Order | Planning Order | Operation Order | Alert Order | Execute Order / Deployment Order |

Figure 5.3 JOPES Process Contingency and Crisis Action Planning. wjtsc10_wgjkddc_jdtc-3

range in detail from those which deal with the most probable contingencies and those with the greatest amount of risk (the OPLANs) to the least probable with the least amount of risk (CONPLAN without TPFDD). In the ideal world of the military planner, there would be no surprise contingencies. But these do happen on occasion. This brings us to a consideration of the second planning process in JOPES, Crisis Action Planning (CAP).

In the ideal world a crisis develops and/or is identified in the NSC. At this point the SECDEF, through the CJCS, issues a Warning Order to the GCC.[12] The Warning Order is designed to trigger a review of current plans for this particular contingency. Is there a plan? Is it an OPLAN, a CONPLAN with or without TPFDD? Depending on the answers, the GCC planners begin to consider what might be needed to make the plan fit the current crisis. In an earlier version of JOPES, these actions were called "Situation Development" and "Crisis Assessment."[13] If the crisis continues, the SECDEF issues a planning order and the GCC planners begin to act in earnest. In the earlier version this phase was called Course of Action Development.[14] What this actually means for the planners is that after verifying the type of plan that exists, they make the revisions necessary. For an OPLAN, this is minimal and involves revising the basic plan and annexes based on development in the situation and the terms of the Planning Order as well as revising the TPFDD if necessary. For a CONPLAN with TPFDD it involves the same actions by the planners plus developing the annexes to the plan that had not been drafted before. For a CONPLAN without TPFDD the planners must also develop the TPFDD. Generally, crises develop in short order and CAP usually takes place in a matter of days, not weeks. The product of the planning phase is an Operations Order (OPORD).

The previous discussion assumes that a plan existed. While this is usually the case, there are crises that arise for which no plan has been developed. One that was recently in the news was revealed in an interview with the CJCS, GEN Martin Dempsey on public television's *Frontline*, May 26, 2015. Dempsey was asked by the interviewer if there had been a plan to deal with the Islamic State's attack and seizure of Mosul in 2014. Dempsey was forced to answer that there was no such plan. Nor was there one for the more recent Islamic State seizure of Ramadi. Nor did we have a plan to go after Al Qaeda in Afghanistan in 2001. This "no plan" scenario, while relatively uncommon, is clearly not unheard of. If no plan exists then the GCC is responsible for building one from scratch. In that case, planning begins with Course of Action Development and flows to Course of Action Selection leading to the basic order. This is followed by developing the TPFDD, and all the annexes just as a staff would do in building an OPLAN, but clearly with a special sense of urgency. Again, the end product is an OPORD. Once the OPORD is complete, the GCC waits for subsequent orders. These may include an Alert Order telling the GCC that execution is imminent, a Deployment Order sending units and equipment to the theater of operations, and/or an Execute Order directing to GCC to undertake combat operations.[15] As we will see in the next two chapters, reality is often quite different.

INTERFACES

To bring this chapter to its conclusion we need to consider the interfaces among the several systems. First, there is the relationship among the defense planning systems. Second is the relationship between those systems and other governmental planning, in particular the NSC system.

With the Defense Planning Systems

When we taught defense planning systems at the Army Command and General Staff College at Fort Leavenworth back in the 1990s, we showed the relationship among them with a slide we called "The Rolling Donuts" (see Figure 5.4). Each system, PPBE (then PPBS), JSPS, and JOPES was represented as a large donut or wagon wheel, symbolizing that planning was always cyclical. The PPBE donut was on the left side of the slide, while the JOPES donut was on the right. In the middle was JSPS. PPBE was intertwined with JSPS, as was JOPES, but neither PPBE nor JOPES directly intersected with each other.

The first key interface between systems is the strategic guidance that drives PPBE. This comes from the QDR, the NDS, and, most important, the

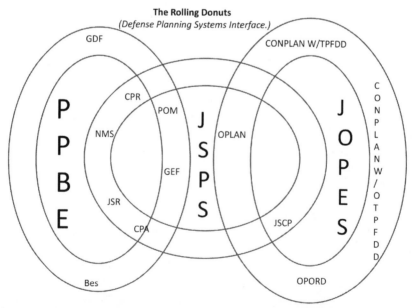

Figure 5.4 The Rolling Donuts. Karina C. Fishel derived from AFSC Pub 1 1997

NMS. The NMS, a product of the JSPS, also drives the Chairman's Program Recommendations (CPR—another JSPS product) that directs the services, defense agencies, and USSOCOM on where the NMS demands that they focus their POMs. The second key interface is the Chairman's Program Assessment (CPA—another JSPS product), where the CJCS reviews the POMs for compliance with his strategy, the NMS, and guidance, the CPR. If the POMs are not supporting the NMS, the chairman raises the issue to the SECDEF if he cannot obtain a satisfactory resolution directly through discussion with service or agency principals or with SOCOM.

The other interfaces are between the JSPS and JOPES. Once again, the NMS is one of the key pieces of strategic guidance for planning. The other is the JSCP, which translates the NMS into specific planning directives and identifies some of the required resources. Those resources, it should be noted, are produced over time through the PPBE system.

The critical player in all of this is the CJCS. He is the principal military advisor to the SECDEF and, therefore, has major input to the NDS as well as the QDR. He intervenes three times in PPBE: with general guidance in the NMS, with specific program recommendations in the CPR, and with a critical assessment of the resourcing of the 11 MFPs in his review of the POMs in the CPA. He also initiates the Contingency Planning process with his NMS and then the JSCP. And he (through the Joint Staff and direct coordination with the GCCs) reviews, influences, and approves each plan produced under JOPES. Moreover, he is intimately involved in Crisis Action Planning, whether it is the conversion of an existing OPLAN or CONPLAN to an OPORD or the creation of one from scratch in a "no-plan" scenario.

With Other Strategic Planning Systems

Although the DOD does share some of its planning with other agencies, especially those with which it works closely, none of them are fully integrated into all the planning systems. One area where there is direct involvement in JOPES planning by other agencies is in efforts to control smuggling into the United States of both drugs and people, especially by sea. Here is the case of Joint Interagency Task Force—South (JIATF-S) operating out of Key West, Florida, as a subordinate agency to USSOUTHCOM. Its director is a two-star U.S. Coast Guard admiral (rear admiral upper half) who commands navy, coast guard, and air force elements along with DEA, ICE, and Border Patrol personnel on a regular basis. JIATF-S is often augmented by army and National Guard elements as well as other U.S. government agencies and ships from allied countries.[16]

The main point of interface between the defense planning systems and other U.S. government planning is with the NSC system. The DOD is represented at all levels of the NSC. The SECDEF is a statutory member of the NSC proper, while the CJCS is one of two statutory advisors. In the Principals Committee (PC) both the SECDEF and the CJCS are full members with both voice and vote. Likewise, on the Deputies Committee (DC) the DEPSECDEF and the vice chairman of the JCS (VCJCS) are both full members. On the subordinate committees (currently called Interagency Policy Committees—IPCs) the Office of the SECDEF (OSD) and the Joint Staff each have a senior representative, usually a member of the Senior Executive Service (SES) from OSD and a flag-rank officer from the Joint Staff. It should be noted that the DOD is the only department that has two representatives at each level of the NSC system and, thus, has two votes if OSD and the Joint Staff are in agreement (which they are most of the time).[17]

Because of the participation of OSD and Joint Staff members at all three levels of the NSC system, the DOD has major input to the written products of the NSC, which include Presidential Policy Directives (PPDs), Executive Orders (EOs), various memoranda, several national strategies, and, most important for defense planning, the national security strategy (NSS). Typically, the managing editor of the NSS is a military officer (usually a colonel or navy captain) serving as a senior director of the NSC staff.[18] The NSS is the document that sets the parameters for all supporting strategies and plans. It is the driver for the NDS and the NMS. It provides strategic guidance for PPBE and through the NMS for the JSCP and JOPES plans.

TRANSITION

The discussion of interfaces brings us to the end of the basic considerations of Part II. To recap, briefly, Part I addressed the underlying theory—or theories—of international relations that actually condition the way policy makers and executors see the world. That focus has strong deterministic elements and serves to explain many of the reasons why policy choices are made.

Part II addressed the nuts and bolts of the national security policy process. Chapter 2 focused on the legal authorities under which policy makers and executors operate. These both enhance and constrain what is viewed as legitimate to do in the world. Chapter 3 addressed the government departments and agencies that provide the capabilities of policy. Simply put, government cannot do something where it does not have the capability. Thus, the organizations of government both enable and constrain what policy can be. Chapter 4 discussed the NSC system, how it works, how it is supposed to work (not the same thing), and the products (documents) it produces. The documents are important because they direct government agencies to do certain things. How clear they are is obviously important. The more ambiguous the document, the more subject to interpretation is the guidance. Finally, Chapter 5 discussed the three key defense planning systems, how they interface with each other and with other systems, and how they are expected to produce capabilities and plans for national security contingencies.

As the old English proverb states, "There is many a slip twixt cup and lip." The reality is often far different from the way the textbook tells us things are done or should be done. Thus, Part III looks at specific cases and shows how they both conformed to the model put forth in Parts I and II and how they differed and changed that model.

NOTES

1. The State Department has a partial and incipient planning system but not nearly so robust.

2. This section is drawn from my experience as the chief of policy and strategy in the J-5 of USSOUTHCOM in 1988 and 89.

3. DOD Directive 7045.14, January 25, 2013.

4. Jeffrey D. Brake, "Quadrennial Defense Review (QDR) Background, Process, and Issues." Library of Congress Congressional Research Service. June 21, 2001.

5. DOD, *Glossary of Defense Acquisition Acronyms and Terms*, December 2012. https://dap.dau.mil/glossary/pages 2192.aspx.

6. CAPE is the successor to the Office of Program Analysis and Evaluation (PA&E), which had its origin in Secretary McNamara's Office of Systems Analysis—the home of the so-called Whiz Kids—back in 1961.

7. This section is taken, except where otherwise cited, from a U.S. Army War College PowerPoint presentation, "Description of the Joint Strategic Planning System (JSPS)," dde.carlisle,army.mil/LLL/DSC/L13_JSPS.pdf. July 2009.

8. This was an issue during my tenure as chief of policy and strategy in the USSOUTHCOM J-5 in the late 1980s.

9. JSPS_pdf.

10. Remember that the JSCP is a classified document, so it is simply not possible to give any concrete examples.

11. Unless GCC staffs have increased in size and capability tremendously since I was a planner in SOUTHCOM, the six-month review will be lucky to happen on a yearly basis. Less often is more likely.

12. Mike McDaniel, "Joint Individual Training Challenges: Training for Integrated Operations." Joint Deployment Training Center, Briefing for the Worldwide Joint Training and Scheduling Conference, March 29, 2010, #6.

13. JFSC Pub 1, Figure 4–2.

14. See McDaniel and JFSC.

15. McDaniel.

16. See John T. Fishel, "The InterAgency Arena at the Operational Level: The Cases Now Known as Stability Operations." In Gabriel Marcella (ed.), *Affairs of State: The InterAgency and National Security*. Carlisle, PA: 2008, Strategic Studies Institute. 409–446.

17. This comment reflects the experience of a deputy J-5 who attended innumerable IWGs during the Clinton administration and made these remarks to a course on defense planning at the Center for Hemispheric Defense Studies, ca. 2000.

18. For the final NSS of the George H.W. Bush presidency (January 1993) the managing editor was Army COL Geoff Jones, who had commanded the 4th PSYOP Group during Desert Shield/Storm. I got to know Geoff in Panama during Just Cause when he commanded the 8th PSYOP Battalion. He was a particularly competent officer and strategic thinker.

Part III

THE CASES

Chapter 6

Panama: National Security Policy from Below

The "Panama crisis" was long running, spanning two presidential administrations and culminating in the invasion of Panama, Operation Just Cause. Yet its roots go back much farther than the Reagan administration to the Carter–Torrijos (Panama) Treaties of 1977. Perhaps, it dates back to the Canal Zone riots of 1964, or even to Panama's independence from Colombia in 1903 aided and abetted by Teddy Roosevelt who made the claim, "I took Panama." For the purposes of this chapter the story begins with a murder mystery. Before telling that story, some background is in order.

THE PANAMANIAN ENVIRONMENT

From independence in 1903 until the 1950s (at least), Panama was totally dominated by the Canal and the United States. Panama had no army and its police force was headed by a superintendent who was an American. That changed with a series of political appointees culminating with the appointment of Jose Antonio Remon. Remon, who had graduated from the Mexican military academy, had the goal of turning the Panama National Police into a true military, something he accomplished, when, as president in 1953, he achieved increased funding from the U.S. Military Assistance Program and renamed the police, the *Guardia Nacional* (National Guard). Even after Remon's assassination in 1954, the *Guardia* remained the dominant political institution in Panama. Indeed, it would only become stronger over the next three decades.

In January 1964, pent-up Panamanian frustrations boiled over in a major riot that was provoked by the raising of the American flag at Balboa High School in the Canal Zone against the orders of the governor and the retaliatory effort by Panamanian students to raise their flag in the same location. In the ensuing melee, the Panamanian flag was torn and major rioting ensued with deaths and wounded on both sides.[1] (Significantly more Panamanians than Americans were killed and hurt.) The riots led to negotiations to revise the Panama Canal Treaty, which finally bore fruit in 1977 but also led to the coup of October 11, 1968. That coup resulted in the relatively popular dictatorship of BG Omar Torrijos Herrera, which lasted until his death in an airplane accident in 1981.

The Carter–Torrijos Treaties[2] left a confused American interagency map in Panama.[3] Normally, the American ambassador is responsible for the activities of all U.S. government agencies operating in country. The treaties, however, resulted in three separate U.S. government institutions operating autonomously. First, the Panama Canal Treaty (one of the two treaties in the package), created a new U.S. government institution, the Panama Canal Commission (PCC), in Washington that was responsible for running the Canal until December 31, 1999. A majority of the commissioners were American, while the rest were Panamanian throughout the duration of the treaty. On the ground, the running of the Canal was the responsibility of the administrator and his deputy. Until December 31, 1989, the administrator was to be an American while the deputy was to be a Panamanian, each nominated by the respective governments but appointed by the PCC. On January 1, 1990, the nationalities of the two positions were to switch. Serving as the American administrator for the first decade of the treaty was the former commander of the U.S. Southern Command (USSOUTHCOM) Lt. General (retired) Dennis P. ("Phil") McAuliffe, while the deputy administrator was the well-respected Panamanian Fernando Manfredo. Many of the issues involved in the running of the Canal required some direct interaction with the government of Panama, while others required coordination with SOUTHCOM. In many of these instances, the embassy might very well be left outside the discussion.

Equally complex was the role of SOUTHCOM. Both the Panama Canal Treaty and the Defense Treaty created a mechanism for coordination of all matters involving these issues between the two governments known as the Combined Board. Membership on the Combined Board was limited to SOUTHCOM and the *Guardia Nacional* (later the PDF); the civilian government of Panama and the American Embassy had no role to play. Because of the creation of the Combined Board both SOUTHCOM and the *Guardia/ PDF* had outsized roles in the conduct of bilateral U.S.-Panama relations. The fact that normal interstate relations were conducted by three separate U.S. government agencies and two Panamanian ones made it less than clear who was in charge both de jure and de facto in each country.

For the United States, the relationship between the commander of USSOUTHCOM[4] and the ambassador depended almost entirely on the personal chemistry between the two. The PCC administrator, both because his functions were limited and because he had previously commanded SOUTHCOM (as a three-star), was generally close and amicable with the GCC. To demonstrate the role personality played in all this consider how GEN John Galvin (GCC from 1985 to 1987) described it in his recent memoir:

> As soon as I started to talk with the U.S. ambassador to Panama, Ted Briggs, I knew we would work out as a team. I acknowledged that he was the president's representative in the country while I was the regional U.S. military commander and that anything I did on the military side in Panama I would clear through him. He said, "I'll be glad to work things out together." I responded, "Yes, but you are in charge." And that's the way it went. I told my staff and commanders that, when it came to Panama, we were on the ambassador's turf, and that he had to know about everything we were doing. No surprises for Ted Briggs, I said.[5]

While Galvin and Briggs clicked with respect to their personalities, the general's relationship with the administrator of the PCC reflected their mutual military background.

Another player on the American side was retired lieutenant general Phil McAuliffe. When in 1979 Phil retired as commander in chief, Southern Command, he accepted an appointment as head of the PCC, a position he held for ten years. A veteran of World War II and Vietnam, he had commanded in Panama for three years and, at this point, with 13 years in the Canal Zone under his belt, he had plenty of experience, and was a great source of advice on Panama, on the region, and on relations with Washington.[6]

Nevertheless, the role of the embassy added to the complex nature of Panama. First, as part of the ambassador's country team there were several military components. As with all embassies in Latin America, the Panama embassy had a defense attaché office that reported directly to the Defense Intelligence Agency (DIA) as well as to the ambassador. Likewise, there was a security assistance office, called a MILGROUP (MILGP) that reported both to the ambassador and the GCC. Then, as in all embassies, there were the Marine Guards who worked for the ambassador reporting to his regional security officer (RSO) but also to the head of the office of all marine security detachments in Latin America, a lieutenant colonel who was a full member of the country team. This was just one of several agencies that had regional offices as part of the Panama Country Team, including the Drug Enforcement Administration (DEA).[7] As a further complication of the interagency environment, the CIA had its station in the embassy but also had a separate and independent presence on the SOUTHCOM staff. Panama was not in any way the usual American Embassy among all of those in Latin America.

ANTECEDENTS TO THE CRISIS

A critical factor leading up to the Panama crisis was the death of Gen. Torrijos in an airplane crash in July 1981. Immediately, rumors surfaced that it was not an accident but rather that Torrijos had been murdered. The usual suspects included the CIA, drug traffickers, and his rivals for leadership of the *Guardia*.[8] Initially, the transition of command took place smoothly. The second-in-command, COL Florencio Flores, simply moved up, as did the next three officers in the hierarchy of the *Guardia*. Then the machinations began. Deputy commander COL Ruben Dario Paredes, G-2 LTC Manuel Antonio Noriega, and LTC Roberto Diaz Herrera signed a pact agreeing to oust Flores and regulate the succession to both command of the *Guardia* and the presidency of the republic among themselves.[9]

Soon after Flores was ousted, Paredes promoted himself to general and Noriega and Diaz Herrera to colonel. Noriega became deputy commander of the *Guardia*, while Diaz Herrera moved into the number three slot. Presidential elections were scheduled for 1984 and, under the constitution, the commander of the *Guardia* had to retire a year before to stand for election. This Paredes did to comply with both the constitution and his agreement with his co-conspirators. With that, Noriega became commander of the *Guardia* and Diaz Herrera his deputy. Like Paredes, Noriega promoted himself to general, but he also arranged for the Legislative Assembly to pass a new law, *Ley 20*, expanding the *Guardia* to incorporate all police and security forces as the Panama Defense Forces (PDF), with formal autonomy from the civilian government, and himself as not only the sole general but also the only four-star general with the rank of general of the forces. What a year 1983 was!

In early 1984, retired general Paredes declared his candidacy for president of Panama expecting the new PDF to fully support his bid. Instead, Noriega threw PDF support to economist Nicolas Ardito Barletta against the perennial candidacy of Arnulfo Arias. Barletta won by fewer than 5,000 votes in a subtly rigged election.[10]

THE CRISIS: FIRST INTIMATIONS

In early 1985, GEN John R. Galvin replaced GEN Paul Gorman as commander of USSOUTHCOM. On September 13, Dr. Hugo Spadafora, a protégé of Omar Torrijos and an enemy of GEN Noriega, crossed into Panama from Costa Rica on a bus. PDF officers removed him from the bus. Several days later, his headless body was found in a U.S. Mail bag on the side of the road in Costa Rica; his head was discovered in a separate location. On the date of Spadafora's disappearance, Noriega was in Paris.[11] Nevertheless, most observers believed that Noriega had ordered the killing.[12] The Spadafora family, which was quite prominent, pressed the issue and President Barletta, believing he was in charge in the country, decided to order an honest investigation. Shortly after he announced the investigation, in the wee hours of the morning, Barletta resigned the presidency on national television.[13]

There were several consequences to this sequence of events. First, the relatively amicable relations with the American Embassy and with SOUTHCOM suffered some important deterioration. Second, Noriega had signaled that there were serious—fatal—consequences to being too overtly opposed to his rule through the PDF. Third, while the first vice president, Eric Arturo Delvalle, succeeded to the presidency, it was clear that the president was subordinate to GEN Noriega.

In February 1986, Ted Briggs left Panama, replaced by Arthur Davis as ambassador. Davis, unlike Briggs, was not a career FSO but a political appointee. However, he had previously been ambassador to Paraguay. During his service there, his wife was killed in an airplane accident. As a result, his adult daughter served as his official hostess in Panama. Davis was assisted by his deputy chief of mission (DCM), John Maisto, a career FSO who had served in the Philippines in the early 1980s and as chief of Philippine affairs at the State Department during the People Power movement that toppled the government of Ferdinand Marcos that year. The experience had a profound impact on Maisto. Throughout the crisis, these three—Ambassador Davis, his daughter, and DCM Maisto—would be the regime scapegoats, epitomized by a huge poster with their photographs in the park across the main avenue from the American Embassy captioned, "These gringos are non grata."[14]

In the summer of 1986, Seymour Hersh of the *New York Times* produced a series of articles purporting to expose GEN Noriega as a thoroughly corrupt leader, drug trafficker, and the author of the murder of Hugo Spadafora, all the while having a strong relationship with the CIA, the DEA, and the U.S. military.[15] Noriega reported on both Cuba and Nicaragua to the CIA, cooperated with the DEA with regard to some traffickers, and provided support for the training of Nicaraguan contras at U.S. military bases in Panama.[16] According to Hersh and his sources, Noriega was also reporting to Cuban intelligence on U.S. activities, and cooperating with some drug traffickers while apprehending others. In short, he was playing both sides.[17] As big a story as this was in the *Times*, nothing much came of it, and by fall 1986, it had all, apparently, blown over.

FRED WOERNER TAKES COMMAND
AND THE CRISIS BURSTS FORTH

On June 1, 1987, GEN Galvin had just five more days before he turned command of SOUTHCOM over to his successor, GEN Fred Woerner. Woerner was well qualified for the position, having commanded the army component of SOUTHCOM, the 193rd Infantry Brigade, under Galvin's predecessor, Paul Gorman. Woerner, like Galvin, was fluent in Spanish and he had served much of his career in Latin America. In fact, he was the army's highest-ranking Foreign Area officer. On June 1, however, GEN Noriega executed another of his double-crosses. He had been due for retirement in 1986[18] but had arranged to be extended as commander of the PDF for an additional five years. Now he dropped the other shoe on his former co-conspirator and erstwhile ally, PDF second-in-command, Colonel Roberto Diaz Herrera, summarily retiring him.

Diaz Herrera refused to go quietly. He called a press conference where he accused Noriega of everything Seymour Hersh had accused him of the previous year, and more. In addition to the murder of Spadafora, drug trafficking, collusion with Castro and the Sandinistas, Diaz Herrera stated that Noriega was guilty of sabotaging Omar Torrijos's airplane bringing about his death. This was no accident, according to the ousted colonel, but rather a political assassination, however far-fetched that appeared given the evidence.[19]

Although Diaz Herrera was under house arrest, he was still talking to the press and opposition to Noriega was taking to the streets. On June 9, Noriega's anti-riot companies, known as the *Dobermans* and *Centurions*, used force against the protesters for the first time. On the 10th, the opposition formally organized as the National Civic Crusade (NCC).[20] The centers of leadership of the NCC were the Chamber of Commerce and the Christian Democratic Party, the latter with some key adherents inside the PDF itself.[21] The show of force, nevertheless, had its desired effect and, for a little while, protests died down. Then, in July, they ramped up again.[22]

On June 26 the U.S. Senate passed a resolution, 84–2, calling for a number of actions by the government of Panama to restore constitutional rights and freedoms.[23] Four days later a pro-government mob vandalized the American Embassy while the PDF looked on.[24] "An outraged Ambassador Davis angrily denounced the attack, demanded compensation (which was later paid), and recommended the suspension of economic and military assistance to Panama."[25] Aid, both military and economic, was suspended during the fall of 1987, putting some U.S. pressure on Noriega and his puppet president. Also, during that fall, and unbeknownst to State Department, the DOD, the American Embassy, SOUTHCOM, the PCC, or even the attorney general of the United States, Edwin Meese, U.S. attorneys in Tampa and Miami, Florida, had convened grand juries to investigate Noriega on allegations of drug trafficking. Both grand juries announced indictments on February 5, 1988.[26]

GEN Fred Woerner, was in Washington, DC, having a meeting with Elliott Abrams, assistant secretary of state for inter-American affairs, that day when Abrams received a phone call. When he hung up, Abrams said to Woerner,

"They just indicted Noriega."[27] As soon as he left Abrams's office, Woerner called SOUTHCOM on a secure line, told his chief of staff what had happened and asked him to convene a senior staff meeting as soon as he returned to Panama. Then, he headed for Andrews Air Force Base (AFB) and boarded his aircraft for the return trip. At the meeting he convened on his return to Panama, GEN Woerner directed his staff to plan for a contingency in which the PDF was the threat. Soon after, he called the chairman of the Joint Chiefs of Staff, Admiral William Crowe, and asked him to direct the planning that Woerner had just ordered.[28]

PLANNING: 1988

To fully understand the planning process it is necessary to put this in the context of the time. In 1986, Congress had passed both the Goldwater-Nichols Act and the Cohen-Nunn Amendment to the Defense Appropriations Act, which reorganized the DOD. What this meant for SOUTHCOM was that: (1) the deputy commander was relieved of his second post as commander of USAF South and became the full-time deputy; (2) the positions of SOUTHCOM Chief of Staff, J-2 (Intelligence), J-3 (Operations), and J-5 (Policy, Plans, and Strategy) were elevated to general/flag officer ranks; (3) the army component, the 193rd Infantry Brigade upgraded to U.S. Army—South; and (4) Special Operations Command-South (SOCSOUTH) was established as a sub-unified command. In addition, SOUTHCOM chose to transfer its Plans shop from the J-5 to the J-3. All this took place after Woerner took command but before Noriega was indicted.

Thus, when GEN Woerner ordered his planners to begin planning for operations against the PDF, the Plans division was in a new directorate, one that at the joint level normally did not have responsibility for strategic planning. This was also a time of doctrinal flux in which the U.S. military was just beginning to become fully comfortable with the operational level of war—the intermediate level between the tactical and strategic. Woerner gave his planners a month to prepare the new plan; they were to brief him on March 5. On February 28, the Joint Chiefs of Staff (JCS) issued a formal planning order directing GEN Woerner to do what he was already doing.[29] The planning order was interesting in that it directed Woerner to conduct his planning within the Crisis Action Planning (CAP) subsystem of the Joint Operations Planning System (JOPS—the predecessor of JOPES), which would produce an Operations Order (OPORD) as its end product. Thus, the planning process would produce an order that, psychologically, creates a sense of urgency that no OPLAN has; the planners had a sense that the OPORD they were producing would be executed in the very near future.

On Saturday, March 5, 1988, the planners briefed GEN Woerner. Their OPORD, codenamed Elaborate Maze, had four phases. Phase I was a buildup of U.S. forces scheduled to be deliberate and taking about two weeks. Phase II was a noncombatant evacuation operation (NEO) that could be executed in either a permissive or nonpermissive environment. Phase III was defensive operations against the PDF, while Phase IV was offensive operations. Woerner listened intently; when the briefing ended, he asked, "Where is my post-conflict phase?" There wasn't one.[30]

Sunday morning, deputy director of the J-5, Colonel David Holdsworth, brought the two senior members of his Civil Affairs section in to work. He asked them if they had ever heard of Elaborate Maze, which, of course, they had not. Then he took them to the Tunnel—the secure location built into the side of Ancon Hill at SOUTHCOM headquarters, where they were read on to the plan. Holdsworth then directed them to have a draft Phase V (post-conflict) ready to brief to GEN Woerner by 5:00 PM that day. Their one question was whether the plan should be for an occupation similar to the post–World War II occupations of Germany and Japan or more along the lines of the civic assistance operations SOUTHCOM was then conducting in conjunction with the training exercises it was undertaking with friendly militaries in the region. The response was "occupation." The Civil Affairs officers briefed the outline of a plan to GEN Woerner and ended with a request that a full Civil Affairs planning cell be brought in from the Reserve Civil Affairs unit that supported SOUTHCOM. The cell would work during the next few months. Woerner approved the request.[31]

In his supervision of the drafting of Elaborate Maze, the one thing GEN Woerner stressed more than any other was that each and every phase of the plan must be capable of being executed sequentially, simultaneously, and/or independently of all the other phases. Once the planning order came down from the JCS on February 28, Elaborate Maze was regularly sent to Washington for review and approval by the Joint Staff (the post Goldwater-Nichols formal name for the JCS staff). At one point, the SOUTHCOM planners sought to include a Carrier Battle Group under the operational control of GEN Woerner. The navy pushed back arguing that naval forces were never under the operational control of a land force commander, although they could be put in support of the latter. The difference is critical; forces in support can be diverted to other missions by the decision of their tactical commander (i.e., the commander of the Carrier Battle Group), while if they are under the operational control of the GCC, they can only take on another mission with his consent. This deadlock went up the chain to the chairman of the Joint Chiefs of Staff, Admiral William J. Crowe, U.S. Navy, who resolved the issue in favor of GEN Woerner. Later versions of the plan made the issue moot as the Carrier Battle Group was no longer included.[32]

As the planning progressed through the spring and summer, supporting plans had to be drafted. Each of the service components had its own supporting plans, as did Joint Task Force-Panama, constituted by GEN Woerner around the staff of the army component, U.S. Army-South (USARSO). In addition, SOCSOUTH, the sub-unified special operations command, built its supporting plan. As would be expected, these were coordinated with the service staffs in Washington while SOCSOUTH's was coordinated with the U.S. Special Operations Command in Tampa, Florida.

During the spring of 1988, following a JCS review of Elaborate Maze, Woerner was directed to split the plan into a family of separate plans, each one following a phase of Elaborate Maze. Collectively renamed the Prayerbook, each OPORD had an independent identity: Phase I became Post Time; Phase II, Klondike Key; Phases III and IV were consolidated as Blue Spoon; and Phase V became Krystal Ball and later Blind Logic after the former codename was compromised.[33] Like the phases of Elaborate Maze, each order (plan) was capable of being executed in sequence, concurrently, or independently of any other order. It appears that the change to a "family of plans" was the result of some experimentation with the JOPS process. The experiment would not be repeated.

CRISIS EVENTS: SPRING AND SUMMER 1988

Soon after the indictment, Assistant Secretary of State for Inter-American Affairs Elliott Abrams met with the president of Panama, Eric Arturo Delvalle, secretly in Miami. The result of the meetings was that Delvalle agreed to fire General Noriega as commander in chief of the PDF. On February 25, Delvalle did so in a pretaped television statement, by which time he was in hiding.[34] That evening, Noriega convened the Legislative Assembly, which retaliated by removing Delvalle and his vice president from office. At 4:00 AM the next morning they swore in minister of education, Manuel Solis Palma, as minister in charge of the presidency, in effect as acting president.[35] The protesters were soon back on the streets and the United States tightened sanctions to some extent. The indictments followed by increased U.S. pressure changed the nature of the conflict from one internal to Panama to an international one involving the two countries directly. According to Secretary Schultz, the United States continued to recognize Delvalle as the legitimate president of Panama and, "at his instruction, impounded in the United States all the funds that would otherwise have flowed to the government of Panama from the operation of the Panama Canal."[36]

The effect of the impounding of funds was immediate and caused a sudden and drastic decline in economic activity in Panama that was especially vulnerable to this and other economic sanctions due to its use of the U.S. dollar as its currency. On March 16, elements of the PDF working with key leaders of the Christian Democratic Party (some with ties to the National Civic Crusade opposition) attempted to resolve the political-economic crisis by launching a coup d'état. The nominal leader of the coup was the chief of the police component of the PDF, Colonel Leonidas Macias, but the real leader was MAJ Fernando Quesada, a popular officer who had recently left command of the Urraca Company that provided security for PDF headquarters known as the *Comandancia*.[37]

Although contemporaneous comment, pushed by Noriega's propaganda operations, pointed to the amateurish nature of the coup and its rapid collapse, the real story came out later and showed it to have been closer to success than previously thought. This hinged on Quesada's role and his assumption that his former troops in the Urraca would remain loyal to him even if he only sent emissaries to the *Comandancia* and did not appear in person. Instead, the company rallied to their new commander, MAJ Moises Giroldi, and the coup collapsed. Its perpetrators were captured, beaten, and thrown into prison.[38]

Only two days after the coup attempt failed, Washington acted. Secretary Schultz sent William Walker, one of Elliott Abrams's deputies and Michael Kozak, a State Department lawyer who had been instrumental in negotiating the Panama Canal treaties a decade before, to Panama to try to get Noriega to leave office. This would be the first of many such trips between March and the end of May.[39] To apply greater pressure to Noriega, on April 8, in response to the advice of Abrams, the embassy, and Schultz, President Reagan invoked the International Emergency Economic Powers Act (IEEPA) against Panama. This action prohibited all American government agencies and individual Americans in Panama from doing any business at all with any entity of the Panamanian government that involved any payment of funds. Since there were some 35,000 American citizens living in Panama, not on the military bases, many of whom worked for the embassy, SOUTHCOM, or the PCC, and were totally dependent on Panamanian government agencies for electricity and telephone, the IEEPA sanctions were largely disregarded.[40]

During the various Kozak visits and the imposition of the IEEPA sanctions, GEN Woerner independently convened interagency discussions with embassy, PCC, and SOUTHCOM personnel at his headquarters in an effort to develop a coordinated plan to put pressure on Noriega. The focus was on exploiting the "fissures" within the PDF and between the PDF and Noriega's civilian supporters; indeed, Woerner called the plan "Fissures."[41] When he sent the plan forward through JCS channels, he heard a deafening silence. In May, Woerner sent a revised plan, "Fissures II," asserting that the plan needed to be executed as a whole and not piecemeal. Of course, he was told to execute individual paragraphs.[42]

Despite Woerner's perception that his "Fissures" plans had no significant impact, Schultz reports in his memoir that Deputy Secretary of State Michael Armacost put forth an interagency plan that had all the hallmarks of "Fissures."[43] While the efforts at negotiations and the pressures of economic sanctions played out, Noriega's PDF made a series of armed probes onto U.S. defense sites. The main location of the majority of these probes was the Arraijan Tank Farm (petroleum storage facility) near Howard AFB, Rodman Naval Station, and Fort Kobbe. In the first incident a U.S. Marine was killed by "friendly" fire; in others there were indications of PDF casualties but none were confirmed.[44]

Finally, toward the end of May, the NSC met one last time. As described by Abrams and Schultz, it was a very contentious session. The decision was to make a final try for an agreement with Noriega with only Schultz and the president in favor.[45] Nevertheless, when the final offer was laid on the table, Noriega would not accept it due to the refusal to withdraw the indictments. The failure of negotiations led to a lull in the crisis as the American presidential election campaign began to heat up and nobody wanted to rock the boat for vice president George Bush, who would become the Republican candidate. Indeed, despite the political and economic sanctions on the regime and the firefights on the edge of the jungle, the one constant refrain from the president, secretary of defense, and CJCS in their guidance to GEN Woerner was, "Don't get us into a war with Panama."

THE ELECTORAL "LULL"

During 1988 there had been a modest increase in U.S. forces in Panama, mostly military police. SOUTHCOM basically believed that this increase was sufficient to deal with the threat, which was mostly harassment. As the American presidential campaign got into full swing, the crisis in Panama stayed largely on the back burner. When Vice President Bush won the election he was primarily focused on putting his administration together. That proved harder to do than in the past due mostly to a more stringent vetting process that took, as its major casualty, Bush's first choice for secretary of defense, Senator John Tower. When that failed the president nominated Congressman Dick Cheney, who did not take office until March, almost three months after the inauguration. These delays carried over into subcabinet appointments. Thus the new administration was only beginning a major policy review for Panama when the next events of the crisis broke.

As a result of the IEEPA sanctions, American individuals and agencies could do no business with any entities of the Panamanian government. This meant, among other things, that when the U.S. government withheld taxes from its Panamanian employees, the money did not go to the government but into an escrow account. The result was that these Panamanians were deprived of evidence of having paid their taxes, could not renew license plates, and so on. This problem also affected the private school bus companies that were under contract with the U.S. Navy to transport schoolchildren to and from DOD Dependents Schools (DODDS). To avoid the problem, the navy provided the buses with U.S. government plates, contrary to Panamanian law. This provided Noriega with an excuse; on March 3, the PDF detained 21 school buses with children on board. Although the incident was resolved in about two hours, it left many Americans living in Panama, military and civilian, bitter toward GEN Woerner, SOUTHCOM, the U.S. government, and President Bush.[46] In the wake of the school bus incident, PDF harassment of American military personnel ticked up even more than it had all year.

Meanwhile, the Panamanian election process was proceeding toward the May 7 election day. As that process moved forward, the Bush administration's review of Panama policy progressed in parallel. For once, the embassy and SOUTHCOM were on the same page having coordinated their positions. Both argued for a reduction of U.S. personnel in Panama, increased pressure on Noriega, support for the opposition, action to drive a wedge between Noriega and the PDF, and full assertion of treaty rights, especially the right of free movement of American forces anywhere within the country. Woerner also proposed an additional buildup of troops, including some units designated in the Post Time OPORD.[47]

The election took place on May 7 and was surprisingly honest and peaceful. Noriega did try to steal it but in a way so inept that it appeared incredible. He, in the best Chicago political style, voted the PDF early and often, but they voted overwhelmingly against his handpicked candidates. This was confirmed by the tally sheets turned over to the Catholic Church for security.[48] The election was observed by both an international delegation led by former president Jimmy Carter and a U.S. delegation that included Senators John McCain and Connie Mack, and Representative John Murtha. While the Carter delegation was officially welcomed by the Panamanian government, the McCain, Mack, and Murtha team had come in without Panamanian permission. This resulted in a warning from GEN Woerner that he could not protect the delegation under international law if it did not have visas. Meanwhile, Ambassador Davis was assuring the delegation that all would be well as his diplomats secured the required visas.[49]

Carter, after observing the election and the stopping of the vote counting on Noriega's orders, publicly asserted that the election was being stolen. On their return to the United States the three members of Congress urged that Woerner be replaced.[50] In the wake of the elections and the violent repression of a peaceful demonstration by the winning opposition candidates on May 10,

President Bush approved executing the remaining measures recommended by Woerner and Ambassador Davis. Nevertheless, the underlying guidance to avoid going to war remained the same.

NIMROD DANCER, BLADE JEWEL, SAND FLEAS, AND PURPLE STORMS

Post Time was the plan to augment American forces in Panama in advance of or in the event of military operations against the PDF. Initially, it had been Phase I of Elaborate Maze, now, in mid-May 1989, it was essentially being executed, in part, as Operation Nimrod Dancer. The main force augmentation was a brigade of the 7th Infantry Division sent to the Atlantic side, a battalion of the 5th Mechanized Infantry Division attached to Army South, and a company of Marine Light Armored Vehicles, augmenting the marine forces on the West Bank of the Canal.[51]

The second element of enhanced pressures on the regime to be executed was, what was euphemistically called, return of off-post personnel. This involved the movement of command sponsored military and their families from apartments in Panama to American bases. It also involved the return to the United States of most of the dependents of those military personnel and the reduction of nonessential embassy staff, including most regional offices, and their departure from Panama. In short, what was going on was a "permissive" noncombatant evacuation operation (NEO), one of the contingencies called for in OPORD Klondike Key. In this case, it was executed as Operation Blade Jewel.[52] Interestingly, Klondike Key was the only OPORD that had been fully coordinated with the embassy.[53]

The third change was the effort proposed by Woerner and his staff to assert treaty rights, especially freedom of movement. These rights had been often allowed to apparently lapse as the United States did nothing to assert them and the PDF began to act as if they had been abrogated. Conducting exercises that would assert those rights by taking U.S. forces into places in Panama where they had not gone for a long time and at the same time stressing the capabilities of the PDF to respond as well as keeping them off balance, all without causing a shooting incident. The exercises also served to rehearse pieces of the Blue Spoon OPORD so that troops would be ready to execute if the order to do so ever came. Over the late spring and summer, the exercises became both more common and more intense and came to be known as Sand Fleas and Purple Storms. Much of the credit for this approach goes to Woerner's J-3 (Director of Operations), BG Marc Cisneros, who would soon be promoted to two stars and take command of Army South and JTF-Panama.[54] Planning for and approval of these exercises began even before the elections, but final approval from the JCS and the National Command Authority (NCA—the president and secretary of defense) was not given until a major freedom of movement exercise was approved for May 22.

SOUTHCOM REORGANIZED, NEW PLAYERS, AND A NEW COMMANDER

When Fred Woerner took command of SOUTHCOM in June 1987, the command underwent a reorganization that moved the Plans Division from the J-5 to the J-3. Two years later it was apparent that the experiment had failed and Plans moved back to the J-5. That meant that the Prayerbook would also move from the J-3 to the J-5, hardly a major issue except for one OPORD, Blind Logic. It was the responsibility of the Civil Affairs section of the J-5, which was very current operations oriented. As a result, Civil Affairs would move to the J-3 to function under current operations. The Civil Affairs officers coordinated their recommendation with the chief of the Policy and Strategy Division as well as with the two directors, Brigadier Generals Marc Cisneros (J-3) and Jim LeClair (J-5). At a briefing for GEN Woerner on May 18, they recommended that Blind Logic stay with the J-5 and be updated.[55] Woerner approved.

These events took place at a time of major changes in personnel at SOUTH-COM and its subordinate components. A new J-2, BG Michael Schneider, with no language or regional experience, replaced BG John Stewart, a Latin America Foreign Area officer. BG William Hartzog replaced Cisneros in the J-3 and Brig Gen Benard Gann replaced Brig Gen Jim LeClair in the J-5 (the latter two were USAF officers). Cisneros, on the promotion list for major general, replaced Bernard Loeffke as commander of USARSO and JTF-Panama. This left only Cisneros and Woerner as Spanish-speaking regional experts in the higher echelons of the command. In early July, the other shoe dropped when the chief of staff of the army personally visited and told Woerner he was being replaced. Although this change was not announced publicly until July 20 and Woerner would not relinquish command until September 30, it clearly diminished the knowledge level at the top.

On July 22, President Bush finally issued NSD 17, the policy statement pressed for by Woerner and Ambassador Davis, that authorized the intensified exercises. Sand Fleas, Purple Storms, and other exercises all had their desired effect. Freedom of movement and other treaty rights were reestablished, and the PDF was both stressed and off balance. Even after his announced retirement, Woerner's was the steady hand that guided the military actions with the strong support and intuitive understanding of how the PDF would react showed by Cisneros both as J-3 and after he took command of JTF-Panama.

Nevertheless, the problem of Panama was not resolved; it appeared that the crisis might go on indefinitely.

When Woerner's retirement was announced on July 20, GEN Maxwell R. Thurman was named as his replacement. Thurman was the senior-most four-star in the army; he had been vice chief of staff, was responsible for the success of the all-volunteer force, and currently commander of the Training and Doctrine Command. Due to retirement that summer, the new position would extend him beyond his mandatory retirement date for a full general. Thurman was known as a very demanding general who often knew more about any subject of interest than his staff did.[56]

THE SECOND COUP

On September 30 GEN Woerner turned command of SOUTHCOM over to GEN Thurman at the change of command ceremony at Fort Clayton, the headquarters of Army South. The next morning, on his first full day on the job, Thurman was informed of a planned coup by PDF MAJ Moises Giroldi, commander of the Urraca company responsible for security at the *Comandancia*.[57] Multiple aspects of the information seemed suspicious to GEN Thurman and his team as they heard the details. First, the information came from Giroldi's wife to her next-door neighbor, and friend, a young woman who handled all SOUTHCOM commercial travel arrangements. She, like many long-term SOUTHCOM employees, was a Zonian (an American citizen born in the former Canal Zone), who had been recommended by the SOUTHCOM commander's secretary who had served in that post since the late 1970s.[58] Unfortunately, the commander's secretary did not yet have a real relationship with her new boss, so she told the officer who was the liaison between the outgoing Woerner team and Thurman, one of the few SOUTHCOM officers who had the confidence of both commanders. He reported this up his chain, and Thurman held a series of meetings to ascertain the validity of the information and decide what to recommend to Washington.

Other issues about the proposal also did not sound "kosher" to Thurman and his senior staff, all of whom had little experience in the country.[59] One of these was that Giroldi was the officer who had saved Noriega from the March 1988 coup; he was also known to be close to Noriega who was the godfather of his son. Moreover, the plans as they were explained by the CIA officers who met with Adela Giroldi sounded half-baked. Thurman was especially concerned that this was all a ruse designed to embarrass and discredit him in his first days in command. Indeed, this interpretation was not totally far-fetched, given Noriega's expertise in psychological operations and experience in intelligence. Nevertheless, the one senior officer in the command who had sufficient experience in Panama and with the PDF to make sense of all this, MG Marc Cisneros, the new commander of Army South, was not called in until fairly late and was not asked to provide any expertise.

What Giroldi wanted from SOUTHCOM was that two major routes from PDF bases into Panama City be blocked so that loyal reinforcements could not make their way to PDF headquarters in the *Comandancia*. He also asked that safe haven for his family and the families of other coup plotters be arranged on American bases. After much deliberation, the hard charging Thurman made recommendations even more cautious than those of Woerner in his conversations with Chairman of the Joint Chiefs of Staff (CJCS) Colin Powell. The NCA agreed with the reluctant recommendation to block one road and be prepared to block the other. Then word came that the coup was postponed. The next word was that the postponement was only until the next day.

On the morning of October 3 the coup went down at 8:00 AM. Soon after, it was fairly clear that Giroldi had control of the *Comandancia*, but not much else was clear. Eventually, Thurman gave the order to close of both of the requested routes into the city, actions approved by the president and secretary through the CJCS. By the time that both routes had been secured, a PDF relief force had been airlifted to the military side of the international airport and was making its way into the city by yet another route. At that, wavering PDF units joined the countercoup. By 3:00 PM the coup was over and soon after that Giroldi and several of his co-conspirators had been summarily executed. U.S. policy toward Panama was nonexistent. Neither the decision makers in Washington, nor Thurman in Panama, had any real sense of how the PDF would react to the coup and, therefore, what SOUTHCOM could do to effectively support it. The one individual who did, Cisneros, in command of Army South and JTF-Panama, was not consulted or listened to. Just how effective Cisneros was in dealing with the PDF was demonstrated when Giroldi sent two of his captains to see Cisneros and not to SOUTHCOM to meet with Thurman.

The failure of the coup resulted in a number of actions. Sand Flea, Purple Storm, and other exercises were ramped up and focused on Blue Spoon targets. Changes in Blue Spoon, begun during the summer, were made more rapidly and the XVIII Airborne Corps was given the war planner and executor mission as JTF-South. The Bush administration determined that it would not be caught by surprise again, and the president appeared ready to give the execute order if there was any reasonable justification. But then, things in Panama quieted down, at least between U.S. institutions and the PDF.[60]

Following the coup all travel into Panama City from the bases was prohibited, except for official business and by local hire U.S. civilians who worked on the bases. As December arrived, the command began to think about allowing personnel to go into the city for dinner, shopping, or just sightseeing. Nearing the middle of the month SOUTHCOM reasoned that, as Christmas was fast approaching (indeed the decorations were up all over town), there would be no incidents. Thus, Saturday, December 16 was selected as the day to lift many of the travel restrictions. However, on December 15, Noriega called a meeting in the Legislative Assembly building of municipal representatives (the *coregidores*) to replace the acting presidency. During the meeting, Noriega gave a virulently anti-American speech in which he declared, "It is as if a state of war exists in Panama because of the North American aggression."[61]

This statement of pure political theater would later be cited as Noriega's "Declaration of War" against the United States. Although meant to rouse the crowd's anger at the United States it was, in no way, a declaration of war. The assembly then named Noriega "Maximum Leader of the Panamanian Revolution and Head of Government," the first time in his career he had ever assumed formal control over the civilian government of Panama. The apex of his career would last all of five days.

THE KILLING OF LT PAZ, THE HARASSMENT OF THE CURTISES, AND OPERATION JUST CAUSE

On the evening of December 16, while most of the senior staff of SOUTHCOM and JTF-Panama were attending gala Christmas events at various officer's clubs, four mid-level and junior officers had gone into the city for dinner. All were new in country, having arrived either just before or soon after the limitation on going into the city except for official business went into effect. Thus, none of them were familiar with the rabbit warren of streets in the city. On their return, the driver, a marine captain, took a wrong turn and ended up at a road block in front of the *Comandancia*.[62] A mixed group of civilians and PDF approached the car in what the driver took to be a menacing manner. On the spur of the moment he decided to run the roadblock, and the PDF manning it opened fire hitting Marine Lt Robert Paz, sitting in the backseat. Sadly Paz bled to death before they could reach the hospital.[63]

As if that were not enough, Navy LT Adam Curtis and his wife, who were walking nearby and witnessed the incident, were detained by the PDF. In the police station for questioning LT Curtis was badly beaten and his wife was sexually threatened and fondled before they were released.

When word of the shooting reached SOUTHCOM and JTF-Panama, all the festivities ended and officers moved quickly to their duty stations. Both incidents were rapidly reported to the JCS and by CJCS Powell to the secretary and President Bush. Even more than the killing of Lt Paz, the beating and harassment of the Curtises incensed the Americans in both Panama and Washington. The next day President Bush issued the order to execute Blue Spoon as Operation Just Cause. On Monday, December 19, TV news cameras caught military transport plane after military transport plane leaving from Pope AFB, North Carolina, adjacent to Fort Bragg.[64] At 00:45 hours on December 20, Operation Just Cause formally began.

CONCLUSION

The title of this chapter covers the essence of the development of national security policy in this crisis. Throughout, Washington actors were rarely initiators of action. Whether it was the reporting of Seymour Hersh (fed by sources in Panama), the actions of the two independent U.S. Attorneys who indicted Noriega without informing anyone in Washington, or Woerner's decision to begin planning, as soon as he heard about the indictments, key actions were made at the lower end of the chain of command. What Washington did, under both Reagan and Bush, was to set a key limit on the actions SOUTHCOM and the embassy could take. That limit was defined by the words "Don't get us in a war."

The limit constrained all the actions SOUTHCOM took to put pressure on Noriega and the PDF. It limited responses to military probes of U.S. bases, the rules of engagement for asserting treaty rights, and how the United States responded to the two coup attempts. With regard to the March 16, 1988, attempt, there is no indication that anybody in the American government knew that it would take place. It was clearly a totally Panamanian affair, so there was no immediate U.S. response. In contrast, the October 3, 1989, coup was coordinated with the U.S. military but nobody in SOUTHCOM headquarters (or the local CIA station) quite understood what was going on. The one person who had a good grasp, and gave indications that he would have handled it differently, was the new USARSO/JTF-Panama commander, Marc Cisneros. GEN Thurman, however, did not trust Cisneros and, therefore, failed to make use of his expertise and insights.[65]

In the end, the decision to go to war was made by President Bush, in response to the clear danger to American military and civilians in Panama from the PDF and the paramilitary Dignity Battalions. Another striking aspect of the decision making is the change of players on the American side throughout the critical spring of 1989. A new U.S. president was inaugurated along with a new set of actors at the top of the administration, all of whom had little time to get their hands around the Panama situation. Continuity was in Panama itself—in the embassy, SOUTHCOM, and the PCC. But the embassy had, by that time, been largely marginalized because of the U.S. de facto nonrecognition of the Noriega-controlled government. The PCC role was limited at best. That left SOUTHCOM and its subordinate headquarters as the critical players.

Just as Washington began to settle in with its new senior officials, changes began to take place in SOUTHCOM. Part of this was normal rotation with the new J-2, 3, and 5 along with Cisneros's promotion and taking command of USARSO/JTF-Panama. The critical change, however, was the relief of Woerner and his replacement by Thurman. Thurman's choices, when confronted by the unexpected coup from an unexpected source, were overly cautious and were ratified by the equally cautious new administration. Not only was Thurman only a day into his new job but Colin Powell, the new CJCS, was almost as new as he was. Despite his prior experience as Reagan's national security advisor, Panama had never been his portfolio. The result was a missed opportunity for a peaceful (from the American perspective) resolution of the Panama crisis. It also made war significantly more likely.

NOTES

1. In the post-conflict period after Operation Just Cause I served with a U.S. officer who had been one of the American high school students who had initiated the flag incident. I also served with another officer in Panama who, as an enlisted soldier, had had to spirit his wife to safety in the Canal Zone during the riots. Clearly, this was not a one-sided event.

2. I follow U.S. practice in discussing the treaties with President Carter's name going first. Panama calls then the Torrijos-Carter Treaties. Indeed, the official English text follows U.S. practice, while the official Spanish text follows Panamanian practice.

3. The next several paragraphs are drawn from my article "The Interagency in Panama 1986–1990," in K.D. Goff (ed.) *U.S. Army and the Interagency Process.* Fort Leavenworth, KS: 2008, Combat Studies Institute Press. 65–77.

4. Prior to the G.W. Bush administration, unified commands were led by commanders in chief, abbreviated CINCs. SECDEF Donald Rumsfeld said that there was only one CINC, the president, and decreed that the former CINCs would henceforth be known as combatant commanders. This term has been abbreviated COCOM (which, however, also means combatant command) and for geographic commands like SOUTHCOM as GCCs. I will use commander and GCC interchangeably.

5. John R. Galvin, *Fighting the Cold War: A Soldier's Memoir.* Lexington: 2015, University of Kentucky Press. 298–299. Notice, however, that Galvin carefully states that this applies to what we were doing in Panama, not the region as a whole.

6. Ibid. I served in SOUTHCOM under General Galvin in 1986 and 1987 in his Strategy, Plans, and Policy Directorate (J-5) and his Small Wars Operations Research Directorate (SWORD). He was, by far, the most competent four-star general I ever met. In this quote, however, he makes a couple of errors. First, LTG McAuliffe was

the Panama Canal Commission Administrator, not the head of the PCC itself. Second, the Canal Zone no longer existed as a legal entity after 1979.

7. The marine lieutenant colonel who headed all the marine security detachments was one of my two best friends in Panama; the other was a DEA pilot who operated from Panama into Peru, Bolivia, and Colombia. Both regularly attended country team meetings.

8. After the invasion, on an official trip around Panama, I was told by the secretary to Panama's new first lady that the CIA was responsible for Torrijos's death. In the early stages of the crisis, Noriega would be accused of the "murder" by his rival, Roberto Diaz Herrera. My colleague on the faculty of the army FAO course, LTC Bob Anderson, who had investigated the crash (himself a helicopter pilot) told me that the crash was simply an accident caused by flying in bad weather in the mountains.

9. I was shown the document by Richard Millett, a well-known scholar of Central American militaries, in 1990 after the invasion.

10. Barletta, who had been a student of Secretary of State George Schultz's at the University of Chicago, never accepted that the election was fraudulent, and Schultz did attend his inauguration.

11. Lawrence A. Yates, *The U.S. Military Intervention in Panama.* Washington, DC: 2008, Center for Military History. 12.

12. See Galvin, 308. During my tenure in SOUTHCOM, I was skeptical of Noriega's responsibility. My sense was that he had nothing to gain from killing Spadafora, while Diaz Herrera, who had broken with Noriega, had everything to gain if he could pin the responsibility on Noriega. Needless to say, I did not have access to GEN Galvin's memoir that would have changed my view.

13. "Wee hours" is the best translation for the Spanish word *madrugada*, which is when the resignation took place—between 2:00 and 3:00 AM.

14. I would run past this picture daily while working out before going to work at SOUTHCOM headquarters.

15. See Yates, 12–13.

16. Ibid.

17. My DEA friends told me at the time that everybody in DEA agreed that Noriega did work both sides of the street but that the special agent in charge, Alfredo Duncan, was convinced that his cooperation with the DEA was more valuable than his cooperation with traffickers. I was also told that the attitude of the CIA station was similar to that of the DEA.

18. Galvin, 304.

19. Yates, 14–15.

20. Ibid., 18.

21. I later came to know several PDF officers who were active Christian Democrats.

22. Protests often took place during the noon hour with participants gathering in front of a major church near two significant shopping areas (and not far from PDF headquarters, the *Comandancia*), lining the streets, banging pots and pans. When the *Dobermans* showed up, the demonstrators would light tires on fire. By 4:00 PM or so, the only indication of the protests would be burning tires in the street as I returned to my quarters in the city from SOUTHCOM HQ in Quarry Heights an hour later.

23. Yates, 19.

24. Ibid. About this same time, another mob set fire to the U.S. Information Service Library (across the street from my apartment), gutting it and resulting in its closing.

25. Ibid.

26. Ibid., 28.

27. Interview with GEN Fred F. Woerner, Boston, Massachusetts, May 6, 1991. In a phone interview with Elliott Abrams on June 15, 2015, he said he did not recall the meeting with Woerner; however, he did confirm that nobody in Washington had been consulted or was even aware that the indictments were imminent. Abrams did say that as a result the DOJ changed its policy and began requiring all U.S. attorneys to at least inform the department when they were convening a grand jury to investigate a high official of a foreign government. See also George P, Schultz, *Turmoil and Triumph: My Years as Secretary of State.* New York: 1993, Charles Scribner's Sons. Chapter 48.

28. Woerner interview.

29. LTC William C. Bennett, "Just Cause and the Principles of War," *Military Review*, March 1991, 9–10. Author's interviews with SOUTHCOM planners, April–May 1991. Woerner interview.

30. Interviews with planners and GEN Woerner.

31. Interview with LTC Robert S. Rodrigues (telephone), May 8, 1991. In 1988 Rodrigues was a major and one of the two Civil Affairs officers called in that Sunday. At the time (and even today) most of the expertise in Civil Affairs was in the Army Reserve.

32. Interviews. This incident is included because a similar case will be addressed in Chapter 7.

33. Bob Woodward, in *The Commanders*, argues that this was a major revision; it was not. New York, 1991: Simon & Schuster. 85. See also John T. Fishel, *The Fog of Peace*. Carlisle, PA: 1992, Strategic Studies Institute. 10

34. Yates, 31, Fishel, 2, and Schultz, location 21574 (Kindle edition). Contemporaneous reports and interviews conducted by the author indicated that Delvalle was hiding at the residence of the U.S. ambassador.

35. Yates, 31.

36. Schultz, location 21580.

37. Interview with LTC (Ret.) Fernando Quesada, May 1, 1991.

38. Quesada interview. Interview with MAJ (Ret.) Francisco Alvarez April 25, 1991.

39. Yates, 98–102. Schultz, Chapter 48.

40. I was one of those affected, and I paid both my electric and telephone bills. The embassy, which rented apartments for its U.S. employees (from all agencies), chose to ignore the bills. On April 21, embassy apartments found their electricity cut off. Soon after, the embassy caved and State granted exemptions for basic services.

41. Woerner interview. Yates, 97–101.

42. Ibid.

43. Schultz, location 21678.

44. Yates, 70–97. Schultz, Chapter 48. On one occasion, I was called out to supervise some of the patrols of the Tank Farm during the period of these incidents.

Unfortunately, at no time were we able to definitively prove that the PDF probes were taking place, although I am convinced they were very real.

45. Abrams interview. Schultz, location 21978–22052. Abrams told me that the cited passage in Schultz is taken directly from his notes of the meeting where he was Schultz's notetaker.

46. Yates, 145.

47. Yates, 150–155.

48. Contemporaneous discussions with Panamanians, some of whom served as poll watchers.

49. Yates, 166–167.

50. Ibid.

51. Yates, 156–189, is the source for much of this section, unless otherwise stated.

52. My family and friends were ordered home under Blade Jewel, and I was ordered to move on post.

53. Interview with embassy political counselor, Michael Polt, April 3, 1991.

54. Interview with MG Cisneros, April 15, 1991.

55. I was the chief of policy and strategy and would inherit Bind Logic under this plan. The story is told in my *The Fog of Peace: Planning the Restoration of Panama.* Carlisle, PA: 1992, Strategic Studies Institute.

56. I was told at the time by one of the deputy directors of the J-5 who had worked for Thurman that he was tough but fair; I was also told that when briefing him, if I didn't know something to say so but never to "tap dance" because that was truly the cardinal sin.

57. Much of this discussion is drawn from Yates, Chapter 9, along with my own conversations with officers from SOUTHCOM and USARSO who were at the meetings on Sunday, October 1, 1989. I was informed of the planned coup as a team of us, led by a deputy director of the J-5, were leaving by commercial air on a trip to coordinate with U.S. Special Operations Command in Tampa, Florida. Since the coup was planned for that morning, there was a possibility that we would be caught in its wake at Panama's international airport.

58. Mary Coffee had been hired by then MAJ John Waghelstein, who was the commander's aide-de-camp at the time. Conversation with retired COL John D. Waghelstein, n.d. A Zonian is a U.S. citizen born and raised in the former Panama Canal Zone.

59. BG William Hartzog had arrived in June to take over as J-3; BG Michael Schneider that summer became the new J-2, and BG Benard Gann, the new J-5, had arrived in August. Schneider, who replaced John Stewart, a Latin American Foreign Area officer, who spoke fluent Spanish and was particularly well rounded in all intelligence disciplines, was noted as a SIGINT specialist with no language skills.

60. They were sufficiently quiet that I was approached by an officer in the J-2 to see if I could touch my friends in Panama City, where I had lived before Blade Jewel, to see if I could make contact with any PDF officers and get a message to them. The message was that the United States still saw a role for the PDF in a democratic Panama.

61. Translation by the author and LTG Marc Cisneros based on witnessing the speech on radio and watching it on TV both live and on videotape.

62. I had flown out that morning on commercial air, the first time since October 3 that this was permitted. Having lived in Panama City for three years by that time I still occasionally took a wrong turn in that part of town.

63. I did not know until later that the officer who was killed was Rob Paz until I heard the story from his boss, Marine Col Len Fuchs, a good friend.

64. I saw this on TV in Georgia and immediately drew the conclusion that we were going to war. I would get a call that night, around 1:00 AM, from a marine friend, that the operation had launched. Not until December 26 would I be able to make contact with anybody in Panama when I finally talked with my roommate at 5:00 AM who said, "John, get your ass back here, they are executing your plan!"

65. Just how attuned Cisneros was to the PDF can be assessed by his actions in the latter stages of Just Cause. No part of Blue Spoon addressed how to deal with the PDF garrisons around the country, outside of the Panama City–Colon Canal Area. Cisneros undertook that, with what became known as Operation Ma Bell, involving telephone calls from a PDF commander who had fought well before he surrendered to overwhelming forces, to the commanders of those garrisons. When reached, those commanders then spoke directly to Cisneros, who told them just how to surrender to the Special Forces units that would be arriving shortly. Every one of the PDF garrisons surrendered as a result of talking to Cisneros without a shot being fired. Interviews with LTG Marc Cisneros and CPT Amadis Jimenez (PDF).

Chapter 7

"I Love It When a Plan Comes Together"[1]

MIDDLE EAST BACKGROUND

Iraq was created out of the wreckage of the Ottoman Empire in the wake of World War I. Given to the British under the Mandate system of the League of Nations; the state became a monarchy ruled by King Faisal, in response to promises made, in part, by T. E. Lawrence (Lawrence of Arabia). Iraq received its independence in 1932, and the monarchy was overthrown by a revolution in 1958. Following that revolution, the Baath Party came to dominate the state and by the late 1970s, the party fell under the sway of Saddam Hussein, and thus, he became the dictator of Iraq.

In 1961, the small emirate of Kuwait, just south of Iraq, became fully independent of the British. An oil state, like Iraq, Kuwait shares the huge Rumaila deposit that runs beneath both countries. Following the Iranian Revolution in 1979, relations between Iraq and Iran deteriorated until, in September 1980, Saddam declared war on Iran and invaded it. Driven out of Iran in 1982, Iraq was on the defensive until the war ended in 1988. Kuwait, along with other gulf Arab states, supported Iraq. Kuwait's support was mainly in the form of large loans. After the war with Iran ended, Kuwait made it clear that it wanted the loans repaid.

THE KUWAIT CRISIS

In the spring of 1990, Saddam began to put pressure on Kuwait to forgive the loans. He also began complaining that Kuwait was flooding the market with oil and that, at least, some of that oil was from slant drilling in the Rumaila field under Iraqi territory. All through the spring and into the summer the

113

rhetoric of crisis ramped up. Nevertheless, no one seemed to think that Saddam would attempt to resolve the issue by war.

On July 16, 1990, DIA's national intelligence officer for the Middle East, retired army colonel Walter "Pat" Lang, viewed satellite photographs of southern Iraq opposite the Kuwait border. "Where there had been empty desert . . . the day before. He saw the beginning of a brigade of an Iraqi tank division of T-72 tanks, the top of the line heavy tanks supplied to Iraq by the Soviets."[2] Three days later, on July 19, Iraq had three of its elite Republican Guard divisions on the border with Kuwait.[3] Meanwhile, on July 17, Saddam had accused both Kuwait and the United Arab Emirates of exceeding OPEC oil production limits to drive down prices, and he warned that Iraq would take "effective action to put things right."[4]

It is worth noting here that the Bush administration in July 1990 was not focused primarily on the Persian Gulf or even the greater Middle East. Europe was in the midst of major changes. President Bush had expanded the "War on Drugs" with NSD 18 in August of the previous year. Panama was still an issue as the administration sought to make sure that the new democratic government had a good chance of success. At home, there was the very bruising budget battle with Congress. As a result, the Kuwait crisis was just one of many international situations the NSC and the various agencies of the government were monitoring.[5]

On July 25, American ambassador to Iraq, April Glaspie, was suddenly summoned to the Presidential Palace to meet with Saddam. Afterward, she sent a summary cable reporting her talks and indicating her belief that Saddam was worried. "He does not want to further antagonize us," she wrote.[6] Glaspie was much criticized for how she handled this meeting, but President Bush notes that Saddam lied to her and that she made very clear to him that the United States would not condone the settlement of the dispute with Kuwait and the UAE by anything other than peaceful means.[7]

Following the meeting with Glaspie, diplomatic efforts by the Arab states seemed to be making headway. Saddam had assured Glaspie that Iraq was not about to attack Israel and wanted that assurance passed on to the Israelis, which it was. The ensuing reduction of tensions secured Saddam's flank. In the meantime, the Iraqi buildup on the Kuwait border continued. On July 30, Pat Lang sent a long memo to the director of DIA, in which he concluded that Saddam was not bluffing and was preparing to invade Kuwait. Although he disagreed with his senior analyst, the director passed the memo on to the rest of the intelligence community.[8] No one agreed with Lang. The reason, as Secretary of State Jim Baker, would later write was:

> Furthermore, without exception, our friends in the region consistently argued that Saddam was only posturing and that confrontation would simply make matters worse. Simply put, the reason why nobody believed Saddam would attack is because no realistic calculation of his interests could have foreseen a full-scale invasion of Kuwait.[9]

INVASION

Two days later, on August 1, the three Iraqi armored divisions had uncoiled and were in attack positions. The next day, they struck. Kuwait fell within hours. The emir and his family barely escaped to Saudi Arabia. Before the day was over the Iraqi army was within easy striking distance of the Saudi border. Over the next several days, the Iraqi army consolidated its control of Kuwait and had positioned itself to move on into Saudi Arabia. Moreover, additional reinforcing Iraqi divisions continued to move into Kuwait. The threat to Saudi Arabia, as seen in U.S. satellite photography, was obvious. On the ground both inside Saudi Arabia and from short reconnaissance penetrations into Kuwait, there was nothing to be seen.

RESPONSE: THE PRESIDENT AND THE NSC

At 5:00 AM on August 2, NSA Brent Scowcroft reported the current status of the invasion to President Bush along with what the United States was already doing about it. The president ordered already alerted American warships at Diego Garcia to head for the Persian Gulf. He wanted to get U.S. aircraft into the area but that would require Saudi agreement to provide them basing. Scowcroft then handed Bush an Executive Order freezing Iraqi assets in the United States.[10] There followed an NSC meeting that was mainly devoted to culling the information gathered and exploring the courses of action that could be considered. Among them was CENTCOM'S OPLAN 1002–90 for the defense of Saudi Arabia.[11]

RESPONSE: OPLAN 1002–90

OPLAN 1002–90 was a product of the military planning process then known as JOPS (and now called JOPES).[12] CENTCOM was created out of the Rapid Reaction Joint Task Force established by President Jimmy Carter in the wake of the Iranian Revolution in 1979. From the beginning, it planned for the defense of Saudi Arabia and its oil fields from attack by Iran and/or the Soviet Union. Later, planning shifted to defending the Saudis from an attack by Iraq.

CENTCOM had been commanded by GEN H. Norman Schwarzkopf since November 1988. In 1990, Schwarzkopf's planners were in the biannual process of updating and revising their principal plans, one of which was 1002. When the revision of the plan had been completed, Schwarzkopf decided to conduct an exercise of 1002, now called 1002–90. This would take place as Exercise Internal Look during June and July. Internal Look was the kind of exercise that the army calls a Command Post Exercise (CPX), which is designed to test staff functions and is conducted without troops on the ground.[13] The purpose of Internal Look was to identify any deficiencies in OPLAN 1002–90 so that they could be revised. The exercise did find deficiencies, and the revisions in the plan were being made when Iraq struck Kuwait on August 2.

RESPONSE: BUILDING THE COALITION

President George Bush was hardly a neophyte in foreign affairs. He had served as the American ambassador to the UN and envoy to China. He had been director of Central Intelligence heading both the CIA and the entire Intelligence Community. As Ronald Reagan's vice president he had conducted a number of delicate diplomatic missions, among them "reading the riot act" to the high command of the El Salvadoran armed forces over their human rights violations. Moreover, Bush had strong personal relationships with a significant number of foreign leaders, including British prime minister Margaret Thatcher, French president Mitterrand, German chancellor Kohl, Soviet leader Mikhail Gorbachev, Chinese leader Deng Xiaoping, Israeli prime minister Yitzhak Shamir, and the Saudi king and Royal Family, especially Saudi ambassador, Prince Bandar Bin Sultan. On top of that, the president had forged a very strong national security team that he was quite close to, especially his national security advisor, Gen (Ret.) Brent Scowcroft, Secretary of State Jim Baker (a close friend and political confidant), and his secretary of defense, Dick Cheney. His chairman of the Joint Chiefs of Staff, GEN Colin Powell, had been both deputy NSA and national security advisor to President Reagan.

The team had the skills needed to assist President Bush in building a solid international coalition designed to turn around Saddam's invasion of Kuwait, if the Saudis could be convinced that the kingdom was really in danger. Thus, the first task in coalition building was to get the Saudis to ask for help. Scowcroft recounts that the key was Saudi ambassador to the United States, Prince Bandar, son of the Saudi defense minister, with the rank of minister in the Saudi government, and King Fahd's chief diplomatic troubleshooter. Scowcroft invited Bandar to his office and offered significant American forces to defend the kingdom. Bandar, however, was less than enthusiastic and, when Scowcroft asked why, recounted instances in the past that had given the Saudis and others in the region the impression that the Americans were not reliable allies.[14] Scowcroft states in *A World Transformed* that "President Bush had thought the issue through carefully, in full recognition of all the consequences. In light of that, I could give him a pledge that, if the troops were offered and accepted, we would stand with them to the end."[15] As a result, Bandar was welcomed at the Pentagon and briefed on CENTCOM's plans. The outcome of that briefing was that a high-level American delegation would go to Saudi Arabia and brief the king.

The delegation, led by Secretary of Defense Dick Cheney, included undersecretary of defense for policy, Paul Wolfowitz, the NSC's Bob Gates, GEN H. Norman Schwarzkopf, CINC CENTCOM, and American ambassador to Saudi Arabia Charles "Chaz" Freeman. It arrived on Monday, August 6, 1990.[16] The delegation briefed King Fahd on the intelligence of the Iraqi capabilities and apparent intentions as well as what the United States was prepared to do about it. Schwarzkopf laid out his entire plan, 1002–90, for the king. Fahd was convinced of both the threat and the seriousness of President Bush to protect the kingdom and reverse the invasion of Kuwait. He gave his blessing to the plan in its entirety.[17]

RESPONSE: INSTANT THUNDER

During this early stage, President Bush, returning from Camp David, said publicly on CNN, "This will not stand; this aggression against Kuwait."[18] With this brief statement, the president committed the administration to reversing the Iraqi invasion, something that would require an offensive option. No such option existed in 1002–90. Finding an offensive option that could be executed without delay thus became an immediate priority within the Defense Department. In fact, it was to be found in a relatively obscure U.S. Air Force planning cell in the Pentagon with the codename Checkmate.[19] Checkmate was headed by the air force's most innovative strategic thinker, COL John Warden, whose book on aerial warfare, *The Air Campaign*, revolutionized thinking about the use of air power. In a crash effort, Warden and his two action officers, Lt Col Dave Deptula and Lt Col Ben Harvey, devised an offensive operations plan based on Warden's concepts that could be executed rapidly with devastating effect on the Iraqis. Called "Instant Thunder," the plan targeted Iraqi leadership, command and control, infrastructure, morale, and fielded forces and was meant to last a matter of a few days. Although Instant Thunder was briefed at the very highest levels, it was seen as a relatively desperate option, one that nobody wished to have to execute. Nevertheless, it became the basis for the air campaign later executed by GEN Schwarzkopf's Joint Force Air Component Commander (JFACC), Gen. Chuck Horner, whose principal planner would be Lt Col Deptula.

DESERT SHIELD

With the approval from King Fahd for American forces in the kingdom, GEN Schwarzkopf received the order to execute 1002–90. CENTCOM planners had been extremely busy through the days leading up to the Execute Order translating OPLAN 1002–90 into an OPORD (Operations Order). Because the OPLAN had been so recently exercised and revised, this process came as close to the ideal as ever happens in the real world. There was, in fact, very little massaging needed, little more than adding a date, changing the heading from OPLAN to OPORD, and giving the operation a name. The name chosen was "Desert Shield."[20]

Executing the plan involved a number of significant actions, many of which would take place simultaneously. These included deploying CENT-COM headquarters forward to Riyadh in Saudi Arabia, air force F-15s to the kingdom and the first ground troops, the 82nd Airborne Division from Fort Bragg, North Carolina, to the Saudi desert. Although the deployment of the 82nd can begin very rapidly—the Ready Brigade can be in the air within 18 hours of being alerted—the entire division takes about two weeks to deploy. The major advantage of the 82nd is its strategic mobility; however, once deployed, it has very limited tactical mobility as well as limited heavy weaponry (artillery). It is only a slight exaggeration to say that once on the ground, the 82nd is merely "foot mobile." Further, the joke at the time was that the division would be little more than a speed bump if Saddam decided to attack with his tanks.

Diplomacy

Even before King Fahd had agreed to accept American troops in the kingdom, President Bush was conducting his own brand of personal diplomacy, working the phones with U.S. allies. On August 3 he spoke with Turkish president Turgut Ozal, "who angrily said Saddam 'should get his lesson.'"[21] Ozal had been talking with King Fahd and shared that conversation with Bush. Later that day, the president spoke with President François Mitterrand of France, who supported Ozal's argument in favor of NATO action as well a working with other allies. Likewise, German chancellor Helmut Kohl and Japanese prime minister Toshiki Kaifu agreed on the necessity of collective action.[22]

Meanwhile, Secretary of State James Baker had been in Moscow holding talks with Soviet foreign minister Eduard Shevardnadze. That same August 3, they issued a joint statement that condemned Iraq's invasion of Kuwait. Scowcroft later noted the importance of this as it showed not only that the Cold War was largely over but that the United States and the USSR were on the same side and that Moscow was not prepared to help its client consolidate what it had gained by naked aggression.[23]

National Security Advisor Brent Scowcroft describes the complexity of the diplomatic issues involved in building the coalition in his joint memoir with President Bush:

Everyone wanted some sort of "cover" to protect themselves against any back-lash. Ozal hoped his moves would be cloaked by NATO. Fahd did not wish to be the only Arab state opposing Iraq. [Australia's] Hawke didn't want to be the single Commonwealth country joining the coalition. Even we needed to demonstrate that this action was not a solo US effort against an Arab state. As countries individually joined up and sent forces, we gained momentum, but the interlocking nature of the requirements for the various members of the coalition illustrated the complicated task of putting it together as well as its inherent fragility. The welcome troop contributions became a challenge to manage, and in the coming weeks and months CENTCOM scrambled to integrate new contingents, some quite small and others (such as the British and French) large into their plans. The diversity symbolized international determination to reverse the invasion, but in practical terms the many smaller, specialized units sometimes left Schwartzkopf's planners scratching their heads.[24]

Despite complexity and difficulties, the diplomacy of the Bush team was highly successful. They accomplished the building of a diverse coalition that was reflected in success within the UN Security Council resulting in a de jure legitimization of the actions that were taken immediately and later against Saddam. They also produced strong military support for the coalition that included such diverse Arab partners as Egypt, Syria, Saudi Arabia, the UAE, and Morocco. Moreover, countries like Japan (whose constitution prohibited contributing military forces) provided major financial support to coalition operations.

DESERT STORM[25]

Over the course of the fall of 1990, coalition forces were built up in Saudi Arabia near the border with Kuwait as part of Operation Desert Shield. At the same time, planning for offensive operations continued with GEN Schwarzkopf calling on planners from the Army Command and General Staff College's School of Advanced Military Studies—dubbed the "Jedi Knights"—augmenting his CENTCOM planning team. The planners developed a sophisticated plan, including deception operations to move the major strike forces out to the west for an enveloping flank attack on the Iraqis. In addition, command and control of coalition forces was established in what was called the C3IC (Command, Control, Communications, and Intelligence Center) in Riyadh, where U.S. and Saudi commanders sat side by side to run the war.

Initially, the United States exercised command and control over all Western forces except the French, who fell under the Saudis. The latter also controlled all the Arab forces. Later, as the date to begin operations approached, the French joined the British under American command. The American forces were under three separate land headquarters: the army's VII Corps, which included the British Armoured Division, the XVIII Airborne Corps that the French division would later join, and a Marine Expeditionary Force, consisting of a marine division and an air wing. The other headquarters was the Saudi-led Arab coalition force.

Desert Storm began with the air campaign when U.S. Army special operations helicopters took out Iraqi early warning radars, and F-117 stealth fighter bombers struck targets in Baghdad at 03:00 AM local time. These actions were followed by round-the-clock bombing raids for 43 days. Lt Gen Chuck Horner, the Joint Force Air Component Commander (JFACC), used a single Air Tasking Order to control all coalition air assets. Although this was near 100% on Day 1, army assets dropped off immediately as they were an integral part of the ground forces campaign. Naval and marine air participated with the marines reverting to a close air support role once the ground campaign began for the same reason as the army aviation did not fall under the JFACC.

During the 43 days of the air campaign, as soon as the Iraqis were blind to any coalition movement, the VII Corps moved sharply to the west, while the XVIII Airborne Corps leapfrogged the VII Corps taking up positions to their west. As this was taking place, marine forces were showing preparations for an amphibious landing, another part of the deception operations.

On February 24, the ground war began. The XVIII Airborne Corps attacked by air assault with the 101st Airborne (Air Assault) division by helicopter to the Euphrates with the 24 Infantry division moving up behind them on the ground and the French division providing the covering force on the Western flank. VII Corps, including the British Armoured division, made its powerful left hook attack on the Iraqi Republican Guard divisions from the west. The marines and Arab coalition forces attacked straight into Kuwait, where Iraqi forces simply collapsed, in part due to the pounding they had taken from the air.[26]

During the 100 hours of the ground war, the allied forces seized a significant portion of southern Iraq and completely liberated Kuwait. Fleeing Iraqi forces were struck from the air on what became known as the "highway of death." Thousands of destroyed Iraqi vehicles were abandoned. Partly because of the perception of a large number of deaths of Iraqi soldiers who no longer had the ability to defend themselves and partly due to the symbolic value of 100 hours, President Bush proclaimed a unilateral cease-fire on February 27.

CEASE-FIRE

When he announced the cease-fire, President Bush stated his terms for a permanent cease-fire:

> Iraq must release immediately all coalition prisoners of war, third country nationals and the remains of those who have fallen. Iraq must release all Kuwaiti

detainees. Iraq also must inform Kuwait authorities of the location and nature of all land and sea mines. Iraq must comply fully with all relevant United Nations Security Council resolutions. This includes Iraq's August decision to annex Kuwait, and acceptance in principle of Iraq's responsibility compensation for the loss, damage, and injury its aggression has caused.[27]

The president also called for a meeting of coalition and Iraqi military commanders to arrange the military aspects of the cease-fire. This meeting was to be held within 48 hours. The cease-fire was conditioned on Iraq's not firing on coalition forces or launching Scud missiles against any state.[28] The president's statement was the sum total of the guidance GEN Schwarzkopf and his staff received before they began their negotiations with the Iraqi generals.[29]

AFTERMATH

In the aftermath of Desert Storm, Shi'ite Arabs in Iraq's South revolted, as did Kurds in the north. While the Kurds took control of the cities of Erbil, Kirkuk, and several others, the Iraqi military used their helicopter gunships—after all they interpreted the terms of the cease-fire to include their flying *all* helicopters—against the Shi'a rebels. Because the United States did nothing, after having verbally encouraged the revolts, Saddam went after the Kurds as well. The Kurdish revolt quickly collapsed, and Kurds began to flee across the international borders to Turkey and Iran. The Turkish–Iraqi border area was mountainous, and the fleeing people took dubious refuge above the snowline where they believed, correctly, the Iraqi army would not follow. They were, however, hardly better off as the weather, lack of food, shelter, clothing, and other supplies left them very much at the risk of their lives.

The dire refugee situation faced the Bush administration with a new set of challenges.[30] Whether acknowledged or not, the refugee exodus had been created by the words of the president urging the Iraqi people to overthrow Saddam. When the Kurds revolted and were met by Iraqi helicopter-borne troops and gunships, they fled and became refugees in the Turkish mountains. Neither the administration nor the involved unified commands, CENTCOM and EUCOM, had planned for a humanitarian relief mission provoked by the revolt they had called for but not participated in. Fortunately, this was not a case of the dreaded "no plan" scenario. During Operation Desert Storm, EUCOM had supported CENTCOM running the air campaign in Northern Iraq out of the airbase at Incirlik, Turkey. Although those air assets were included on CENTCOM's single air tasking order, their missions were largely autonomous.[31] In addition, Special Operations Command, Europe (SOCEUR), under the command of BG Richard Potter, U.S. Army Special Forces, had run the Combat Search and Rescue operations in the Northern

Theater.[32] The plans for these missions were easily adapted to the refugee situation on the Iraqi–Turkish border.

EUCOM commander, GEN John R. Galvin (also NATO Supreme Allied Commander, Europe—SACEUR), tapped U.S. Army Europe, deputy commander, LTG John Shalikashvili, to take command of the entire effort in Turkey and Northern Iraq. Galvin actually made this decision in anticipation of the presidential order establishing the humanitarian rescue mission.[33] Shalikashvili, operating under Galvin and in response to the president's April 5 order directing what would be called Operation Provide Comfort, established two ground task forces, one under Potter and the other under MG Jay Garner. In addition, there was an air component, a support element, and a Civil Affairs command, all headed by general officers or equivalents. There was even an interagency element with a USAID Disaster Assistance Response Team (DART) working out of Garner's headquarters.[34]

Potter's task force was responsible for initial support of the refugees and then moving them off the mountains and into the camps established by Garner's task force. Protecting the camps from the Iraqis was a battalion of infantry commanded by then LTC John Abizaid, who would later command CENTCOM. Abizaid was particularly well qualified since he was a Middle East Army Foreign Area Officer (FAO) and fluent in Arabic. Allied countries also contributed troops to the force that was given the name of Combined Task Force (CTF) Provide Comfort. The plan that the CTF developed was to first stabilize the situation, then provide transit camps in the valley near the cities the refugees had fled, and finally to move them back into those cities, all the while protecting them from a vengeful Iraqi military and police. This was accomplished all without firing any shots in anger.[35]

CONCLUSION

The lesson from this chapter is found in its title. Operations Desert Shield, Desert Storm, and Provide Comfort were a triumph of the defense planning systems that had been developed by the Department of Defense over the years since 1961 (or since the National Security Act of 1947). The NSC worked to provide President Bush with the options he needed to address *the* crisis caused by Saddam's surprise attack on Kuwait. The fact that former president Carter had established what became CENTCOM back in 1979 meant that there was a unified command focused on the region. The Goldwater-Nichols Act of 1986 had made the CJCS responsible for the JSCP, which directs future contingency plans, and the current JSCP directed CENTCOM to plan for the defense of Saudi Arabia. This plan was OPLAN 1002–90, which CENTCOM commander GEN Schwarzkopf exercised during the summer of

1990 with Exercise Internal Look. Thus, the command was ready with a plan and all the supporting plans from both subordinate commands and supporting unified commands (e.g., TRANSCOM and EUCOM).

This is not to say that the planning was perfect. The First Gulf War represents the beginning of a transition in war planning from the old Joint Operational Planning System (JOPS) to the new Joint Operational Planning and *Execution* System (JOPES). JOPS ended with the deployment, while JOPES focuses on what forces are to do—that is, how they will actually fight. As we saw in the previous chapter, GEN Woerner not only addressed the lead-up to and combat operations but also focused on post-conflict reconstruction operations. Although the CENTCOM planners did address post-conflict reconstruction, most of that work was done in Washington by the Kuwait Task Force operating under the supervision of assistant secretaries of defense and state. The integration of the Kuwait Task Force into CENTCOM's operations thus was not nearly as smooth as would have been the ideal.

What was clearly an unexpected development was that President Bush's rhetoric would be taken seriously by the Iraqis—both Shi'a in the South and Kurds in the North—leading to rebellions in both areas. The end of combat operations was largely conducted ad hoc, and the negotiations of the "military aspects of the cease-fire" were equally unplanned. As a result, GEN Schwarzkopf conceded to the Iraqis the use of their helicopters to conduct governmental administrative activities. When the Iraqis interpreted this to mean that they could use their gunships to put down the Shi'a revolt, the United States simply acquiesced. Saddam then took this as a lesson that he could do the same in the Kurdish regions, provoking the refugee crisis and the subsequent rescue, Operation Provide Comfort. Although the refugee crisis was a surprise and there was no explicit plan to address it in place, the EUCOM supporting plan for Desert Storm provided a solid basis for adaptation, resulting in a very clear and long-lasting success.

In short, the First Gulf War demonstrates the wisdom of Hannibal Smith's remark, "I love it when a plan comes together."

NOTES

1. COL John "Hannibal" Smith in the 1980s television series *The A Team*. This was the signature line of each episode.

2. Bob Woodward, *The Commanders*. New York: 1991, Simon & Schuster. 206.

3. Ibid., 206–207.

4. George Bush and Brent Scowcroft, *A World Transformed*. New York: 2011, Vintage Books (Kindle Edition). Location 6332.

5. Ibid., passim.

6. Ibid., location 6360.

7. Ibid., location 6384.

8. Woodward, 216–217.

9. James A. Baker III, *The Politics of Diplomacy*. New York: 1995, G. P. Putnam's Sons. 274.

10. Bush and Scowcroft, Location 6425–6437.

11. Ibid., location 6483. The authors do not mention the number of the plan but that is the correct number.

12. Unless otherwise indicated, the discussion in this section derives from multiple conversations and formal interviews with COL Doug Craft, chief of policy and strategy in USCENTCOM during Desert Shield/Storm. For a discussion of JOPES see Chapter 5 of this book.

13. If troops are used in an exercise, it is called a field training exercise (FTX).

14. Bush and Scowcroft, location 6654–6670.

15. Ibid., location 6670.

16. Woodward, 263–273.

17. Ibid.

18. Ibid., 260.

19. This discussion of Checkmate and its plan, Instant Thunder, comes from and interview conducted with one of the two principal action officers involved, then Lt Col Bernard Harvey. Ben was later promoted to full colonel and unfortunately passed away much too soon.

20. There is much confusion as to where and how operations are named. It is often said that names are generated at random by computer but some seem very carefully crafted. In Panama, neither GEN Thurman nor his J-3, BG Hartzog, was willing to execute Operation Blue Spoon and so it became Operation Just Cause, apparently chosen in SOUTHCOM. Desert Shield may have been selected in CENTCOM or by the Joint Staff in Washington (or even by the president and SECDEF).

21. Bush and Scowcroft, location 6678.

22. Ibid., location 6678–6687.

23. Ibid.

24. Ibid., location 6999–7010.

25. This section is drawn from my *Liberation, Occupation, and Rescue: War Termination and Desert Storm*. Carlisle Barracks, PA: 1992, Strategic Studies Institute. Chapter 4, 31–36.

26. One story told at the time was how a B-52 strike had dropped leaflets over the Iraqi positions telling them that the aircraft would return the next day with bombs. In the words of a character from a wonderful science fiction TV show, *Babylon 5*, the leaflets sad, "If you value your lives, be somewhere else." They were.

27. George Bush, television address, "Suspension of Allied Offensive Combat Operations," February 27, 1991 in *Military Review*, September 1991, p. 86.

28. Ibid.

29. Interviews with CENTCOM staff officers, 1991–1992.

30. Kimbra L. Krueger, "US Military Intervention in Third World Conflict: The Need for Integration of Total War and LIC Doctrine." *Low Intensity Conflict & Law*

Enforcement. Volume 4, Issue 3, Winter 1995: Frank Cass, London. 399–428, especially 420–422.

31. Fishel, *Liberation*, 51–58.
32. Ibid.
33. Ibid.
34. Ibid.
35. Ibid.

Chapter 8

Adventures in Peace Enforcement: The Somalia Tragedy

As the Cold War came to an end in 1992, it appeared that the United Nations Security Council would be able to work as the founders had intended. It had achieved success in the Gulf War with significant cooperation between the United States and the Soviet Union. Now the Soviet Union was gone, replaced by a fragile democracy in the Russian Federation, but one that appeared to want to cooperate with the West in the UN. This new set of circumstances opened the door to an updating of the ability of the UN to undertake peace-keeping operations with the capabilities of the Great Powers in ways that had not been possible before.

THE SOMALI CONTEXT

Somalia was forged from the former British protectorate of Somaliland and the Italian colony of Somalia in 1960. Although formed out of the lands controlled by two different colonial powers—the British in the North and the Italians in the South—the Somalis see themselves as one people. They are united by the common Somali language and the common religion, Islam. In addition, all Somalis reckon their descent from seven clans found throughout the country.[1] The clans are themselves divided into subclans led by elders. Separate from, but drawn from the clans and subclans, are various political factions, many of which field militias operating under warlords.[2]

For two decades prior to 1990, Somalia had been ruled by General Mohamed Siad Barre, a wily and ambitious faction leader. Early in his rule Siad Barre had aligned his regime with the Soviet Union, but in 1977, neighboring Ethiopia overthrew its longtime emperor, Haile Selassie. The new government, led by Lt. Col. Haile Mengistu Mariam, declared itself to be communist and seemed to have a more serious commitment to communism than did Siad Barre. As a result, the Soviets dropped Siad Barre, who, immediately, sought American support. The U.S. support was given. As the Soviet Union began to come apart after 1989, the great game in the Horn of Africa became a matter of far less interest to either of the two superpowers. The United States no longer had any incentive to support Siad Barre's continuance in power, and the domestic factions and clans acted to overthrow him. When he fled the country, Somalia rapidly descended into chaos. "By April 1992, Somalia was a nation in name only."[3]

From January through August 1992, the UN Security Council passed five resolutions relating to Somalia.[4] From January through April the United States was represented by Ambassador Thomas Pickering. After that, the American representative was Ambassador Edward Perkins. During this entire period, and until near the end of August, James Baker served as secretary of state, when he was succeeded by his deputy, Lawrence Eagleburger.[5] The other members of the Bush administration, the president and vice president, Secretary of Defense Dick Cheney, and chairman of the Joint Chiefs of Staff, GEN Colin Powell, were unchanged, as was the vice chairman, Admiral David Jeremiah. This listing is relevant because of the low level of importance the principals have given Somalia in their memoirs.[6] Thus, although the final decision to intervene fell to President Bush and his principals, most of the decision was developed at the second echelon or below.

THE FAILURE OF UNOSOM I

The last two of the five Security Council Resolutions authorized troops to go to Somalia to provide security. UNSCR 767 authorized 500 troops, while 775 authorized 3,000 more. Passed in July and August of 1992, the first 500 UN peacekeepers arrived in September.[7] The first increment of peacekeepers had been negotiated with the parties, militia leaders Mohammed Farrah Aideed and Ali Mahdi, by the UN Special Representative for Somalia, Mohamed Sahnoun. The additional 3,000 had not been mentioned, and Aideed signified that he felt he had been betrayed.[8] As a result, what limited cooperation Aideed and the other faction leaders had been giving the UN was generally withdrawn. The impact on humanitarian aid delivery was entirely negative. Although aid was arriving in country, much of it from the U.S. Air Force, significant amounts were being diverted to the warlords. This was either directly or in terms of protection payments to the faction-led "technicals" (machine gun–mounted pickup trucks).[9]

AFTER DESERT STORM AN ELECTION

Meanwhile, in the United States President Bush, just off his victory in Desert Storm, was contesting the presidential election of 1992. Unfortunately for him, his high approval rates from the Gulf War did not last as the country experienced a recession. Even though the recession was a relatively mild one, Democratic candidate, Bill Clinton, made the most of it with his slogan, "It's the economy, stupid." The result was that Clinton's election to the presidency. The period between election day, the first Tuesday in November, and the inauguration on January 20, 1993, was one of transition, a time when new presidential initiatives in foreign policy are rarely undertaken. This transition was to be different, however.

THE AMERICAN SOMALI ELITE AND CNN

As the election of 1992 was unfolding in the United States, the situation in Somalia was unraveling. The country, which had been without a government for nearly two years, was now on the verge of starving all the while being dominated by the warlords and their militias driving around in pickup trucks armed with machine guns called technicals. Moreover, the humanitarian aid NGOs were less and less able to operate due to being extorted by the militias.

As far back as the mid-1970s better-educated Somalis had been immigrating to the United States. One of the locations, then as now, where these Somalis settled was the Upper Midwest, especially in the Minneapolis area. Among those who ended up there was Dr. Ahmed Samatar, a political scientist who became the dean of Macalester College.[10] He had brought his brother Abdi to the United States and the latter was, at the time, a professor of geography at Iowa State University.[11] Samatar is a clan name and another highly educated professor from the clan was teaching at Rutgers University in New Jersey. These three, along with other Somalis in the United States, were very concerned about events in their home country and sought ways to get the American government to act.

One other Somali in America was the supermodel Iman. She was friendly with Christiane Amanpour, CNN's chief foreign correspondent. Apparently, at the suggestion of the Samatars and others, Iman suggested to Amanpour that there was a story to be had in Somalia and that she should take her camera crew there. Amanpour did so, and starving Somali children began to appear regularly on CNN and other American news shows. The result was significant public pressure on the Bush administration to "do something."

THE BUSH ADMINISTRATION SEEKS TO EXIT
ON A HIGH NOTE

As noted previously, the principals did not put a high priority on Somalia, so this was an issue that rose through the third-tier committees of the NSC system, the Policy Coordination Committees (PCCs). The relevant PCC was headed by assistant secretary of state for political-military affairs, Robert Gallucci.[12] As a result of the increasing public pressure, Gallucci pressed the issue with his boss, Deputy Secretary of State Lawrence Eagleburger (along with the Bosnia crisis). Gallucci's memo to Eagleburger made the case for going into Somalia as "low risk, high payoff."[13] Eagleburger argued the case for Somalia and, according to Gallucci, "said we are going to do Somalia. And he said, you are going to get on an airplane with Admiral [David] Jeremiah and go down and explain to the governor of Arkansas that when he gets into office he is going to find marines deployed in Somalia."[14]

Clearly, the Deputies Committee recommended that the United States lead action in Somalia. Having lost his bid for reelection, President Bush was offered the opportunity to leave office on a high note. Reports at the time said that GEN Colin Powell, the chairman of the Joint Chiefs of Staff, was adamant that (1) the mission was doable and (2) that it needed to be crafted very narrowly. The instructions given to Ambassador Perkins at the UN reflected this view and the Security Council Resolution (UNSCR 794) reflected the narrow focus of the mission. UNSCR 794 called for the United States to lead a multinational force under Chapter VII of the UN Charter to use "all necessary means to establish as soon as possible a secure environment for humanitarian relief operations in Somalia."[15]

THE SECRETARY-GENERAL OBJECTS

UNSCR 794 established the Unified Task Force (UNITAF) with the mission described in the mandate quoted previously. But the meaning of the mandate was in doubt from the beginning.

> SCR 794 "did not require . . . the Unified Task Force to disarm the Somalis but [Secretary-General] Boutros-Ghali subsequently argued that he had an understanding with U.S. President George Bush that the force would disarm the Somali gunmen." The Secretary-General claimed the creation of a "secure environment" presupposed disarming the gunmen and that this would be necessary for the cessation of civil strife, as well as for a U.N. mission to replace UNITAF. President Bush argued that "there was no consideration of disarming the Somali factions."[16]

Given what we know of GEN Powell's approach and the careful manner in which 794 was crafted, we can be certain that President Bush's recollection is correct. This was reflected in the orders given to the UNITAF commander.

CENTCOM's Task

American military unified commands are organized geographically according to the Unified Command Plan (UCP). In 1992, the Horn of Africa was in the area of responsibility of the U.S. Central Command (CENTCOM). During Operations Desert Shield and Desert Storm CENTCOM was under the command of Army GEN H. Norman Schwarzkopf. From its inception under President Carter, command had alternated between the army and the marine corps. Now it was the turn of the marines, and Schwarzkopf had been replaced by Gen Joseph Hoar, U.S. Marine Corps. At President Bush's direction, Secretary of Defense Dick Cheney issued the order for Gen Hoar to establish a joint and combined task force to carry out the mandate in UNSCR 794. This operation would be called Operation Restore Hope, and initial planning would take place at CENTCOM headquarters at MacDill AFB in Tampa, Florida.

When given the task of forming a joint and combined task force, the commander of a unified command—known at the time as the CINC—must decide what organizational base he will use. If the Joint Task Force (JTF) is going to be a large force, then the CINC has only two headquarters capable of controlling it. Both are three-star commands; one is an army corps and the other is a marine expeditionary force (MEF). A corps can control from two to five divisions (commanded by major generals—two stars) plus assorted support forces. A MEF consists of one marine division, a marine air wing, and its logistics elements. With augmentations the corps or MEF staff can command and control significant forces from other services or even from allied nations. Thus, when Gen Hoar was ordered to stand up the JTF for Somalia and be prepared to control allied forces, he had to choose between a MEF and a corps. As a marine, he fell back on the organization and personnel he knew best and made I MEF, commanded by Lt Gen Robert Johnston, the base of his JTF.[17] In addition to the Marine elements—1st Marine Division, the air wing, the logistics command, Johnston was augmented by the army's 10th Mountain Division, air force elements, a navy Amphibious Group, and Navy SEALs.

International elements came from a number of countries, including Belgium, Canada, Italy, and the United Kingdom. France contributed a demi-brigade of the French Foreign Legion, which arrived early from the French base in adjoining Djibouti. The Legion force was particularly effective during the UNITAF operation. In all, UNITAF forces peaked at about 38,000, of which at least 25,000 were American. Gen Hoar decided to exercise operational control of allied forces by giving them specific areas of the country in which they operated, more or less exclusively.

In addition to the allied forces there were numerous civilian agencies from the UN to the U.S. government, to NGOs of all sizes. Among the U.S. government agencies was the USAID Office of Foreign Disaster Assistance with its Disaster Assistance Response Team and the president's special envoy, Ambassador Robert Oakley. Unlike operations in a country where there is an American embassy, in Somalia Oakley's relationship with Johnston was ambiguous, yet, clearly Johnston was in charge of all U.S. efforts.[18]

OPERATION RESTORE HOPE AND UNITAF

The speed at which Operation Restore Hope was launched was, in fact, remarkable. UNSCR 794 was passed on December 3, 1992. Air operations over Mogadishu began on December 5. Then, Navy SEALs followed by marines landed in the early hours of December 9. The speed of the launch indicates that CENTCOM had begun planning in anticipation of receiving orders and was following the Crisis Action Planning protocols of the JOPES process.

A very curious aspect of the landing was that as the SEALs came up on the beach to mark it for the landing craft, they were met by Klieg lights and TV news cameras. It was as if the media had been tipped off.[19] As strange as it appeared at the time, the effect was similar to the effect of military aircraft making low passes over the city during the four previous days. The militias, especially those of Ali Mahdi and Farrah Aideed, saw the arriving troops as a force to be reckoned with and one they did not want to challenge.

Although Gen Johnston did not attempt to disarm the militias, his Rules of Engagement allowed for the confiscation of crew-served weapons (technicals) or their placement in storage. Light weapons were not to be carried openly. And UNITAF troops were authorized to use "all necessary means" to see that these rules were enforced.[20] Indeed, the rules were enforced and the UNITAF force remained large enough that none of the militias, but particularly Aideed's, wanted to get into a fight. By January 1, 1993, hardly any weapons, other than those of UNITAF, were visible anywhere in Somalia.[21] By all indications, Operation Restore Hope was a success.

CLINTON BECOMES COMMANDER IN CHIEF

On January 20, 1993, Bill Clinton was inaugurated as president of the United States. With Clinton came a new national security team. Scowcroft was replaced as NSA by Tony Lake; Eagleburger at the State by Warren Christopher; Cheney in the DoD by former congressman Les Aspin; Perkins at the UN by Madeleine Albright.[22] The only holdover from the old team was Powell (and his VCJCS, Jeremiah). Where professionalism and tenure marked the Bush team, academia and politics marked Clinton's. Moreover, none of Clinton's team had been in government for at least 12 years, again except for Powell.

A trend that complicated transitions, and had first appeared in the Bush transition four years before, was the problem of increased vetting of subcabinet political appointments. This was exacerbated by increased political polarization in Congress. The result was that early in the Clinton administration the only assistant secretary of defense confirmed in office was the Assistant Secretary of Defense for Special Operations and Low Intensity Conflict (ASD-SO/LIC) Allen Holmes, a career Foreign Service officer. Notably the ASD-SO/LIC was the only such position established by legislation. The fact that so many political positions were staffed only by acting office holders from the career government service meant that policy advice from below was tentative at best.

BACK TO THE UN AND SECURITY COUNCIL RESOLUTION 814

From the end of January, the U.S. Mission to the UN, led by Ambassador Madeleine Albright, worked with Secretary-General Boutros Boutros-Ghali to craft a new Security Council Resolution to establish a UN Peacekeeping Force to replace UNITAF. Not surprisingly, given Albright and Clinton's view of "assertive multilateralism," the UNSCR reflected Boutros-Ghali's interpretation of how peace should be enforced. UNSCR 814 was passed in March and it reflected the administration's views on who should command and control the force and how it should be organized.

Although most UN peacekeeping missions had a political head, called the Special Representative of the Secretary-General (SRSG), in most cases the position was not one of command. Under UNSCR 814, however, the SRSG would be the true head of the mission—at American insistence. Not only that, the SRSG would be the American proposed by the United States, Admiral Jonathan Howe, U.S. Navy (retired) and former deputy national security advisor to President Bush. Reporting to the SRSG would be the Force Commander (FC) (often a more or less autonomous position). Again, at American insistence, the FC would be a NATO officer, Lt. Gen. Cevik Bir of Turkey, while the Deputy Force Commander would be another American, MG Thomas Montgomery, U.S. Army, who would wear a second hat as commander of U.S. Forces—Somalia.[23] In short, the command and control of this peace enforcement operation in Somalia—to be called UNOSOM II—was American in everything but name.

ESTABLISHING UNOSOM II

The process of establishing a UN peacekeeping operation only begins with the mandate in the UNSCR. As noted previously, the United States wrote the resolution and insisted on certain command and control relationships. The next step is for the under-secretary-general for peacekeeping operations, at the time Kofi Annan, to call for countries to be force contributors. As states step forward, staff from the Department of Peacekeeping Operations (DPKO) negotiates a contract, called a Terms of Reference (TOR) with each force contributor. The TOR is based on the UNSCR mandate and specifies how many and what kind of forces will be contributed as well as what they will do—and not do. This last is confusing because UN peacekeeping forces always operate under the operational control of the FC. The problem, however, is the meaning of operational control.

In American military parlance, operational control, or OPCON, means a commander can not only give a task to a subordinate unit but he can also attach and detach elements of the unit or other units. In other words, the commander can organize and reorganize his subordinate units for combat. A lesser control element called Tactical Control, or TACON, allows the commander to give a task to his subordinate units but not organize them for combat. In UN peacekeeping missions, however, OPCON (the same word) means, at most, TACON. But it only means TACON if the subordinate commander views the task as falling within his TOR. If he objects, then he refers the issue back to his home government, which, may or may not, tell him to follow the order of the FC. The outcome depends on the policy that the force contributing *government* wants to pursue.

The structure of the UNOSOM II force followed that of similar peacekeeping operations with most of the usual force contributing countries stepping forward. In addition, NATO members Belgium and Italy offered forces, as did the United States. (These countries generally did not participate in UN peacekeeping operations during the Cold War.) The American contribution, in addition to the SRSG and Deputy FC, consisted of a number of staff officers and the Logistics Support Command (which would control and provide logistics support for all of UNOSOM II). In addition, the United States provided a quick reaction force (QRF), a brigade-sized element of 1,100 troops from the 10th Mountain Division under the command of COL William David.

THE BOTCHED TRANSITION

With the passage of UNSCR 814 in March and the naming of the FC and his staff, planning began with the UNITAF staff for the transition to UNOSOM II. For planning purposes, the transition was to take place on or around May 4, 1993. From the point of view of the UNOSOM II command, this was a target date dependent on conditions on the ground, especially the arrival of forces. However, from the vantage point of UNITAF, which very much wanted to return to the United States (a large majority of the force and staff was American), May 4 was soon "carved in stone" regardless of the conditions on the ground.[24]

As May 4 approached, it became clear to the UNOSOM II headquarters that the forces earmarked for the mission would not be in place. UNDPKO had secured promises, but the force contributors would not be able to get many of their forces deployed by that date. In fact, the bulk of the UNOSOM II forces that would be in country by the time of the planned transition would be already there as part of UNITAF. This included the American QRF. Thus, as the planned transition date approached, 28,000 UNITAF forces remained in Somalia on May 3. By the next day that would fall to half, including both forces staying behind and new forces arriving. SRSG Howe, FC Bir, and Deputy FC Montgomery strongly requested, through their various channels, that the transition be postponed until the full force of UNOSOM II could be in place—to no avail.[25] On May 4, 1993, the change of command ceremony was held in Mogadishu. Forces from UNITAF staying for UNOSOM II replaced their national headgear with the blue berets and blue helmets of the UN as the newly arriving forces donned their own blue helmets.

AN INSANE C2 SYSTEM

Force Command took charge and exercised OPCON through assigning sectors of operation for the various national contingents. However, as noted previously, OPCON meant different things to different national forces. National contingent commanders from NATO countries, at least, understood what OPCON means in U.S. and NATO doctrine.[26] But that did not mean that OPCON would be exercised according to American field manuals. Rather, OPCON was exercised by assigning sectors in which to operate and giving the commanders a task to accomplish—in other words, what the U.S. military understands as TACON.

American forces deployed to UNOSOM II in two large contingents: the Logistics Support Command and the QRF. According to American doctrine, both elements should have been under the operational control of the Commander U.S. Forces Somalia, MG Montgomery, whose second hat was that of UN Deputy FC. While Montgomery did have OPCON of the Logistics Support Command, his American higher headquarters, CENTCOM, retained OPCON of the QRF. Gen Hoar released TACON of the QRF to Montgomery for (1) normal training requirements and (2) bona fide emergencies. All other uses of the QRF required a request to CENTCOM.[27] This very strange command relationship was contrary to U.S. military doctrine and normal practice, and had the effect of vitiating the essentially American nature of the UNOSOM II command and control system. This, along with the looser UN version of OPCON, created serious problems for Force Command over the course of the mission. These difficulties would expand as resistance developed.

AIDEED TAKES ON THE UN

As Richard Stewart wrote, in his study of the U.S. Army in Somalia, "It quickly became apparent that Aideed had little respect for the new organization [UNOSOM II], the UN, or Admiral Howe. On 5 June 1993, his Somalia National Alliance forces ambushed and killed 24 Pakistani soldiers assigned to UNOSOM II. Another 44 were wounded."[28] Admiral Howe was livid about the attack and communicated his views to UN Headquarters in New York, the Clinton administration in Washington, and the U.S. Mission to the UN in New York.

SECURITY COUNCIL RESOLUTION 837

June 5 was a Saturday. At the call of the United States, the UN Security Council convened in an emergency session and passed the American-sponsored (drafted) SCR 837 authorizing UNOSOM II to go after the perpetrators of the attack on the Pakistanis by any means necessary. Whether anyone realized it or not UNSCR 837 constituted a major change of mission for UNOSOM II. Under the authority of the resolution, the SRSG and the FC made the decision to seek the arrest of Mohammed Farrah Aideed. Admiral Howe issued the arrest warrant on June 17 after being advised by a UN panel of jurists that Aideed was responsible for the attack.[29] On June 7, the United States augmented its forces in Somalia with four AC-130 (Spectre) gunships, which remained until July 14 carrying out a number of missions, including destroying Aideed's radio station.

ITALY BEGS TO DIFFER AND DISSENT

"The rush to approve and implement UNSCR 837 also failed to gain consensus with the UNOSOM II contributing nations, most of whom were not members of the Security Council."[30] Among the most vociferous in expressing discontent with UNSCR 837 was Italy. Italy, the former colonial power in southern Somalia (its colonial capital was Mogadishu), had not only contributed combat forces but also played the critical role in the UNOSOM II staff of the intelligence officer and head of the intelligence section (U-2). The Italian contingent commander made it very clear from the outset that his government had not signed up to enforce 837; only 814 was covered in the TOR that Italy had signed.[31] After June 7, Italy no longer would carry out any tasks assigned by the FC that, in the judgment of the contingent commander, did not fall within the bounds of its TOR. Moreover, the Italian colonel who was the UNOSOM II U-2 began to pass critical information to Aideed's forces.[32] Other UNOSOM II force contributors also refused cooperation in the enforcement of both 814 and 837 to varying degrees.

TASK FORCE RANGER OR JSOC BY ANOTHER NAME

The focus on capturing Aideed produced a violent reaction on his part, and the operations against him escalated. At the same time, a number of the force contributors reduced their participation in operations directed against Aideed. In August, UN secretary-general Boutros Boutros-Ghali asked President Clinton for additional military support to capture Aideed. On August 22, Secretary of Defense Les Aspin announced that the United States would send a Joint Special Operations Task Force (JSOTF) to Somalia to accomplish this task.[33] The JSOTF would be known as Task Force Ranger.

Task Force Ranger was actually a composite national special operations force under the direct command and control of the Joint Special Operations Command (JSOC) that had been incorporated under U.S. Special Operations Command (USSOCOM) by the Cohen-Nunn Amendment to the 1986 Defense appropriations Act. The JSOC was commanded at the time by army MG William Garrison, who deployed with his JSOC staff to Mogadishu. The major components of TF Ranger were Delta Force (SFOD-D), the army's premier special mission unit (SMU), the 160th Special Operations Aviation Regiment (SOAR), and the 3rd Ranger Battalion of the 75th Ranger Regiment. There were also navy and air force elements attached to the JSOC.[34] According to Stewart, command of the JSOC did not pass to U.S. Forces—Somalia, but, according to the Goldwater-Nichols Act, was retained by

CENTCOM.[35] Thus, MG Garrison did not report to the FC, Lt. Gen. Bir, through USFORSOM commander MG Montgomery (Deputy FC), or through them to the SRSG, Admiral Howe. Although the relevant legislation did envision the unilateral and independent use of the JSOC, it did not anticipate such use contrary to established military doctrine where a strong American command was in place.

Even though MG Garrison was not required to coordinate with Force Command, he soon found it necessary and wise to do so, especially after his troops struck an unmarked UN facility in error. Not only for that reason but because his troops might need support from either the QRF or UNOSOM II if they were in trouble, Garrison met with Bir, Montgomery, and Howe to work out a modus operandi. From the FC perspective, they did not want the JSOC interfering in their activities, so the arrangement was that Garrison would notify FC 30 minutes before an operation was to begin. FC could veto the operation if necessary.[36] Between the end of August and October 2, TF Ranger conducted five operations to capture Aideed's lieutenants. All were tactically successful and did handicap his activities.

Although the JSOC operations were conducted both during the night and the day, as they progressed, more were in the daylight hours. Partly this was due to Aideed's people avoiding the night, which they quickly realized was TF Ranger's preferred operational profile. During this period, Aideed began to receive training and other assistance from a group known as the "Afghan Arabs." These were Arab fighters, organized by Osama bin Laden who had supported the *mujahideen* in Afghanistan against the Soviets and developed tactics that worked well against troops in helicopters. As the JSOC missions progressed toward October, Aideed's militia showed greater tactical proficiency with increased use of rocket-propelled grenades (RPGs) targeting the helicopters of the 160th—both the MH-60s which carried the operators and Rangers and the "Little Birds," which provided fire support from both the aircraft-mounted weapons and snipers. This was the result of the training and operational advice provided by the Afghan Arabs.[37]

"BLACK HAWK DOWN"

The final mission of TF Ranger produced the incident known ever since as "Blackhawk Down," although perhaps the Battle of Mogadishu would be a better name. The mission was a daylight raid on the Olympic Hotel, where a number of Aideed's lieutenants were meeting. It began with the usual tactical success as the Delta operators successfully took their prisoners. As they were withdrawing, however, to exfiltrate by helicopter, Aideed's forces coached by the Afghan Arabs successfully downed a MH-60 Blackhawk and forced another to return to base with significant damage.[38] A dead American pilot was dragged through the streets and another pilot taken prisoner. The Delta operators exfiltrated themselves and their prisoners on foot to the perimeter established by the 3rd Ranger Battalion. The rest of the day and the entire night was spent fighting off attacks by Aideed's militia. Many of those attacks were led by civilians forced into the lead at gunpoint to act as human shields. Including the pilots and Delta operators, 18 American servicemen were killed in the battle and 78 were wounded. Between 300 and 500 of Aideed's forces were killed, some of whom were civilians who had been used as human shields.

From the beginning of the battle, the Rangers requested assistance through the JSOC. This resulted in a call to the QRF from MG Montgomery as the senior American commander. The commander of the QRF, COL Bill David, immediately mounted a rescue mission. However, the rescue force met heavy resistance and, because it was a light infantry force and mounted in thin-skinned vehicles, it was forced to withdraw.[39] The question was whether to try again immediately or seek to plan a rescue with the use of some armored elements. This, in turn, depended on how dire a situation the Rangers found themselves in. Radio communications between TF Ranger and the QRF indicated that none of the wounded were in mortal danger and the force was in a strong defensive position and capable of defending itself until the next morning. This gave COL David the time to plan and organize the rescue. Part of his task was securing armored personnel carriers from the Malaysian contingent and tanks from the Pakistanis.[40]

On the morning of October 4, the QRF mounted a well-planned and well-equipped rescue. All the dead, all the wounded, all the prisoners, and all their rescuers were withdrawn successfully. The Battle of Mogadishu was over. All that remained was getting the captured helicopter pilot back safely and this was accomplished within two weeks.

WHO WILL BLINK FIRST, CLINTON OR AIDEED?

The Battle of Mogadishu was a shock to all sides. The effect on Aideed was immediate as his clan elders were extremely upset by the civilian losses caused by their being used as human shields. They issued him an ultimatum to leave the country and Aideed, having lost his legitimacy with his clan, prepared to comply.[41] The UN was shocked that the mission could have gone so wrong, but Secretary-General Boutros-Ghali had little influence at this point. Mission success or failure depended on the American reaction.

Even as the JSOC deployed in late August, the United States was beginning to have second thoughts. MG Montgomery's requests to bring back the

AC-130s and to bring in armor were rejected by SECDEF Les Aspin. The large number of casualties in the battle and the video of a dead American pilot being dragged through the streets stunned the leaders on the NSC and the American public. The reaction was shock, hurt, and anger in nearly equal measure. President Clinton faced a real choice: Should he try to salvage the mission by reinforcing and taking a hard line or should he simply cut his losses? We know in the aftermath what we did not know at the time: that Aideed had, in fact, been forced to blink. He was, in fact, preparing to leave Somalia under pressure from the clan elders. We just had not seen it. Thus, Clinton took the second option and decided on withdrawal after a brief period of reinforcement but only for the purpose of force protection. Tactically, UNOSOM II no longer undertook offensive operations and TF Ranger was withdrawn as soon as the captured pilot was released. Clinton's blink was the one that was significant.

LESSONS RECORDED AND NOT LEARNED

The very first lesson of the intervention in Somalia is that an administration inheriting an action taken by its predecessor needs to take the time to fully understand the goals, methods, and resources committed. The Bush administration had a clearly developed concept for the operation and had resisted the expansive view of the UN secretary-general. The Clinton administration was sympathetic to the secretary-general's position and discounted the difficulties.

The second lesson is that a UN Peace Operation is not the same as an American or NATO operation. Command and control are both different and weaker. And fielding a force takes far more time. It is not merely a matter of capability but also of what the force-contributing countries are willing to do. In Somalia, this resulted in a conflict over the transition from UNITAF to UNOSOM II that made the change of command happen prematurely. The failure to wait for the full complement of troops left UNOSOM II vulnerable to the aggressive actions of Aideed and sparked the armed conflict.

The third lesson is that the American military needs to follow its own doctrine for command and control. When a commander in the field is named, he needs to have the appropriate command relationship with his national forces. This is normally operational control (OPCON), and any deviation from this doctrinal approach should be fully justified. The deviations with respect to the QRF and TF Ranger simply made no sense and contributed to the strategic defeat (in the midst of a tactical victory) in the Battle of Mogadishu.

Because of the voluntary nature of the building of a UN force, it is critical to include all force contributors in the development of any new mandate. The force contributors, like Italy, had agreed to carry out the mandate of UNSCR 814. They had no input to the development of UNSCR 837, which gave the force a new and expanded mandate, one that they had neither agreed to or that was included in their TOR. The lesson here is how to degrade unity of effort to a point where it is close to nonexistent.

The final lesson is not to react emotionally to a perceived disaster. Despite the high casualty figures in the battle, TF Ranger had accomplished its mission. Cooperation with UNOSOM II was effective and the forces were successfully withdrawn without additional casualties, resulting in a significant tactical victory for UNOSOM II. The question was whether it would be a strategic victory or a strategic failure, and that depended on the political will of President Clinton. As we know now, and would have known at the time had the president waited before he acted, Aideed was on the verge of being forced out of the country by his clan elders. Such would have amounted to a strategic victory for UNOSOM II and might—no certainty here—have given Somalia a chance at being something other than the failed state and terrorist haven that it is today.

NOTES

1. Terrence Lyons and Ahmed Samatar, *Somalia: State Collapse, Multilateral Intervention, and Strategies for Political Reconstruction.* Washington, DC: 1995, Brookings Institute. vii–13.

2. Ibid.

3. Ibid., 177.

4. Ibid., 178.

5. Pickering was one of the most well-respected members of the U.S. Foreign Service, having served in numerous hot spots. His successor, Ed Perkins (whom I had the pleasure to know at the University of Oklahoma when he was director of International Programs), was also a very senior Foreign Service officer having served as ambassador to South Africa (during the Apartheid regime) and director general of the Foreign Service. Baker was a close confidant of President Bush and had served as a cabinet member during the Reagan presidency. Eagleburger was the first, and so far the only, career Foreign Service officer to serve as secretary of state.

6. Baker has only one brief reference to evacuating American citizens in the wake of Siad Barre's fall, while Bush and Scowcroft do not mention Somalia at all.

7. Lynn Thomas and Steve Spataro, "Peacekeeping and Policing in Somalia," in Robert B. Oakley, Michael J. Dziedzic, and Eliot M. Goldberg (eds.), *Policing the New World Disorder.* Honolulu, HA: 1998, University Press of the Pacific. 178.

8. Ibid.

9. Ibid., 178–181.

10. In the 1970s, Ahmed Samatar had studied at the University of Wisconsin-La Crosse, where he was my student.

11. Since then Dr. Abdi Samatar has become a professor of geography at the University of Minnesota.

12. David Rothkopf, *Running the World.* New York: 2005, Public Affairs (Kindle Edition). Location 6470.

13. Ibid., location 6483.

14. Ibid.

15. Quoted in Thomas and Spataro, p. 181.

16. Ibid., 184.

17. During Desert Storm, Gen Hoar had been chief of staff in CENTCOM. From there he went to command I MEF. His successor in both positions was Lieutenant General Johnston. Interviews with COL Douglas Craft, chief of the Policy and Strategy Division, CCJ5, 1991–92.

18. Robert B. Oakley, "An Envoy's Perspective," *Joint Force Quarterly*, Autumn 1993. 44–55.

19. I was a professor at the Army Command and General Staff College at the time and the constant commentary among the majors and lieutenant colonels of the student body and the faculty was whether anybody had ever heard of operational security (OPSEC). In retrospect—and from my perspective as a former psychological operations officer (in the 13th PSYOP Battalion and as the SOCSOUTH PSYOP Officer and acting J-5)—it may well have been purposeful as a show of force to indicate to the militias that they really did not want to confront the arriving American forces.

20. Thomas and Spataro, 185.

21. Ibid., 186.

22. The new group was heavy on academics as Lake and Albright both came from academia. Aspin came out of Congress, where he was the long-serving chairman of the Armed Services Committee. Christopher had held a senior position in the State Department under Carter.

23. Interviews with LTC Thomas Daze, executive officer to the FC and deputy FC of UNOSOM II, 1997. Daze was also one of the principal authors of the *After Action Report*, cited later, issued under General Montgomery's name.

24. Daze interviews.

25. Ibid.

26. Military doctrine is, first, not dogma. It is how the textbook says that we train to fight and, hopefully, we fight as we train. But doctrine is adaptable to the situation on the ground. And in a UN operation, the doctrinal solution is subject to interpretation according to the TOR negotiated for the force contributed.

27. Daze interviews.

28. Richard W. Stewart, "The United States Army in Somalia: 1992–1994," in Center for Military History, *United States Forces in Somalia: After Action Report*. Washington, DC., nd. 9 (PDF). Stewart, a well-respected military historian, is currently the chief of Military History.

29. Ibid.

30. Ibid., 41.

31. Daze interviews.

32. Ibid.

33. Stewart, 10.

34. Ibid.

35. Ibid. Daze, however, indicated that JSOC was actually under the command of USSOCOM as a unilaterally deployed national asset. In any case, it was not formally integrated into the UN C2 structure.

36. Daze interviews.

37. John T. Fishel and Max G. Manwaring, *Uncomfortable Wars Revisited.* Norman: 2006, University of Oklahoma Press. 215, 221–222.

38. Ibid. See also Stewart and *After Action Report.* This section is drawn from these sources.

39. Interview with COL Bill David, Panama, 1995.

40. Ibid.

41. Daze interviews.

Chapter 9

The "Intervasion" of Haiti

THE PREDATORY STATE

The end is the beginning. In 1998, I published the following assessment of Operation Uphold Democracy and the future of Haiti after the United States and the UN ended their mission: "As the UNMIH mission wound down, the indications were that Haiti would most likely revert to the kind of authoritarian regime it has known since it won its independence—what scholars of Haiti have dubbed a predatory regime."[1] To get an idea of what the term "predatory regime" means consider that of 41 Haitian heads of government between 1804 and 1994, 31 died violent deaths, were forced to flee the country, or were forced out of office. They were killed or driven off due to their robbery and oppression of the Haitian people as well as the fear they produced in their rivals that they would not be able to steal their due. None of the remaining ten heads of government served a full constitutional term.[2]

One example that demonstrates the predatory nature of the Haitian state is that of Guillaume Vibrun Sam, president in 1915. His opposition gathered a bunch of thugs from the countryside, known as *cacos*, to oust him. They not only succeeded, but also dismembered him. The ensuing chaos triggered the occupation by the U.S. Marines that lasted from 1915 until 1934. Although the occupation developed Haiti's infrastructure and established a professional constabulary force, the *Garde d'Haiti*, it failed to change the predatory nature of Haitian culture. Succeeding presidents until 1957 resigned their offices, fled, or were overthrown.[3]

In 1957, Dr. Francois Duvalier assumed the presidency. He would not vacate it until his death in 1971, when he was succeeded by his son, Jean-Claude. The elder Duvalier, known as Papa Doc, ruled with an iron fist through a combination of voodoo, the establishment of a militia of modern *cacos*, the *Ton-ton macoutes* (literally, bogeymen), to offset the power of the regular military and police, and the violence of both the *macoutes* and the established security forces. After Papa Doc died in 1971, the dictatorship became somewhat less repressive but still predatory. It lasted until 1986 when Jean-Claude fled to France. Between 1986 and 1990 four different people served as president; one of them, Henri Namphy, served twice, and none served a full term.[4] During this entire period, Haiti remained a predatory state.

THE RISE OF JEAN-BERTRAND ARISTIDE

Born in 1953, Jean-Bertrand Aristide made his name as a firebrand Catholic priest speaking loudly in favor of Haiti's poor and against the dictatorship of Jean-Claude Duvalier. Well educated, able to speak five languages fluently, his sermons were mostly in Haitian Creole, where he railed against Duvalier and his successors. This drew not only the enmity of the mulatto elite but also the wrath of the Catholic Church. In 1988 he was expelled from the Salesian Order, where he was a priest.[5] Nevertheless, Aristide had developed a following among Haiti's poor and ran for president in 1990. He won overwhelmingly and then was faced with the task of governing.

Although Aristide had a strong following, his movement, *Lavalas* (Creole for The Flood), was a movement and not a political party. He had few of Haiti's educated and managerial class willing to collaborate with him to run the government. In fact, between his election and inauguration, he survived two coup attempts, one of which came near murdering him.[6] Among the very few leaders who were willing to work with Aristide were Rene Preval and Smark Michel, both of whom served as ministers in the government and would serve again after the intervention.[7] Another was Lt. Col. Raoul Cedras, a graduate of the first class in the restored Haitian Military Academy, who was promoted to lieutenant general and commander of the *Force d'Armee d'Haiti* (FAd'H).

THE OVERTHROW

Aristide bears a good deal of the blame for his own failure. He had a knack for turning supporters into opponents.[8] As Ballard states:

> Aristide did not speak out against violence, he did not prevent the arrest of his opponents on vague charges, and perhaps most fatal to his chances for success, he antagonized both the military and the rich. Equally as damning, he failed to build any form of political rapport with his legislature, including alienating members of his own Lavalas support group.[9]

As a result of his actions, and the lingering opposition from the elites, Aristide was overthrown in a coup engineered by Lt. Gen. Cedras and Chief of police, Michel Francois, on September 30, 1991.

CRISIS

The coup sparked an international crisis with several dimensions. First was a political crisis in the hemisphere that later expanded to the UN. This was the high point for democratic reform in the Western Hemisphere, and the Organization of American States (OAS) adopted a resolution that supported international action taken to support and/or restore democracy in American states under threat. Thus, the OAS immediately condemned the coup and called for the restoration of Aristide. It was soon followed by the UN Security Council. The OAS appointed an active mediator, Colombian diplomat Augusto Ocampo, who tried to negotiate a restoration of Aristide. Later, UN secretary-general Boutros Boutros-Ghali appointed Argentine diplomat Dante Caputo as his Special Representative to Haiti, with a similar goal to that of Ocampo. In sequence, both diplomats made numerous trips to the country over the year and a half from October 1992 until the spring of 1993. Due to the fact that there were no real consequences for the coup leaders and the political-economic elites, the diplomacy had no real chance of success, not even when coupled with severe economic sanctions.[10]

Haitian elites, including the military and police, did not suffer much from the sanctions but the people did. They soon found it nearly impossible to get the staples needed to live in any decent way. If they were seen as Aristide supporters, which most of them were, they were severely repressed. Soon after the coup, Haitians began to flee the country in rickety and unseaworthy boats, trying to cross the Florida Straits to reach the United States.[11] By the end of January 1992, the U.S. Coast Guard had already picked up more than 14,000 Haitians fleeing the island.[12] Many ended up in Florida, where the governor objected strenuously, largely on health grounds—real or exaggerated—due to the high incidence of AIDS in Haiti.

BUSH ADMINISTRATION RESPONSE

These issues impacted the Bush administration in a number of ways. President Bush and his team were working hard to wind down the aftermath of the Cold War and strengthen the relationship with the fragile new Russian democracy; they were addressing the postwar era in Iraq, beginning to implement No-fly Zones, and sustaining the Kurds in Northern Iraq after the crisis that produced Operation Provide Comfort. Haiti was a distraction, but one that could not be ignored. As a result, the administration initially housed rescued Haitians in camps at the U.S. naval base in Guantanamo, Cuba. Soon they began forcible repatriation on the grounds that the Haitians were economic and not political refugees.[13] "This action soon became entangled in U.S. presidential politics as Democratic candidate Bill Clinton lambasted President Bush for his inhumane and ineffective policy."[14] Then, in November, Bill Clinton won the election. The voters did not care about the Iraq War victory, the Kurds of Northern Iraq, or Haiti and Haitian migrants, except to the extent that they were arriving in South Florida. Voters mainly cared about the economy. President Bush's policy of forcible repatriation put a temporary lid on the migration crisis but on January 20 the United States had a new president.

THE CLINTON ADMINISTRATION
AND ASSERTIVE MULTILATERALISM

The Clinton administration took office on January 20, 1993, faced with a number of issues left over from the Bush administration. As David Rothkopf states:

> Unfortunately, the problems that it faced in rapid succession were knotty ones. [National Security Adviser, Tony] Lake referred to the litany of foreign policy problems as "brown blobs," according to [Sandy] Berger [his deputy], Somalia, Haiti, Bosnia, North Korea. These were the issues floating out there, threatening, demanding attention but eluding solution.[15]

Not only was the new administration faced with all the issues left over from its predecessor, it was not yet fully staffed to deal with them, especially at the subcabinet level. This problem had first surfaced as a significant issue in the Bush administration and would escalate in major ways in all the succeeding ones.

Although candidate Clinton had argued that the Bush policy of forced repatriation was wrong, shortly before his inauguration, president-elect Clinton reversed course saying that the new administration would continue the policy. This was, at least, partly in response to high levels of opposition to Haitian immigration from Florida and its governor, Democrat, Lawton Chiles. Nevertheless, in Washington and among the Haitian community in the United States there were strong countervailing pressures to deal positively and humanely with the Haitian migrants and see that Aristide was restored to the presidency of Haiti.

OAS AND UN

From the ouster of Aristide in September 1991, the OAS took the lead in trying to restore the democratically elected government. Colombian diplomat Augusto Ocampo played the leading role for the OAS making a number of trips to Haiti. In the end, it was to no avail.[16] Over the course of 1992 and early 1993, the lead on Haiti shifted to the UN Security Council. The secretary-general appointed former Argentine foreign minister and diplomat Dante Caputo as his Special Representative. Caputo began to play the same kind of role that Ocampo had, with similar results. In February 1993, General Cedras signaled that he was willing to relinquish power and restore Aristide, under certain conditions. But when Caputo arrived in Haiti to work out the details, he was met "by demonstrations and insults."[17] Caputo soon left having achieved nothing. It was clear that Cedras and the junta were playing a bait and switch game, stalling for time, and doing so quite successfully. Finally, in June, the UN Security Council, having grown tired of the runaround, voted to sanction Haiti by cutting off shipments of petroleum, oil, and lubricants.[18] This caught Cedras's attention since these sanctions would make it much more difficult for the junta to govern.

GOVERNORS ISLAND AND *HARLAN COUNTY*

On June 27, Cedras and Aristide met in proximity talks (separately with UN mediators) to hammer out an agreement for the departure of Cedras and the junta and the return of Aristide. On July 3 the agreement was signed on Governors Island, New York.[19] As part of the agreement, a UN Haiti Assistance Group (HAG) of military and police from the United States and Canada were to go to Haiti to train the Haitian military and police, a unified force known as the FAd'H.

In August, the Department of Defense authorized the establishment of a Joint Task Force, JTF-HAG, under the command of COL J.G. Pulley, U.S. Army, commander of the 7th Special Forces Group at Fort Bragg, North Carolina. A multiservice JTF planning staff was established ad hoc in Norfolk, Virginia, home of U.S. Atlantic Command (USACOM). The staff was made up of officers from several services called up from whatever they were doing and sent to Norfolk on short notice. One such case was that of an army lieutenant colonel who was a military history instructor at the Army Command and General Staff College at Fort Leavenworth, Kansas.[20] What they found was chaos, until they were able to meet with COL Pulley at the Officers Club.[21]

On September 23, the UNSC authorized the dispatch of 1,267 military and police personnel under the terms of the Governors Island agreement; 225

were to travel to Haiti on the USS *Harlan County*, a landing ship, tank, under the command of Commander Marvin E. Butcher, U.S. Navy.[22] Butcher did not answer to Pulley but rather to ACOM through Commander in Chief, U.S. Atlantic Fleet (CINCLANTFLT). Pulley would take charge only when the UN observer force landed in Haiti.[23] The ad hocery and the divided command (contrary to what was envisioned by the Goldwater-Nichols Act) indicated that Haiti was a secondary or tertiary consideration for the administration.

Near the end of September, the *Harlan County* sailed from Norfolk to Roosevelt Roads in Puerto Rico where she was to pick up a U.S. Navy construction battalion (Seabees) and Canadian engineers. Her departure for Haiti was then delayed as Haitian violence increased. Then, on October 3, the Black Hawk down incident took place in Somalia, causing some serious qualms in the Pentagon. Nevertheless, the *Harlan County* had sailed and was en route to Port-au-Prince, while Cedras and the junta, who were following the news carefully, plotted how to avoid having the HAG land.[24]

Meanwhile, COL Pulley had arrived in Haiti by air and was working out of the American embassy and his hotel, the Montana, which catered to foreigners. Among others staying there were the chargé d'affaires, Vickie Huddleston, and academic Dr. Bryant Freeman, a specialist on Haiti from the University of Kansas, serving with the UN International Civilian Mission in Haiti as a human rights monitor.[25] *Harlan County* arrived in Port-au-Prince harbor on October 11 and found her berthing at the dock blocked. Over the next 24 hours a tense stand-off developed as the junta orchestrated mob action on the dock. Harassment by paramilitary boats and Haitian naval boats occurred, with two armored cars mounting 90 mm guns conspicuously placed near the dock. In addition the mob harassed Huddleston, beating on her armored sedan with heavy sticks and shaking the vehicle until she beat a hasty retreat.[26]

In spite of the harassment, both Pulley and Huddleston argued that the force should land as they believed Cedras was engaged in an elaborate bluff. Butcher, however, was not convinced and determined to depart the area without landing the troops. Although there was contact with both Washington and Norfolk, CINCLANTFLT supported the decision of Commander Butcher. It was a resounding victory for Cedras and his junta. As Kretchik reports, Freeman, watching from the Hotel Montana on a hillside, stated, "I watched the ship leave the port and for the first time in my life I was not proud to be an American."[27]

PLANNING IN EARNEST

Before the *Harlan County* incident, USACOM was planning for a noncombatant evacuation operation (NEO). Soon after, the CJCS directed ACOM to shift its planning from a NEO to a forcible entry operation designed to restore

Aristide and remove the junta.[28] ACOM began planning in November and focused on developing both an interagency plan to achieve the goal of restoring the democratically elected government peacefully and helping it achieve success, and a military plan to accomplish the same end. The military plan was given the code name Jade Green. Later, it would evolve into OPLAN 2370.[29] The ACOM planners working on Jade Green checked their archives to see if they had any plan on file on which they could base their new plan. They found a 1988 plan from U.S. Forces Command that fit their needs. Its most glaring deficiency, however, was that while it identified forces and deployments, it gave no indication of how those forces would be used once they arrived in Haiti.[30] This was essentially a function of the JOPS planning system in effect in 1988; the more recent revision of the system, called JOPES, rectified that situation.

While some members of the ACOM staff focused on Jade Green, others were engaged in planning for an interagency response to the crisis. This interagency planning was the first of its kind. Conducted at the instigation of the USA-COM commander, Admiral Paul D. Miller, the plan would be submitted to the Joint Staff for review and then to the NSC Interagency Working Group (NSC/IWG).[31] As described by army planner MAJ Ed Donnelly, assigned to ACOM:

> Essentially, USACOM put together a document that told the interagency working group within the National Security Council what they would be expected to contribute to the operation in Haiti. USACOM laid out the purpose of the operation, the endstate, and defined the criteria for military success. The document went to the JCS and then the NSC, where it was codified. The document then came back with corrections but essentially USACOM wrote the document.[32]

After Donnelly and ACOM J-5, Brig Gen Mike Byron, U.S. Marine Corps, went to Washington, in April, to brief the NSC/IWG, they received approval of the concept.[33] Their understanding of this approval was that the agencies represented in the IWG had agreed to do their part. This was especially important because Byron had made clear that ACOM did not see training Haitian police as a military mission, and so, that mission was assigned to the Department of Justice.[34]

January 1994 arrived and Cedras was still in power in Haiti. At the UN, France and Canada sought to increase the pressure adding more and stronger sanctions, while the United States, concerned about a new influx of refugees, continued its policy of forced repatriation. At USACOM, planners responded to a new planning order from CJCS. Jade Green began to migrate into OPLAN 2370. A key element was the establishment of JTF 180 around the base of the army's XVIII Airborne Corps. Located at Fort Bragg, North Carolina, the corps was under the command of LTG Henry Hugh Shelton and was the parent unit of the 82nd Airborne Division, the key combat element for any invasion of Haiti. A second element would be a Joint Special Operations Task Force (JSOTF). Later a marine corps element was added.[35]

2370, 2380, AND 2375

OPLAN 2370 was a plan for forcible entry. The 82nd Airborne was to jump into Haiti in two Drop Zones near the capital, Port-au-Prince. The JSOTF would hit high-priority targets, and its Special Forces teams would take control of the smaller towns in the countryside. Finally, the Marine Expeditionary Unit (MEU) would seize Cap Haitien, Haiti's second city, on the North coast.[36]

In April 1994, Aristide attacked Clinton and his Haiti policy. Aristide's charges were taken up by key African American supporters of the Democrats both within and out of government, including members of the Congressional Black Caucus. A hunger strike by activist Randall Robinson put sufficient pressure on the administration to change its policy toward Haitian migrants giving them a chance to win asylum in the United States. Then, on April 15, JTF 180 was disestablished as the likelihood of an invasion of Haiti seemed to have been postponed indefinitely.[37] This did not mean that OPLAN 2370 was shelved; work on it continued, especially within the Special Operations community.

Although the status of Haitian migrants was improved by the administration decision to treat each case individually, this only increased the flow of refugees. Again, the administration turned to the UN Security Council and began working on a new resolution. This, in turn, translated into NSC guidance to the secretary of defense and the CJCS to begin working on a new plan. "On June 2, 1994 USACOM notified the XVIII Airborne Corps to begin creating a second option, one that enabled U.S. forces to enter Haiti permissively, with a handover to a United Nations Mission in Haiti (UNMIH)."[38] The new plan, Concept Plan (CONPLAN) 2380, was similar to 2370 but eliminated combat operations against the Haitian armed forces and police. The corps submitted the plan through ACOM for Joint Staff review on June 17. On June 29, USACOM received the reply from the Joint Staff, which both approved CONPLAN 2380 and directed that it be developed as an Operations Order (OPORD) under the Crisis Action Planning mode of the JOPES process. For military planners, this change is significant in that it usually indicates the imminent execution of the plan (although, as we saw in the Panama case, "imminent" took 21 months).[39]

The development of OPORD 2380 was then delegated to the 10th Mountain Division, which, along with the 82nd, is a subordinate element of the XVIII

Airborne Corps. This was something of a problem in that the division staff was not (and is not) robust enough or senior enough to conduct such high-level planning without significant assistance. This meant that planners from both the corps and the division were in constant motion between Fort Bragg, home of the corps, and Fort Drum, New York, where the 10th Mountain Division is located. Added to the issues facing the planners in both organizations developing 2380 was a new requirement that a multination force from the Caribbean Community (CARICOM), made up of platoons from each of the contributing states, be added to the troop list for 2380. The negotiations for the CARICOM force were conducted by the American embassies in each Caribbean country, with the USACOM J-5 coordinating and providing support and military "advice."[40]

Early in September, GEN Shelton's somewhat facetious prediction that the next surprise would be a plan that blended 2370 and 2380 came true. In his capacity as commander of JTF 180, Shelton received orders to develop a plan that bridged the two plans. The new plan was called 2375 and retained the forcible entry of 2370 but transitioned to 2380 more rapidly than previously contemplated.[41] At about the same time, Secretary of Defense William Perry directed USACOM to preposition forces for the invasion of Haiti.[42]

THE ADMINISTRATION DECIDES

With the continuing political stand-off and refugee crisis, coupled with the Black Hawk down and *Harlan County* humiliations of the autumn of 1993, the Clinton administration was slowly inching toward the decisive act of invading Haiti. Much of the decision making was incremental as when the administration established the Haiti IWG and the planning orders to USA-COM, the XVIII Airborne Corps, and their subordinate and supporting units. On September 9, 1994, USACOM had one OPLAN fully developed and approved (2370), one in the final stages of development (2375), and one OPORD fully approved (2380). That day, the corps received an Alert Order from USACOM directing it to activate itself as JTF 180 (again) and the 10th Mountain Division as JTF 190.[43]

The Alert Order also formally approved 2370 and 2380 for execution with the anticipated deployment date of the next day, September 10. On September 11, Maj Gen Mike Byron (he had recently been promoted), ACOM J-5, and LTC Ed Donnelly, his planner, traveled to Washington for a meeting of the NSC Haiti IWG. At that meeting, the two officers briefed the plans, surprising many of the participants.[44] There were two reasons for the surprise: (1) Not all the members of the IWG had been granted prior access to the plan, and (2) there was a high rate of turnover among the participants from the various government departments with principals represented at many meetings by substitutes/subordinates. At one point during the meeting, Byron asked the DOJ representative to brief his plan for reconstituting and training the Haitian police (as the DOJ had agreed to do at a previous meeting). The DOJ representative was shocked, he had never heard of this task, and stated that the DOJ could not do it.[45] Byron immediately called back to ACOM and one of his planners, an infantry LTC, took on the mission and completed it in time for the operation.[46]

On the evening of September 15, President Clinton addressed the nation on the Haiti crisis. He announced he was calling up reservists to support a military operation and further announced he was sending two aircraft carriers to the region. The next day, the president directed Secretary of Defense Perry to implement the military operation that would be scheduled for September 19.[47]

THE SECURITY COUNCIL ACTS

While all this was going on at USACOM, the XVIII Airborne Corps, the 10th Mountain Division, and the NSC, in New York the UNSC wrestled with the Haiti problem. U.S. ambassador to the UN, Madeleine Albright, took the lead for the administration and in the UNSC. UN action came to a head in July where discussions were taking place about establishing a UN Mission in Haiti (UNMIH). On July 12 the Haitian junta ordered UN human rights monitors out to the country. The same day, the United States dispatched the command ship of the U.S. Second Fleet, the USS *Mount Whitney*, to the Caribbean in the vicinity of Haiti. On July 13, the 24th MEU completed a NEO exercise, a rehearsal for an evacuation from Haiti, at the nearby island of Great Inagua.[48]

> On July 14th Madelaine Albright . . . announced that eleven nations had pledged their support for the multinational force (MNF) to be placed in Haiti following the removal of the junta. The following day U.N. Secretary-General Boutros Boutros-Ghali elaborated on the Security Council's authorization of a coalition force of 15,000 to provide peacekeeping capability in Haiti after President Aristide resumed his office.[49]

On July 20, Ambassador Albright asked the UNSC to approve American-led action to remove the junta "by all necessary means" and the council voted in favor.[50] Then on July 31, the UNSC approved UNSC Resolution 940.[51] The heart of UNSCR 940 was in paragraph four, which provided a mandate under Chapter VII of the UN Charter to use "all necessary means" to remove the junta and restore Aristide to the presidency.

THE EXECUTE ORDER

President Clinton's order to Secretary Perry to implement OPLAN/OPORD 2370 should have constituted the Execute order.[52] This direction caused a number of actions to take place. ACOM alerted its subordinate JTF 180. At the same time JTF 190 was alerted that 2370 was authorized for execution with 2380 as the follow-on. JTF 180 alerted the 82nd Airborne Division and air force lift assets moved to Pope AFB adjacent to Fort Bragg. The JSOTF was also alerted, and the 24th MEU was moved into place off Cap Haitien on Haiti's northern coast. The two aircraft carriers moved into position. All was ready to execute in the very early hours of September 19. Then, the unanticipated happened.

JIMMY CARTER PARACHUTES IN

That same day, September 17, GEN Cedras contacted former president Jimmy Carter to see if there was a possible negotiated solution.[53] Carter contacted President Clinton and proposed that he go to Haiti to negotiate with Cedras. Clinton added former CJCS, GEN Colin Powell, and Senator Sam Nunn (D–GA), chairman of the Senate Armed Services Committee, to the team. Carter added his former NSC director for Latin America, Dr. Robert Pastor, one of his senior aides at the Carter Center.[54] Clinton had issued specific instructions to Carter that there should be no discussion of whether an invasion would occur; they were only to negotiate the specific terms of the departure of the junta.[55]

The Carter mission arrived in Haiti on September 17, negotiated the rest of the day, and all day on the 18th and well into the night. Although the discussions were cordial and some progress was made, the outcome remained in doubt. Meanwhile, operational actions were already under way at sea and in North Carolina. At 10:00 PM, ACOM commander Admiral Paul D. Miller turned the command of the operation over to JTF 180 commander, LTG Shelton. USACOM then got authority to issue the Execute Order (EXORD) for 2370 from the president and secretary of defense. Combat operations were to begin at midnight, which meant that the 82nd Airborne was already in the air and other combat elements were on the move.[56]

By the afternoon of September 18, the negotiations had moved to the presidential palace. There, Cedras had been joined by President Jonassaint. At about 4:00 PM Cedras's junta colleague, General Biamby, burst into the room. He had just received a report from his sources near Fort Bragg/Pope AFB that the 82nd Airborne Division was loading into transports and taking off for Haiti.[57] As Pastor described the event,[58] Cedras jumped out of his chair and took off running with Carter, Nunn, Powell, and Pastor in hot pursuit. Cedras soon lost them and as they contemplated what to do next, somebody thought to call Mrs. Cedras. She was able to contact her husband and convince him to return to the negotiating table.[59] Things moved swiftly in the final round of the negotiations as President Jonassaint took charge and agreed to the terms. Cedras had been convinced by the fact that the troops were in the air, and therefore, he was looking for "an honorable way out," which the president gave him.[60]

THE 82ND TURNS AROUND

Rumors began to reach USACOM that the Carter mission had succeeded about the time the 82nd lifted off from Pope AFB. Thirty-five minutes later the rumors were confirmed and ACOM was notified that JTF 180 would make an administrative landing in Haiti, essentially executing OPORD 2380. But 2380 was to be executed by the 10th Mountain Division operating as JTF 190. Since the agreement called for the junta to stay in power until Aristide would return to the presidency on October 15, Admiral Miller decided to leave JTF 180, under LTG Shelton, in control of the operation. This would entail some important revisions to 2380. As a result the landing was postponed until the next day.[61]

Meanwhile, the paratroopers in their C-130s and C-141s, en route to Haiti through some severe storms, were notified they were turning around. Thus the aircraft returned through the same storms they had just encountered, leaving both troopers and aircrew airsick and miserable and they returned to Fort Bragg without even a combat jump to show for their effort.

On the USS *Mount Whitney*, JTF 180 planners worked on developing a new plan that blended elements of 2370 and 2380 to address the new situation in an ambiguous environment where today's enemy would, when dawn came up the next day, be a nominal friend. The new OPORD was dubbed 2380+ but would be executed under the name Operation Uphold Democracy.[62] LTG Shelton approved 2380+ at 1:00 AM, September 19, and the OPORD was issued by 3:00 AM.[63]

"INTERVASION" AND THE 10TH MOUNTAIN DIVISION AND CARICOM

Shortly after 9:00 AM on September 19, a flight of Black Hawk helicopters approached the tarmac at Port-au-Prince International Airport. As they touched down, fully loaded combat soldiers from the 10th Mountain

Division, many of them veterans of Somalia, jumped down, threw themselves down behind their rucksacks with their weapons pointed outward, establishing a defensive perimeter. The command Black Hawk landed in the center of the perimeter and GEN Shelton stepped off, wearing his camouflage uniform with his red, paratrooper beret but unarmed. Walking out from the terminal building to greet Shelton were Ambassador William Swing in a business suit, and a U.S. Army officer assigned to the embassy wearing his short-sleeved, Class B office uniform. The scene was a perfect visual metaphor for what came to be called the "Intervasion" of Haiti. And it was all captured by CNN's cameras.[64]

THE SURREAL WORLD OF THE MULTI-NATIONAL FORCE

The Multi-National Force (MNF) initially consisted of JTF 180, JTF 190, the 10th Mountain Division, the 24th MEU, the JSOTF (as conceived in 2380), which was essentially the 3rd Special Forces Group (Airborne), and the 300-member CARICOM contingent made up of platoons from several Caribbean countries. Later the MNF would be augmented by forces from other countries.

The forces that landed on September 19 were the 1st Brigade Combat Team (BCT) and TF Mountain, built around the division artillery, all in Port-au-Prince, the 24th MEU in Cap Haitien (in the north), and Special Forces teams moving into the outlying villages and population centers. The 2nd BCT would replace the 24th MEU by September 28.[65]

Almost immediately confusion as to purpose reigned. GEN Shelton wanted the forces to posture professionally as both collaborative with the Haitian Armed Forces (FAd'H) and police but be seen as clearly in charge. However, MG David Meade, commanding the 10th Mountain Division, interpreted the rules of engagement (ROE) so strictly that soldiers from 1BCT did not intervene as FAd'H troops beat peaceful protesters, including at least one beaten to death. In contrast, a patrol of the 24th MEU opened fire on Haitian police who threatened the patrol with their weapons. The police suffered ten killed and there never was another threat to U.S. forces in Cap Haitien.[66] Meanwhile, in Port-au-Prince, the signals sent by 1BCT and TF Mountain, along with those of GEN Meade, commander of JTF 190, remained ambiguous.

Throughout the MNF operation, there were several disconnects between 2BCT, JTF 190, and the JSOTF. JTF 190 continuously interpreted the ROE in ways that focused on force protection over mission accomplishment. By contrast, 2 BCT and the Special Forces, even more, aimed at establishing a safe and secure environment for the newly empowered Haitian government.[67] To accomplish this, 2BCT, under the command of COL Jim Dubik, conducted extensive small unit patrols in the northern part of the country, in contrast to the operations of 1BCT operating out of the capital.[68] The Special Forces operated in all of the smaller towns of the country, getting as close to the people as possible, and dispensing with helmets and body armor in the process.[69] The ambiguity continued until the 25th Infantry Division replaced the 10th Mountain Division as JTF 190 on March 31, 1995.[70]

TRANSITION TO UNMIH

The UNSC passed Resolution 975 on January 30, 1995, establishing the UN Mission in Haiti to replace the U.S.-led MNF on March 31, 1995. The UNSCR was drafted by the United States, which also insisted that the force commander be an American general.[71] MG Joseph Kinzer was nominated by the United States to be force commander (FC) of UNMIH to serve until February 29, 1996.[72] Kinzer would also wear a second hat as commander, U.S. Forces, Haiti, keeping the command of American military entirely within the U.S. chain of command. As UNMIH FC, Kinzer reported to the secretary-general through his Special Representative, Algerian diplomat Lakhdar Brahimi, while as commander of U.S. Forces, he reported to the new commander of USACOM, Gen John Sheehan, U.S. Marine Corps.

> The MNF had been assigned the missions of facilitating the return and proper functioning of the government of Haiti [President Aristide], improving Haitian security, establishing a secure environment, and efficiently transferring responsibility to the United Nations.[73]

The MNF had accomplished this and so, on March 31, 1995, MG Kinzer and UNMIH replaced the MNF. The UNMIH missions followed from those of the MNF but with a shift in emphasis. UNMIH was charged with fostering democratic stability by holding a series of elections, recovering the basis for Haitian politics and economic viability, and improving the capacity of the new Haitian security forces. The election series would culminate with a presidential election on December 17, 1995.[74]

MISSION: HOLD THE ELECTION AND GO HOME

MG Kinzer put the main focus of his mission on holding elections. As he put it to his aide-de-camp, MAJ John Charlton, "I'm here to hold an election and go home."[75] Ballard puts it that "the successful completion of presidential elections was the acknowledged endstate goal of UNMIH."[76] Unfortunately, this narrow definition of democracy as the holding of free and fair elections indicated a lack of understanding on the part of the U.S. government of just how complex a system democracy really is. Although UNMIH, under the leadership of General Kinzer accomplished this task—and did so despite President Aristide's efforts to extend his term in office—the equating of democracy with elections sowed the seeds for future problems in Haiti.

TRANSITION TO CANADIAN LEADERSHIP

Following the election of December 17, Rene Preval, the new president, requested an extension of UNMIH. Clearly, this request had been anticipated and the UNSC approved a four-month extension under Canadian leadership. Canadian Forces Brig. Gen. Pierre Daigle was designated as the new FC. He was on the ground by early January 1996.[77] The UNMIH force level fell during the transition to around a total of 6,000 troops as most of the Americans left the country. What remained was a U.S. Support Group, Haiti, of several hundred military personnel under the command of COL David Patton, U.S. Army.

THE AFTERMATH AND PREDICTING THE FUTURE

Unfortunately, Haiti quickly began to revert to an ungovernable state. Before UNMIH left in July 1996, President Preval was already stymied by his Congress and former president Aristide, neither of whom would allow any forward movement on policy. Part of the reason was the splintering of Aristide's Lavalas movement into Aristide and Preval factions such that legislative gridlock ensued through the end of Preval's term in office. Not only was there gridlock but the security situation deteriorated with increasing political killings each year.

AND THEN THERE WAS ARISTIDE AGAIN . . . MINUSTAH

President Preval's term ended on February 7, 2001. On that date, after winning the presidential election in December 2000, Aristide began his second term as president.[78] The second Aristide term saw the same kind of excesses as the first term, but in spades. Political violence increased continuously, much of it fostered by Aristide himself and his supporters. Finally, in February 2004 the United States and France called on the UNSC to act and it passed UNSCR 1529, which authorized a Multinational Interim Force led by the

United States for a period of three months. Aristide resigned under pressure and left the country. On June 1, 2004, the force was replaced by a UN peace-keeping force called MINUSTAH, led by Brazil, which provided the FC.[79]

As for what was accomplished by Operation Uphold Democracy—the 1994 "Intervasion"— the following words I wrote in 1996 sum it up:

> In simple terms, a bunch of thugs was finally removed from Haiti, and the government was returned to the Haitian president who had been elected by the people. A series of free and relatively fair elections were held to legitimize the holders of legislative and municipal offices, and finally, a new president was elected who took office peacefully from his elected predecessor—the first such transition for Haiti since 1804. But democracy is more than free and honest elections, and the efforts to restructure the economy and judiciary of Haiti have lagged far behind, while the international community, led by the United States, has been rapidly losing interest in the Haitian experiment. As the UNMIH mission wound down, the indications were that Haiti would most likely revert to the kind of authoritarian regime it has known since it won its independence—what scholars of Haiti have dubbed "a predatory regime."[80]

Today, a dozen years after the international community ousted a Haitian predatory regime, led by the president it had restored a decade before, MINUSTAH is still on the ground—an international tutorial force as the only real alternative to the Haitian norm of predation. Unfortunately, it appears that for the foreseeable future there are no other alternatives.

NOTES

1. Walter E. Kretchik, Robert F. Baumann, and John T. Fishel, *Invasion, Intervention, "Intervasion:" A Concise History of the U.S. Army in Operation Uphold Democracy.* Fort Leavenworth, KS: 1998, U.S. Army Command and General Staff College Press. 176.
2. Ibid., 251–252.
3. Ibid.
4. Ibid.
5. John R. Ballard, *Upholding Democracy.* Westport, CT: 1998, Praeger. 46–47.
6. Ibid, 48.
7. Ibid, 55.
8. Ibid, 49.
9. Ibid.
10. Ibid, 50–51.
11. Kretchik et al., 20.
12. John T. Fishel, *Civil Military Operations in the New World.* Westport, CT: 1997, Praeger. 211.

13. Ibid.

14. Ibid.

15. David Rothkopf, *Running the World.* New York: 2005, Public Affairs Books. Location 6601.

16. Ballard, 50.

17. Kretchik et al., 33.

18. Ibid., 34.

19. Ibid.

20. Ibid., 35.

21. Ibid.

22. Ibid., 36.

23. Ibid.

24. Ibid., 37–38.

25. Ibid.

26. Ibid.

27. Ibid., 41.

28. Ibid., 43.

29. Ibid.

30. Ibid., 43–44.

31. Ibid. In Panama, just five years previously, where I was the principal planner for the post-conflict plan (Blind Logic), I was specifically told I could not coordinate planning with the State Department or any other USG agency located in the U.S. embassy.

32. Quoted in ibid., 44.

33. Ibid., 45.

34. DOJ was the logical choice because they had an organization, staffed by senior FBI agents, called ICITAP, that had precisely that mission and had undertaken it in El Salvador, other countries of Central America, and, most especially, Panama.

35. Kretchik et al., 45–49.

36. Ibid.

37. Ibid., 56.

38. Ibid., 57.

39. Ibid. See also Chapter 6 of this book.

40. Ibid., 57–65.

41. Ibid., 69.

42. Ibid.

43. Ibid., 70.

44. Ibid., 71.

45. Ibid. The account in the text is an abbreviated version. Kretchik told me that as Donnelly had described the meeting, the discussion had taken place as indicated earlier. One should also remember that this is the first ever interagency contingency plan.

46. Ibid.

47. Ibid., 73–74.

48. Ballard, 86.

49. Ibid.

50. Ibid.

51. UNSCR 940 quoted in its entirety in Ballard, pp. 241–243.

52. There is, under JOPES, a transition from a plan to an order as noted earlier with respect to 2380. This same transition took place sometime prior to the implementation of 2370, so the direction given by President Clinton was for the OPORD.

53. Kretchik et al., 74.

54. Conversations with Bob Pastor at a Conference on Haiti in Puerto Rico, 1995.

55. Ballard, 97.

56. Ibid.

57. Ibid. There is a vantage point near Pope AFB where loading operations at Green Ramp can be seen as well as the string of aircraft taking off. I watched this in real time on CNN when the troops were launching for the invasion of Panama on December 19, 1989.

58. Conversation with Pastor.

59. Conversation with Pastor.

60. Ballard, 97–98.

61. Kretchik et al., 76.

62. Ibid., 77–78.

63. Ibid.

64. Ibid., 78–79. I watched the entire scene on CNN and where this account diverges from that in Kretchik et al. it is the scene that I witnessed on CNN.

65. Ibid., 95–101.

66. Ibid.

67. Ibid. Also, interview with COL (later LTG) James Dubik, July 17, 1995, Fort Leavenworth, Kansas.

68. Interview with COL Dubik (later LTG) at Fort Leavenworth, Kansas.

69. Interview with COL Mark Boyatt, commander of the 3rd SFG (A) Fort Bragg and observations/discussion with SF teams in Haiti, 1995.

70. Ibid., 136.

71. Ballard, 162.

72. Ibid.

73. Ibid., 165–166.

74. Ibid., 167.

75. Conversation with Charlton at Fort Leavenworth, Kansas, 1997.

76. Ibid., 169.

77. Kretchik, Baumann, and I were in Haiti during the first two weeks of January 1996, conducting interviews and observing the transition. Although Ballard seems to indicate that the transition was rushed, our interviews and observations showed that it had been planned well in advance. General Daigle's arrival in early January was just one indicator.

78. Walter E. Kretchik, "Haiti's Quest for Democracy," in John T. Fishel and Andres Sainz (eds.), *Capacity Building for Peacekeeping: The Case of Haiti.* Dulles, VA: 2006, Potomac Books. 28.

79. Ibid.

80. Kretchik et al., 176.

Chapter 10

"Some Damned Foolish Thing in the Balkans!"

Prince Otto von Bismarck

THE COLLAPSE OF YUGOSLAVIA

As the final decade of the twentieth century began, the world we had known for over 40 years was changing dramatically. The Soviet Union was on its last legs. The UN had actually worked more or less as intended in Kuwait. Democracy was on the rise in Latin America but Haiti was about to blow up. Somalia, a Cold War pawn, was turning into a disaster—all of these "crises" dealt with in previous chapters. Then, in the Southern part of Europe, Yugoslavia, which had been a quasi-ally of the West during the Cold War, was suffering the strains of ethnic nationalism, dormant under the long rule of Marshal Tito, whose 1980 death awakened the sleeping tiger. As the "iron chancellor" of Imperial Germany had predicted before the First World War, the next conflagration in Europe would be the result of "some damned foolish thing in the Balkans."[1]

As was the case in the chapters on Somalia and Haiti, the Balkans crisis overlapped the Bush and Clinton administrations. That they represented different political parties was less an issue than that there was the overlap, and that the Clinton administration inherited each one just as it was gaining its sea legs. The Balkans differs somewhat in that deep American involvement began later in the process—after Clinton had learned some hard lessons in both Somalia and Haiti.

As suggested previously, the collapse of Yugoslavia was a slow process. It began with the death of Tito in 1980 and did not really pick up speed until 1990. By this time, there had been violent ethnic clashes in Kosovo, an autonomous region within the Serbian Republic with a mostly Albanian population.[2] Croatia and Bosnia-Herzegovina soon followed, each seeking independence.[3] In 1990, after several failed attempts to either adjust the nature of the federation that had been Yugoslavia or break it apart under the extreme rhetoric of nationalist politicians like Slobodan Milosevic of Serbia and Franjo Tudjman of Croatia, in June 1991, Croatia and Slovenia declared their independence.[4] This immediately prompted a short war with the Yugoslav National Army (JNA), won by the Slovenians, which confirmed their independence.

The Croatian declaration of independence also produced a war with the JNA but with very different results. Parts of Croatia with large Serb populations were controlled by the JNA before their advances were stopped by the Croats. Another result was that Bosnia-Herzegovina saw little reason to remain in a federal Yugoslavia to be dominated by Serbia. Thus, its leader, Aliya Izetbegovic, declared independence, prompting the Serb minority in the Western part of the country to resist. Similarly, the Croat minority, in the parts of the country bordering Croatia, resisted and sought union with that independent state. By the end of summer, 1991, there was a three-sided and very uncivil war going on in Bosnia and Croatia with the strings of the Serb side being pulled by President Slobodan Milosevic, the Serb who was president of a Yugoslavia that now consisted of Serbia and Montenegro (Macedonia having declared independence as well).

The official position of the Bush administration was that Yugoslavia should remain a united country. However, neither President Bush, his national security advisor, Brent Scowcroft, nor Secretary of State James Baker wanted to really deal with the issue. They, along with Deputy Secretary of State Lawrence Eagleburger, were happy to leave the Yugoslav crisis to the Europeans, who said they could handle it, and wanted to handle it, without significant American help.

EUROPE TRIES TO LEAD

Under the leadership of the European Commission, the European Communities (EC) attempted to guide the separate Yugoslav republics to an accommodation. Unfortunately, the EC was unable to decide whether that accommodation should involve the peaceful dissolution of Yugoslavia or the continued existence of the federal system. Although the EC sent signals that the country should stay together, the individual member states were divided on the issue. Britain and France were most inclined to support a single state, while Germany was more inclined toward independence. So, too, were the Austrians. Thus, when Slovenia declared independence in June it was soon recognized by EC countries.[5]

This was accompanied by the defeat of the JNA in Slovenia and the decision by Serbian President Milosevic to let that secession stand. The same could not be said for Croatia or Bosnia. EC diplomacy was unable to state clearly whether it would or would not accept the independence of any of the republics even after Slovenia had successfully seceded. The result was that the Croatian and Bosnian secessions went forward and the JNA took the war to them.

CROATIA AND BOSNIA-HERZEGOVINA

Although Croatia was mainly a land of Croats, there were areas with large Serb populations, especially Eastern Slavonia and the Krajina. There were other areas, bordering on parts of Bosnia that had significant populations of Bosnian Muslims. Bosnia-Herzegovina had a Muslim plurality with a nearly equal number of Serbs. The remainder of the population, less than 20%, was Croat. The JNA initially invaded both Croatia and Bosnia but, even more important, gave the Serb militias in both countries training, weapons, and resupply. To make things even more complicated, Croat militias in Bosnia made war on their Bosnian Muslim neighbors. The net result was a civil war between the rump Yugoslavia, made up of Serbia and Montenegro, and Croatia and Bosnia-Herzegovina but also civil wars within Croatia and Bosnia between Croats, Serbs, and Muslims. To illustrate, the man who would become the commanding general of the Bosnian Serbs, Ratko Mladic, began the war as a lieutenant in the JNA.

THE BUSH ADMINISTRATION

In June 1991, Secretary of State James Baker made his only visit to Belgrade just a few days before Slovenia and Croatia declared independence. Baker's analysis was simply wrong and, according to Richard Holbrooke, may well have accelerated the rapid slide into chaos. Holbrooke quotes American ambassador to Yugoslavia, Warren Zimmerman, reflecting on the events: "The refusal of the Bush Administration to commit American power early was the greatest mistake of the entire Yugoslav crisis."[6] Nevertheless, the United States continued to support a united Yugoslavia long after the state had come apart.

Holbrooke comments on how strange this was since both National Security Advisor Brent Scowcroft and Deputy Secretary of State Lawrence Eagleburger had significant experience in Yugoslavia. Scowcroft had been the air attaché in Belgrade during his air force service, while Eagleburger had served as ambassador to the country. Scowcroft responded to a question about this state of affairs posed to him in 1995:

> Eagleburger and I were the most concerned here about Yugoslavia. The President and Baker were furthest on the other side. Baker would say, "We don't have a dog in this fight." The President would say to me once a week, "Tell me what this is all about."[7]

This is not to say that the president and his secretary of state ignored the problem but rather that their analysis was faulty and they believed they had more important issues to address at the time. Baker simply did not see the breakup of Yugoslavia as an issue that should consume the United States, and Bush was focused on the post-Soviet world and the threat posed by Saddam Hussein in the Persian Gulf region. By the time the Gulf War ended, the Europeans had taken the position that they could handle the fallout of Yugoslavia without American help and the administration was more than willing to let them do so, with only the most minimal U.S. involvement.

UNPROFOR

As the Yugoslavia crisis heated up in late 1991 and early 1992, the UN Security Council passed its first resolution, 713, calling for an arms embargo to the area. Soon after, the UN secretary-general, at the request of the Yugoslav government, began preparations for a peacekeeping force. This was followed by UNSCR 743 of February 21, 1992, which established the UN Protection Force (UNPROFOR). In March, the first elements deployed to Croatia.[8]

The purpose of UNPROFOR was to implement the peace plan developed by the secretary-general's special representative, former U.S. secretary of state Cyrus Vance. The mandate in the UNSCR was to "create the conditions for peace and security required for the negotiation of an overall settlement to the Yugoslav crisis."[9] As stated by former deputy commander of UNPROFOR, Canadian Maj. Gen. John Arch MacInnis,

> The specific tasks set out for UNPROFOR were to verify the withdrawal of the JNA, to ensure that the UN Protected Areas (UNPAs) were demilitarized through the withdrawal of all armed forces and that all persons in them were protected from fear of armed attack, to monitor the formation of local police to ensure nondiscrimination and full respect for human rights, and to facilitate the return of displaced persons.[10]

This was a tall order and very nearly impossible with the forces available, the mandate under Chapter VI of the UN Charter, and the expansion of the war and the mission from Croatia into Bosnia-Herzegovina.

In Croatia

From March 1992 until March 1994, the only significant success of UNPROFOR in Croatia was the removal of the JNA forces. Otherwise, UNPROFOR operated in an ambiguous environment of civil conflict between Serb majorities in parts of the country and the Croatian army attempting to defeat them. The ambiguities increased with UNSCR 815 of March 1993, which called for the UN Protected Areas to be seen as integral part of the Republic of Croatia in contrast to the original mandate that specified a negotiated end to the Yugoslav crisis.[11]

A year later, there was a major breakthrough in the situation. The Croatian government and the de facto Serb government in the Serb regions of the country reached an agreement that allowed for a cease-fire to take effect and be policed by UNPROFOR.[12] Of course, this agreement would only be temporary, but it would introduce a modicum of calm to Croatia, allowing attention to shift to Bosnia.

IN BOSNIA

All during the Croatian war, a not dissimilar conflict was developing in neighboring Bosnia. But where the Croatia fight was between Serbs and Croats, the Bosnia conflict pitted Bosnian Serbs against the plurality of Bosnian Muslims, with Bosnian Croats battling the Bosnian Muslims for control of places like Mostar. As bad as the fighting became between the Croats and Bosnian Muslims it never achieved the ideological intensity of the war between the Bosnian Serbs and the Bosnian Muslims. Ethnic cleansing was rampant in the Serb areas as they drove the Bosnian Muslims from their homes and into becoming refugees in their own country. All this was clearly aided and abetted by Serbia and its leader, Slobodan Milosevic.

Thrust into this messy conflict with an inadequate humanitarian mandate to provide assistance to certain "protected" Bosnian Muslim populations was UNPROFOR. Such a mandate is appropriate for traditional peacekeeping under chapter VI of the UN Charter.[13] Included in the mission was the protection of Bosnian Muslim enclaves in the cities of Srebrenica, Zepa, and Gorazde. NATO responded to this Bosnian Serb offensive with air attacks that had minimal impact, amounting to little more than pinpricks, according to Richard Holbrooke.[14] The Serbs responded by taking UNPROFOR peacekeepers hostage and holding them as human shields. While it is unclear what the negotiated terms of their release were, in its wake Secretary-General Boutros-Ghali took control of the authorization for NATO bombing from his force commander, British general Sir Michael Rose. The net effect was a significant reduction in the NATO "air campaign."

THE CLINTON ADMINISTRATION EDGES
TOWARD THE FRONT

The various issues of the UNPROFOR operation prompted calls for the UN to withdraw from the mission. By June 1995, French president Jacques

Chirac, who had been among the most hawkish of the Europeans, began to make the case for greater American involvement. Without that involvement, Chirac indicated he would support UNPROFOR withdrawal. This put significant pressure on the Clinton administration.[15] Adding to the pressure was a U.S. military operations plan, OPLAN 40–104, already approved by the NATO Council, to use 20,000 American troops to extricate the UNPROFOR forces. This plan had not been briefed to Secretary of State Warren Christopher, or President Clinton, although the president had pledged U.S. forces to facilitate a UN withdrawal. Somehow, Richard Holbrooke, then assistant secretary of state for Europe (with the Bosnia portfolio), got wind of the OPLAN and requested (perhaps "demanded" is a better word) a briefing. On receiving it he informed Christopher and arranged for him to receive the briefing as well.[16]

Chirac visited Washington on June 14. During the presidential pre-brief that day, Clinton was informed of the OPLAN but, in Holbrooke's view, in a way that was misleading. When he attempted to present an alternate understanding of the automatic nature of the OPLAN, the president cut him off. It was not until that evening that Holbrooke and Christopher were able to tell the president exactly what the United States was committed to—this conversation took place not in the situation room, but in the ceremonial rooms of the White House after the dancing that followed the State Dinner for Chirac.[17] The president "began to press his advisors for better options; he understood how odd it would be to send troops to Bosnia to implement failure."[18]

In July the Bosnian Serbs renewed their offensive targeting Srebrenica, Zepa, and Gorazde. In all three they committed major atrocities but the world watched Srebrenica in particular. There, in a city ostensibly under the protection of UNPROFOR, with Dutch soldiers on the ground, the Serbs massacred nearly 8,000 Muslim men, while the Dutch troops did nothing and were virtual prisoners. The United States pressed for air strikes, to no avail. The Europeans had had enough and were afraid of losing their soldiers in the fighting that would ensue. Then, British prime minister John Major proposed to convene a conference in London on July 21. Although neither Major, Chirac, nor anyone else had any idea of what such a conference might accomplish, the proposal sparked a flurry of activity, particularly on the part of the United States.

The chairman of the Joint Chiefs (CJCS), GEN John Shalikashvili, immediately left for London. He was soon joined by Secretary of State Christopher and Secretary of Defense William Perry. Christopher was joined by a team that included Holbrooke's deputy and the director of the Policy Planning Staff.[19] On the plane, the team drafted a set of conclusions for the conference. The key ones were: (1) NATO would "draw a line in the sand" around

Gorazde; and (2) the decision to use air power to defend Gorazde would be made by NATO alone without UN participation.[20]

THE KRAJINA OFFENSIVE AND THE ROLE OF MPRI

Back in April 1995, the American private military company (PMC) Military Professional Resources Inc. (MPRI) was awarded a contract by the Croatian government to train their army and organize their Ministry of Defense. Founded by retired senior U.S. military officers, MPRI was then headed by former U.S. Army chief of staff, GEN Carl Vuono. The contract was approved by the State Department and the DOD, so there is no question that MPRI had the full support of the U.S. government (USG). However, the contract was with Croatia, not a USG entity, and the potential for conflicts of interest between the PMC and the USG certainly existed. Nevertheless, MPRI carried out its programs with skill and left Croatia with a military far more capable than it had before. In August, after MPRI left, Croatia launched Operation Storm to take back the Krajina from Serb forces, this in an area that bordered on Bosnia and had significant influence on events taking place there.[21] "It was a dramatic gamble by President Tudjman [of Croatia]. When it finally took place—still against our advice—it was a complete success."[22] Contrary to the expectations of the Americans and British, Serbian president Milosevic did not come to the aid of the Serbs in Croatia.[23]

DECISIONS

As the Croatian offensive came to an end, President Clinton held a Balkans policy review on three successive days. This was the NSC system at work, although the State Department was represented by the deputy secretary because the secretary was traveling in Asia. The meetings were representative of the interagency approach to an issue but with the highest level of intensity due to the president's direct involvement. Not taken into account—at least not to the extent warranted—was the success of the Croatian offensive. As would later become clear, it changed the facts on the ground in such a way as to set new parameters for subsequent negotiations.[24]

The outcome of the policy review was a two-stage strategy with a seven-point policy initiative. The first stage involved sending National Security Advisor Tony Lake and Under Secretary of State Peter Tarnoff to Europe as presidential emissaries with a proposed framework for peace, that is, the seven-point initiative. Stage two would hand off the implementation to Holbrooke, the assistant secretary of state for Europe, and his interagency team.

HOLBROOKE TAKES THE LEAD

Holbrooke's original team suffered tragedy on its first shuttle mission to Bosnia when a vehicle carrying three members, Robert Frazure, from the State Department, Joseph Kruzel, from the DOD, and Col S. Nelson Drew, USAF from the NSC staff, went off a cliff on Mount Igman, killing all three. Just prior to the funeral at the Fort Myer Chapel in Washington, Holbrooke met with Secretary Christopher and his senior staff in the secretary's office, to reconstitute the team and prepare for a meeting of the Principals Committee (PC) that would take place after the funeral. Present, along with Christopher and Holbrooke, were Undersecretary for Political Affairs Tarnoff, Chief of Staff Tom Donilon, Deputy Secretary Strobe Talbott, and a couple of others. They decided to name Christopher Hill, a senior Foreign Service officer, to replace Frazure and leave the DOD and NSC representatives to Secretary of Defense William Perry and Tony Lake, respectively. They also added one of State Department's senior international lawyers, Roberts Owen.[25]

Immediately after the funeral, the PC convened in the Situation Room in the basement of the White House. As discussed in a previous chapter, the PC is the NSC less the president and vice president and is chaired by the national security advisor. Although it is supposed to be a major decision forum, Holbrooke notes that the PC is usually much less.

> In theory, the views of the senior officials, including any disagreements, were then brought to the President for final policy decisions. In fact, if a clear consensus was not reached at these meetings, the decision-making process would often come to a temporary halt, which was followed by a slow, laborious process of telephoning and private deal making. People hated to take their disagreements to the President; it was as though a failure to agree somehow reflected badly on each of them. . . .[26]

In this instance, however, the PC acted effectively because President Clinton had made clear his sense of urgency for the development of a well-crafted, effective policy to bring the war in the Balkans to an end.[27] The PC reviewed the issues for a meeting with the president the next day. At the end, Lake told Holbrooke that he intended to appoint army BG Donald Kerrick to replace Nelson Drew. Shortly thereafter, SECDEF Perry named army LTG Wes Clark, director of Policy and Plans on the Joint Staff (J-5), as his military representative and James Pardew, director of the Balkan Task Force in the Office of the Secretary of Defense (OSD), as the civilian representative.[28]

The next day, following a memorial service at Fort Myer, the team and senior officials met with President Clinton informally in a room in the

Chapel. The bottom line was that the president gave his blessing and directed Holbrooke to work the forthcoming shuttle diplomacy until he had a solution.

NATO

The European NATO allies had been the primary force contributors to UNPROFOR. That was both a blessing and a curse. The blessing was that they had stepped up to the plate; the curse was that they were very casualty averse. As a result, they were less than fully committed to forceful military action by NATO, even though that is precisely what they had committed to in London. On August 28, the day the Holbrooke team arrived in Paris, the Bosnian Serbs mortared a marketplace in Sarajevo killing 35 and wounding some 85 more. Acting Secretary of State Strobe Talbott called Holbrooke saying that the attack called for a strong military response. He wanted to know what the team thought. According to Holbrooke he asked what effect retaliatory air strikes would have on the negotiations, saying, "Your advice could be decisive. . . . There is a lot of disagreement here."[29]

> I did not need to think about my reply. The brutal stupidity of the Bosnian Serbs had given us an unexpected last chance to do what should have been done three years earlier. I told him to start NATO air strikes against the Bosnian Serbs—not minor retaliatory "pinpricks," but a serious and, if possible, a sustained air campaign, which was authorized by the "London rules." It would be better to risk failure in the negotiations than let the Serbs get away with another criminal act. This was the most important test of American leadership since the end of the Cold War, I said, not only in Bosnia, but in Europe.[30]

This event demonstrated that the old soldiers' saying that the enemy always has a vote applies. The Serb attack established the conditions that the American leaders in Washington and the team in Paris exploited to get NATO to act decisively under the "London rules."

Among the oddest features of this decision-making process was that, except for UN ambassador Madeleine Albright, all the "principals" (including the president and vice president) were on vacation at the end of August. Thus the PC, attempting to "forge a united front with our NATO allies and the UN" was made up entirely of deputies and their deputies. Led by Deputy NSA Sandy Berger, it included Deputy SECDEF John White, VCJCS Admiral William Owens, acting CIA director George Tenet, and Undersecretary of State (the number 3 position) Peter Tarnoff. Also attending were Albright and Under SECDEF for Policy (again the number 3) Walter Slocum.[31] And the system worked—the PC made up of the deputies succeeded.

BACKSTOPPING HOLBROOKE IN WASHINGTON

Operation Deliberate Force, the NATO air campaign under the "London rules," began on August 30. It continued well into September with pauses. On September 11, the PC met again, this time with President Clinton in attendance part of the time. It is worth noting that Holbrooke, by his rank as an assistant secretary of state, much too junior to even sit along the wall in the Situation Room, was at the table as a full participant. Membership in the NSC and its committees varies with the need and inclination of the president and his NSA. Clinton's participation clearly facilitated a number of decisions, but the bottom line was that the bombing campaign had a very limited time to pressure the parties into an agreement. As is often the case, there were significant differences between the departments and organizations represented on the NSC, with the most profound being between Defense and State. The DOD, in many ways, held the upper hand because it controlled the information about what it could and could not do in executing its war plans.[32] The DOD also made its weight felt in these meetings because it invariably had two principals (or deputy)-level representatives at all of these meetings, whereas State (and the other agencies) had only one. If OSD and JCS were in agreement—and they usually were and had coordinated before the meetings—their united voice was very powerful.[33]

Holbrooke makes the case that the success of the negotiations was due to the backup his team received from Washington. The key to that support was the flexibility given to the negotiators in the field and the lack of interference from the Washington bureaucracy. As an example of what could have happened, Holbrooke points to the efforts by USAID to insert itself into the negotiating team on the grounds that success required winning the peace, which was USAID's job. Efforts like this were thwarted by Christopher and Deputy NSA Sandy Berger, who protected the flexibility of the team. Micromanagement from the NSC would have greatly hampered and may well have resulted in the failure of the negotiations. Holbrooke also credits President Clinton who gave the team a mission, expressed his confidence in them, and made it clear to one and all that they had his confidence.

DAYTON

Events moved rapidly through the rest of September and into October. Holbrooke's team was able to bring the Europeans, NATO, and the Russians on board with help from the White House. Again, the president's involvement was decisive but he was a resource that could only be deployed on occasion. Too much, and he lost his effectiveness.[34] The team focused mainly on the three Balkan presidents, Izetbegovic, Milosevich, and Tudjman. The effort finally produced a cease-fire, coupled with the impact of the Croatian offensive and the NATO air campaign. Several agreements were reached at levels below the presidents but including NATO, the EC, and the UN. By the middle of October, the ground had been laid for a final peace conference.

The first issue was where it would be held. The Europeans wanted it in Europe; the French were the most insistent. This prompted Holbrooke to ask Vice President Gore to intervene. The outcome was a call from President Clinton to President Chirac, with the decision to hold the conference in the United States with a final ceremony in Paris. Location for the conference ended up being a collaboration between State and DOD with three sites in the running after Camp David was ruled out as too small. These were the Naval War College in Newport, Rhode Island, Langley AFB near Norfolk, Virginia, and Wright-Patterson AFB in Dayton, Ohio. Dayton, although Spartan and somewhat out of the mainstream, was chosen partly because of those features.

If Dayton were to turn out a success, then the next order of business would be the nature and role of the peacekeeping force to be deployed. This issue was complex because it involved the European NATO allies, who were also force providers for UNPROFOR, which included its British commander, General Rupert Smith. In addition to NATO it was desirable that the peacekeeping force include the Russians, who refused to serve under NATO command. Not only did this issue involve the international partners but it also marked sharp divisions between State and the JCS. Holbrooke discusses two "high-level" meetings involving the president and his national security team held on October 25 and 27 designed to settle the issues.[35]

Prior to the October 25 meeting, the DC, led by Sandy Berger, had met and narrowed the issues. Nevertheless, 11 significant issues remained between State and the Pentagon. State took an expansive view of the role of the peacekeeping force, while the JCS favored a narrow interpretation. Although the NSC meetings did not resolve all the issues, the fact that CJCS, GEN Shalikashvili, offered some creative compromises went a long way toward their resolution.[36] Holbrooke still felt that the compromise had not gone far enough and the Pentagon military representative on the negotiating team, LTG Clark, agreed. Clark "and his staff added a 'silver bullet' to the military annex" to the proposed Dayton accord. "Although phrased in bureaucratese, it gave the IFOR commanders the freedom to use force whenever they felt it was necessary without recourse to civilian authorities."[37]

Dayton was a difficult negotiation but it was well prepared. It concluded with an agreement that was finally signed in Paris to keep the French and other Europeans happy. But it could not have been concluded except for the leadership of the United States. That leadership was exercised by a team of diplomats and soldiers who were allowed the freedom to operate and protected by key leaders in Washington. While most of the key players in both DC and on the negotiating team were career government officials, several were drawn from the political side. These included both the NSA, Tony Lake, and his deputy, Sandy Berger, SECSTATE Warren Christopher and his chief of staff, Tom Donilon, and Richard Holbrooke. This is not to say that these individuals were inexperienced but rather that they were foreign policy professionals who had built careers as foreign policy experts for their political parties and who came into office when their party won the White House. Of interest, both Lake and Holbrooke had begun their careers as Foreign Service officers in Vietnam.

AFTERMATH: IFOR, SFOR, KFOR

The aftermath of Dayton was the implementation of the agreement. The peacekeeping force, known as IFOR, was under the overall command of NATO Supreme Allied Commander Europe, GEN George Joulwan. But Joulwan was also commander in chief of the U.S. European Command and the Russian contingent served under his command wearing his American, and not his NATO, hat. Congress had authorized funding for, and U.S. military participation in, IFOR for a limited time. That this limitation on the length of the commitment would risk the success of the entire effort prompted President Clinton to ask for and receive long-term support from Congress. The new authorization resulted in a new name for the force, SFOR (or Stabilization Force).

The success of these operations in Bosnia set a pattern for how to deal with the next Balkan crisis, Kosovo. This largely autonomous province of Serbia was inhabited mainly by ethnic Albanians, who desired independence. The Serbs, however, saw Kosovo as the historic heart of Serbia and were not about to let it go. The result was yet another war and another American-led peacekeeping force known as KFOR.

EPILOGUE

In many ways, the Balkans marked the coming of age of the Clinton administration's national security apparatus. The process of getting to Dayton and beyond involved the development of a relatively strong team. Jelling the team was helped by the succession of William Perry as secretary of defense, replacing Les Aspin, and the low-key but strong CJCS, John Shalikashvili. The loss of three of the original team members on Mount Igman galvanized the new team and made for a special closeness among the State, OSD, JCS, and NSC staff members. This was enhanced by the solid working relationship between the two army generals on the team, Wes Clark representing the JCS and Don Kerrick representing the NSC staff. Helping it all come together were the Secretary of State Warren Christopher, who was really in his element as an international lawyer, and Deputy NSA Sandy Berger, who was a very effective facilitator.

Christopher and Berger played especially important roles in allowing the negotiating team to maintain its flexibility and avoid micromanagement from the NSC. Although Holbrooke makes no overt criticism of his old friend Tony Lake, the NSA, in this regard there is a subsurface sense that Lake wanted to exercise more control from the White House. That he did not is evidence of his professionalism, respect for Holbrooke and the NSC Principals, and his solid relationship with his deputy.

In spite of institutional differences between the State Department and the DOD, by this late period in Clinton's first term, the two departments had found effective ways of working together in mutual support. Where there were difficulties, they were often within a department rather than between departments.

Finally, unlike the cases of Somalia and Haiti, the Balkans achieved a great deal of visibility to President Clinton and piqued his interest. Once that happened, Clinton was engaged and ready to make the efforts needed to make things happen within the U.S. government and with foreign leaders. The president set the tone and the objective to be achieved and made himself available as the instrument to be used when no other would do. Critically, President Clinton was there when he was needed but was not there to micromanage. He stated his objectives clearly, exercised oversight, but allowed his subordinates the leeway to achieve his policy goals.

NOTES

1. As quoted in Barbara Tuchman, *The Guns of August*. New York: 1963, Dell. 91.

2. Kosovo was of great historical importance to the Serbs because that is where Serbia lost its independence to the Ottoman Turks.

3. Saadia Touval, "Lessons of Preventive Diplomacy in Yugoslavia," in Chester A. Crocker, Fen Ostler Hampson, and Pamela Aall (eds.), *Managing Global Chaos*. Washington, DC: 1996, U.S. Institute of Peace. 403–418.

4. Michael J. Dziedzic and Andrew Bair, "Bosnia and the International Police Task Force," in Robert B. Oakley, Michael J. Dziedzic, and Eliot M. Goldberg (eds.), *Policing the New World Disorder*. Washington, DC: 1998, National Defense University Press. 253–314.

5. Touval, 407–412.

6. Richard Holbrooke, *To End a War.* New York: 1998, The Modern Library (Kindle Edition). Location 675.

7. Ibid., location 680.

8. Dziedzic, 254.

9. Quoted in John A. MacInnis, "Piecemeal Peacekeeping: The United Nations Protection Force in Former Yugoslavia," in John T. Fishel (ed.), *"The Savage Wars of Peace:" Toward a New Paradigm of Peace Operations.* Boulder, CO: 1998, Westview Press. 114.

10. Ibid.

11. Ibid., 115.

12. Ibid., 116.

13. Ibid., 120–122. General MacInnis goes into significant detail on the nature of the conflict and UNPROFOR's role that is only background to the American decision making.

14. Holbrooke, location 1402–1407.

15. Ibid., location 1494.

16. Ibid., location 1494–1507. This lack of coordination between the DOD and the State Department is not all that surprising. War plans are tightly held within the DOD itself and not always shared by the JCS with the civilian side of the building. According to a Pentagon civil servant, in a private conversation, the military side of the house during the Clinton administration was totally dominant over the Office of the Secretary of Defense (the civilian side).

17. Ibid., location 1543.

18. Ibid., location 1550.

19. Ibid., location 1621. The latter was James Steinberg, who would become deputy national security advisor in Clinton's second term.

20. Ibid., location 1621–1627.

21. The role of MPRI is addressed by Deborah Avant in *The Market for Force: The Consequences of Privatising Security.* New York and London: 2005, Cambridge University Press. 103.

22. Holbrooke, location 1639.

23. Ibid.

24. Ibid., location 1639–1662.

25. Ibid., location 1738–1743.

26. Ibid., location 1760–1765.

27. Ibid., location 1771.

28. Ibid., location 1771–1803.

29. Ibid., location 1986.

30. Ibid., location 1986–1991.

31. Ibid., location 2022–2028.

32. Ibid., location 3059–3104.

33. Briefing to Center for Hemispheric Defense Studies class by the Deputy J-5 in the Pentagon, 1998. It is also worth pointing out that military officers serve on the NSC Staff and, although they do not represent the DOD or their services, they do bring both those perspectives and the current thinking of the DOD and the JCS to the principals as they get ready for NSC, PC, and DC meetings.

34. Holbrooke, location 4570–4624. This is Holbrooke's view of presidential effectiveness in Dayton.

35. Ibid., location 4570–4624. Although Holbrooke does not call these NSC meetings, that is exactly what they were, especially when the statutory makeup of the NSC is remembered.

36. Ibid.

37. Ibid., location 4629. IFOR is the name given to the peacekeeping force for Bosnia.

Chapter 11

9/11 and the Invasion of Afghanistan

THE BIN LADEN THREAT AND THE CLINTON
ADMINISTRATION RESPONSE

As discussed in Chapter 8, Osama bin Laden had played an important, if behind-the-scenes, role in the battle of Mogadishu. His Afghan Arabs had provided important training to the militia forces of Mohammed Farrah Aideed, such that they were able to track the Task Force Ranger helicopters and bring two down. They also organized the assault on the Rangers and the use of civilians as human shields. This attack on the Americans in October 1993 followed years of bin Laden activity in Afghanistan, where he had supported the Mujahedeen against the Soviets and would make common cause with the Taliban in their successful takeover of the country.

Bin Laden was clearly an Islamist militant but he was hardly the only one. That same year, Islamists led by Ramzi Yousef, had organized the first attack on the twin towers in Manhattan. The attack killed several people, wounded more, and did some damage to one of the towers. Later, Youssef would be implicated in a plot to blow up several transpacific airliners nearly simultaneously. Another Islamist plotter was the so-called Blind Sheikh, Omar Abdul Rahman, who would be arrested, tried, and convicted for a plot to blow up various New York City landmarks.

President Clinton and his national security team slowly began to address the threat of terrorism, in particular Islamist terrorism, by establishing the organizations within the national security community to focus on the issue. One of the first steps was to create within the NSC an Interagency Working Group (IWG) on counterterrorism. Clinton had inherited the NSC committee structure created by George H.W. Bush's NSA, Brent Scowcroft, of the Principals Committee (PC) and Deputies Committee (DC). Below that was a third tier that the Bush team had called Policy Coordinating Committees (PCC) and Clinton renamed IWGs. To head the counterterrorism IWG—later named the Counterterrorism Security Group or CSG—he chose NSC staffer Richard A. Clarke, a longtime national security professional who had worked in both the State and Defense departments.[1]

One of Clarke's first tasks was to get the FBI to share intelligence with the NSC, a practice that was made more difficult by the decentralized nature of both the FBI and the Justice Department. The FBI field offices work closely with the regional U.S. Attorneys but have an arm's-length relationship with their own headquarters. Likewise, the U.S. Attorneys are fairly autonomous with respect to the Department of Justice.[2] Clarke, accompanied by NSA Tony Lake, discussed the issue with Attorney General Janet Reno, who agreed that terrorist intelligence developed by the FBI could be shared with designated members of the NSC if there was some foreign connection.[3]

Over the years of the Clinton administration's two terms the CSG acquired significantly greater importance. It was the only IWG with responsibility for both domestic and international security issues. Given the increasing terrorist threat largely from bin Laden and his crew of radical Islamists, it was little wonder that the CSG received more responsibility. The greater the influence of the CSG, the higher the visibility of its leader became. By the end of the Clinton presidency, Dick Clarke was the *czar* of counterterrorism and was a regular member of the PC. This role for a third-tier player clearly was not what Scowcroft had in mind when he developed the modern NSC structure. Nevertheless, organizations adapt to facts on the ground and clearly so did the NSC by elevating the CSG.

The other organizational innovation on counterterrorism during the Clinton years was the creation of the Counterterrorism Center (CTC) at the CIA. Within the CTC, the CIA established a "virtual" station. Initially focused on terrorist finances and called Terrorist Financial Links or TFL, it soon began to focus on the actions of a radical Islamist activist and financier, Osama bin Laden. Officially the UBL station, it was given a code name by its first director, Michael Scheuer, "Alec Station," named for his son.[4]

In spite of the institutional changes to deal with terrorism, the Clinton administration was both hesitant and cautious. First, it tended to see terrorism as a law enforcement issue. This was compounded by the fact of two domestic terrorist incidents, the Oklahoma City bombing and the bomb placed at the Atlanta Olympics. Second, following the Al Qaeda attacks on American embassies in Kenya and Tanzania, it retaliated only with cruise missiles into the Afghanistan desert. When Al Qaeda attacked the USS *Cole*, the administration could not bring itself to go after Al Qaeda because it could not prove them to be responsible. The November 2000 election changed all that. After 35 days of dispute, the Supreme Court ruled against the Gore campaign, effectively making George W. Bush president-elect. The incoming administration planned to take a tougher stance.

THEY CALLED THEMSELVES THE "VULCANS"

In a normal presidential election there are around 75 days between the election and the inauguration for the new president to nominate, vet, and get his nominees confirmed by the Senate. After the election dispute in 2000, there were only 39 days for that to happen. The shortened period caused by the electoral dispute compounded the problem of staffing a new administration that had only increased since the election of George H. W. Bush in 1988. Although all of George W. Bush's cabinet nominees were confirmed on January 20, 2001, many subcabinet appointments were held up. For example, deputy secretary of state, Richard Armitage, was not confirmed until March 23.

The difficulties of filling the government did not mean that preparations had not been made. In 1999, Condoleezza Rice, then Provost of Stanford University, was asked to join Bush's campaign as foreign policy advisor. Rice, with a doctorate in political science from the University of Denver where she had studied under Clinton's secretary of state, Madeleine Albright's father, Joseph Korbel, was a veteran of the Bush 41 NSC staff. She had then held the portfolio on the Soviet Union and had greatly impressed the president. Rice put together a team beginning with Paul Wolfowitz, who had served as ambassador to Indonesia in the Reagan administration, as the undersecretary of defense for policy in the Bush 41 administration, and was now the dean of the School of Advanced International Studies of Johns Hopkins University.[5] Rice invited Wolfowitz to co-chair the group.[6]

Another member was Richard Armitage, who had served in the Reagan administration as assistant secretary of defense for international security affairs and briefly in the Bush administration.[7] Armitage was also Colin Powell's best friend. Other members of the group were Stephen Hadley, Robert Zoellick, and Robert Blackwill. Rice also asked Richard Perle, from the right wing of the Republican Party and a former defense official in the Reagan administration, to join the group.[8]

Developing their Pentagon reform plans was Dov Zakheim, another former defense official.[9] As James Mann notes of the group, "Their wellspring, the common institution of their careers, was the Pentagon."[10] Rice says of the group, "Just for fun we decided to adopt a nickname and called ourselves the Vulcans, after the Roman God and the symbol of my home city of Birmingham, Alabama. The name meant nothing more than that, but many a conspiracy theorist tried to divine some deeper significance."[11]

In the top tier, above the Vulcans, the president selected many of the senior foreign policy leaders of the party. Dick Cheney was his vice president, Colin Powell his secretary of state, and Don Rumsfeld his secretary of defense, while Andy Card became White House chief of staff and Rice, herself, was named NSA. Despite public identification of the top and second tiers of the administration as "neo-cons" only Wolfowitz fits the criteria.[12] The rest were traditional conservatives, most with a penchant toward realism in their view of international relations.

The Vulcans were not a new phenomenon in the staffing of presidential administrations. The common practice is to draw from people who have served in previous administrations of their party. Thus the Clinton administration was staffed largely by people who had served in the Carter administration as well as a few older members who had served in the Kennedy–Johnson era. The Vulcans, for the most part, were veterans of the Reagan and Bush 41 teams. Some of the older players like Rumsfeld and Cheney harkened back to the Nixon and Ford years. Similar to career public servants, these political appointees held successively higher offices in each succeeding administration with major breaks in public service when the other party won the White House. This phenomenon would reappear when the next party turnover took place in January 2009.[13]

CHATTER

When the new administration took office in January 2001, terrorism was only one of many items on its national security plate. Relations with Russia, China, North Korea, and Iraq all raised significant potential for conflict. President Bush wanted to put greater emphasis on U.S.-Latin American relations, starting with Mexico, where President Vicente Fox was the first president from outside the official party, the PRI, since that party had been founded in the 1920s.[14]

Among other things occupying the new administration was the organization of the NSC and the NSC staff. Rice was a veteran of Brent Scowcroft's NSC staff in the Bush 41 administration. She attempted to re-create its structure and method of operation. In doing so, she did not have to modify the basic structure except for replacing the more ad hoc IWGs with the more formal Policy Coordination Committees (PCCs).[15] The PCCs were of two types, regional and functional. Regional PCC were chaired by the appropriate regional assistant secretary of state, while functional PCC chairs came from among the senior directors on the NSC staff. One functional PCC that was retained intact was the CSG, under the leadership of Dick Clarke.

Early in the new administration, Clarke gave NSA Rice an informal briefing in his office. They had worked together in the Bush 41 administration, and now she was his boss. As Clarke recounts it, "She said, 'The NSC looks just as it did when I worked here a few years ago, except for your operation. It is all new. It does domestic things and it is not just doing policy, it seems to be worrying about operational issues. I'm not sure we will want to keep all of this in the NSC.' "[16] In this incident, we actually see the origin of the Bush administration's organizational approach to homeland security after September 11.

Within the administration, the CIA was especially focused on terrorism. Its focal point was in the CTC, an element of the Directorate of Operations and the parent organization of Alec Station that targeted Osama bin Laden and Al Qaeda. The CTC was headed by Cofer Black, a longtime clandestine service officer. Black and the CTC had very good relations with Clarke and his CSG but much less strong with the FBI, which was still not well organized for counterterrorism. Moreover, the bureau was hampered by what was, in effect, a wall between its intelligence side and its law enforcement side. Due to bureaucratic interpretation, the "wall" extended beyond the FBI to its relations with other intelligence agencies like the CIA and the National Security Agency. It even extended to DOJ prosecutors in the U.S. Attorneys' offices.[17]

In the Spring and Summer of 2001, there was a major increase in terrorist threat reporting.[18] CSG chief Dick Clarke had approached Rice early on with the urgency of addressing the terrorist threat posed by bin Laden and Al Qaeda. DCI George Tenet had both echoed and reinforced Clarke, especially with his direct access to President Bush during his daily 8:00 AM Presidential Daily Brief. Through July, as the 9/11 commission report said, Tenet had stated that "the system was blinking red."[19] Unfortunately, the blinking lights were all over the place. There were reports of plans to attack American embassies abroad, to attack Israel, India, and other U.S. allies and interests. There were reports of planned attacks in June and again in July but not specifically where. There were reports of attacks planned in the United States, including in New York City, but not when or how. Some reports spoke of kinds of attacks but not where or when. In July the CIA received intelligence that a major planned attack had been delayed but not where it would take place or the type of attack. In short, the chatter picked up from all sources focused on the Islamist terrorists indicated a real threat but not its location, timing, or method. And, because of some of the constraints between the FBI and the rest of the intelligence and law enforcement communities, some information that was inside the system was not being shared between agencies and, therefore, did not reach the decision makers.

In spite of the spike in threat reporting, the wheels of the national security policy apparatus ground at their normal pace. A National Security Presidential Decision (NSPD) was being prepared to address the terrorist threat. By summer, it had been approved by the deputies. On September 4 it went to the PC and was to go to President Bush the following week, tentatively September 10 (but Bush was traveling to Florida that day).[20]

THE ATTACK

Tuesday morning, September 11, 2001, dawned bright and clear on the East Coast of the United States.[21] For most Americans, the world—and the United

States—was at peace. For the NSC, CSG, and the intelligence community, they were already engaged in a long twilight war with Islamist terrorists.[22] As with many ongoing conflicts, the participants on both sides were planning their moves. As indicated previously, the NSC had developed a "war plan" (the NSPD) that was about to be approved when the enemy struck first.

That morning, President Bush was in Florida walking into the elementary school where he was to engage second graders in reading "when Karl Rove [political counselor] mentioned that an airplane had crashed into the World Trade Center."[23] Bush spoke with Rice by phone who told him that the plane was a commercial airliner. The president went into the classroom and participated with the teacher and kids in the reading lesson. After a bit, the President wrote, "I sensed a presence behind me. Andy Card [White House Chief of Staff] pressed his head next to mine and whispered in my ear. 'A second plane hit the second tower,' he said. 'America is under attack.' "[24] In all, four planes were hijacked. Two struck the Twin Towers of New York's World Trade Center, where approximately 3,000 people died. One hit the Pentagon, home of the DOD and America's military headquarters. At the Pentagon, 125 personnel were killed, as were all 59 people (including the hijackers) on the plane. Casualties in the Pentagon were relatively light because the hijacker flying the aircraft aimed it directly at the long, flat wall of the outer ring of the building on its West side. As a result, it plowed through the E ring, the space between the E and D ring, the D ring, finally coming to rest having just penetrated the space between the C and B ring. Had it struck one of the corridors connecting the rings, the casualties would likely have been much higher. The last aircraft crashed in the fields of Pennsylvania, when the passengers and some crew members attempted to regain control from the hijackers.

The immediate response to the attacks was to get people to safety and find out exactly what was happening. The president was rushed to Air Force One, which flew him to Barksdale AFB in Louisiana. From there he flew to Offutt AFB at Omaha, Nebraska, where he would hold a NSC meeting by video teleconference from headquarters, Strategic Command, before returning to Washington. Most of the White House was evacuated except for the national security team, which was divided between the President's Emergency Operations Center (PEOC) below the East Wing and the bunker next to the Situation Room in the basement of the West Wing. Vice President Cheney and NSA Rice operated out of the PEOC, while key NSC staff worked in the bunker under the leadership of Dick Clarke.[25] Laura Bush was whisked to a safe location in Washington, while the Bush daughters were made safe in Connecticut and Austin, Texas, where each was attending college. SECDEF Rumsfeld was in the Pentagon when the attack happened, and he soon joined the first responders in their rescue efforts. Secretary of State Powell, in Lima, Peru, for a meeting of the Organization of American States, immediately boarded his airplane to return to Washington.

INITIAL RESPONSE

One of the first questions that needed to be addressed was what to do about all the aircraft in or en route to American airspace. In addition, the FAA and the FBI believed that as many as six airplanes may have been hijacked. Vice President Cheney called President Bush on Air Force One and recommended that the air force be given the order to shoot down any aircraft that posed a threat.[26] Bush agreed and the order was issued. At about the same time, the FAA grounded all flights within American airspace and closed entry to that airspace.

At 3:30 PM, the president convened a NSC meeting by VTC from Offutt AFB. DCI George Tenet stated that it was a near certainty that the attacks had been conducted by Al Qaeda. The proof was that three key Al Qaeda operatives were on the passenger manifest of American Airlines #77 that had hit the Pentagon. The NSC told Bush about the grounding of all flights. Little was decided except for the fact that the president would return to the White House against the advice of the Secret Service.[27]

Bush returned to the White House about 7:00 and met with his speechwriter, Michael Gerson, and with Rice to go over the speech he was to deliver on national television at 9:00 PM. Included in the speech was the phrase, "We will make no distinction between the terrorists who committed these acts and those who harbor them."[28] Here in the speech was a major policy decision, made by the president, not fully vetted through the NSC system. It was a lesson that the system for communicating policy is also a policy making tool in its own right. It was also a lesson—if one were needed—that the NSC is there to advise and assist the president it is not, itself, a policy making body.

In the days immediately following 9/11 President Bush met with his NSC multiple times to develop his policy and give guidance. One key factor is that the Bush NSC—which became known as the "War Cabinet" —was very close to the original statutory design of the NSC. Its membership consisted of the president, vice president, SECSTATE, SECDEF, CJCS, DCI, NSA, and White House chief of staff. All but the last two are statutory members or advisors. In addition, the State and Defense deputies along with the VCJCS were often invited to attend.

As noted previously, one issue addressed at this level was how to communicate policy. President Bush relied on his communication team, which included his speechwriters, his counselor Karen Hughes, and Rice. Two speeches in this time period are particularly important. The first was the speech at the National Cathedral on September 14, where Bush spoke one exceptionally memorable line: "This conflict was begun on the timing and terms of others . . . It will end in a way, and at an hour, of our choosing."[29] The second critical speech was to Congress and the American people, as well as the world audience, the night of Wednesday, September 19. President Bush ended, saying, "I will not forget this wound to our country and those who inflicted it . . . I will not yield; I will not rest; I will not relent in waging this struggle for freedom and security for the American people."[30]

On the diplomatic front, multiple steps were taken. One of the first was not initiated by the U.S. government; it was the decision by NATO to invoke Article V of the North Atlantic Treaty, which states that an attack on one member is an attack on all. An extremely important action, entrusted to SEC-STATE Powell and his deputy, Rich Armitage, was to make sure Pakistan came on board. Powell and Armitage drew up seven demands for Pakistan's president, General Pervez Musharraf. These included stopping Al Qaeda operatives at the border, basing rights for the United States, blanket overflight rights, and a pledge to break relations and end support to the Taliban if they continued to harbor bin Laden.[31] Armitage delivered the demands to Pakistani intelligence chief, General Masoud, who was in Washington, to be passed to Musharraf. Early that afternoon, Powell called Musharraf, who surprised him by accepting all seven demands, without any reservations.[32]

At his NSC meeting on September 17, President Bush stated that he wanted an ultimatum issued to the Taliban that day. Powell asked for time to craft it and determine if they needed another day so that Pakistan could deliver it. The president agreed.[33] The ultimatum was issued on Thursday, September 20, and made public the next day. It demanded that the Taliban turn over the terrorists "or share their fate."[34]

THE IRAQ QUESTION AND DISTRACTION

Perhaps, the most significant NSC meeting early in the crisis took place at Camp David on Saturday, September 15. At that meeting, SECDEF Rumsfeld and his deputy, Paul Wolfowitz, seriously raised the issue of attacking Iraq in response to 9/11. There was little support for their position beyond the two of them, although for Vice President Cheney and, perhaps, Bush himself, it was a matter of timing and coalition support. Rice and Powell were adamantly opposed and the CJCS, GEN Shelton, sided with them. In the end, President Bush decided to keep the focus on Al Qaeda, the Taliban, and Afghanistan.[35] To that end, much of the action shifted to the CIA, with much of the rest to the DOD and U.S. Central Command.

JAWBREAKER

Wartime operations generally fall under the Department of Defense and the particular combatant command with that area of responsibility (AOR).

Afghanistan is in the AOR of U.S. Central Command (CENTCOM), whose commander at the time was GEN Tommy Franks. In most cases, indeed in all that have so far been considered in this book, the relevant combatant command had in place an OPLAN or CONPLAN that could be modified to address the operational need following the Crisis Action Planning (CAP) element of JOPES. Afghanistan, however, was a "worst case scenario" for which no plan existed. As a result, the CENTCOM planners had to start their CAP planning from scratch. By contrast, the CIA, although it did not have a plan on the shelf, had assets and a concept that could be deployed quickly.

The CIA had been an active player in Afghanistan for a long period but especially since the Soviet invasion in December 1979. The agency had worked closely with Pakistan's ISI to support the mujahideen in their war against the Soviets. During the decade of that fight, CIA had established strong relations with various mujahideen factions. After the Soviets left Afghanistan in 1989, the U.S. government, as a whole, lost interest, but not the CIA, which did maintain its contacts. This was especially true with a number of warlords of the northern tribes who would form the Northern Alliance under Ahmed Shah Masood, against the Taliban after 1995. Masood was assassinated by Al Qaeda operatives on September 9, just prior to the 9/11 attacks.

By late afternoon on September 11, the CIA had confirmed that the 9/11 attackers were Al Qaeda operatives whose leadership was based in Afghanistan. This was due, in part, to the establishment during the Clinton administration of the CTC and its subordinate, virtual Alec Station, targeted on bin Laden and Al Qaeda. On September 13, DCI George Tenet presented President Bush a list of expanded authorities designed to give the agency the ability to conduct operations against Al Qaeda and other terrorists worldwide (although not in the United States). The list was expanded at the NSC meeting on September 15 at Camp David and approved by the president on September 17. According to Tenet, the president said, "I want the CIA to be first on the ground."[36]

Gary Schroen, who had been deputy head of the Near East/South Asia Division in the Directorate of Operations (a three-star equivalent position), had just entered the 90-day retirement program on September 11.[37] Late on September 13, Schroen received a phone call from Cofer Black, head of the CTC, who wanted to meet with him the first thing the next morning. When they met the next morning Black said,

> Gary, I want you to take a small team of CIA officers into Afghanistan. You will link up with the Northern Alliance in the Panjshir Valley, and your job is to convince them to cooperate fully with the CIA and the U.S. military as we go after bin Ladin and al-Qa'ida. You will also evaluate their military capabilities and

recommend steps we can take to bring the Northern Alliance forces to a state of readiness so they can effectively take on the Taliban forces, opening the way for our efforts against UBL.[38]

Schroen, of course, accepted the mission. As Tenet had pointed out at the NSC meetings, the American role would not be one of conquest. Rather, the CIA would be the insurgents—later complemented by Army Special Forces.[39]

On September 19, Schroen's team of eight CIA operators departed for the long, roundabout trip to Afghanistan by way of Germany, Uzbekistan, and Tajikistan. They traveled by C5-A, chartered bus, and a CIA-owned Russian MI-17 helicopter that the agency had refurbished and upgraded, especially its avionics. The team, code named Jawbreaker, arrived in the Panjshir Valley on September 26, linking up with the Northern Alliance.[40]

While Jawbreaker was deploying, CAP planning and execution were under way in Tampa, Florida, at both CENTCOM and U.S. Special Operations Command (SOCOM), at Army Special Forces Command headquarters at Fort Bragg, North Carolina, and at Fifth Special Forces Group (5SFG) at Fort Campbell, Kentucky.[41] Commanding 5SFG was COL John Mulholland, a veteran of 7SFG operations in Latin America, SFOD-D (Delta Force), and a graduate of the Army Command and General Staff College and the National War College.[42] It was 5SFG that would provide the Special Forces (SF) teams (ODA Operational Detachment Alpha or A Teams) that would work with the CIA in Afghanistan.

In September, the chain of command for 5SFG was hazy at best. It ran from USSOCOM through USASOC and Army SF Command to Mulholland. But the theater commander was GEN Tommy Franks at CENTCOM, who was charged with running the war. Thus, 5SFG would need to be detached— chopped, in military slang—from the SOCOM chain to CENTCOM, where it would fall under the sub-unified SOCCENT (Special Operations Command, Central Command). This would create some difficulties since CENTCOM leadership was not entirely comfortable with how SF groups operate. Moreover, there were relatively poor communication links between CENTCOM and the CIA along with issues over command relationships between the CIA and DOD assets. These issues existed between the national bureaucracies, at the operational level, and between operators in the field—although the farther away from Washington, the easier it was to resolve them.

5SFG, codenamed Task Force Dagger, established itself at K2 airbase in Uzbekistan in late September, about the time Jawbreaker arrived in Afghanistan. Coordination with CIA headquarters and with the Jawbreaker team was a problem, and it was not until the second week in October that the first SF team would be inserted and link up with Jawbreaker.

SPECIAL FORCES ODAS 555 AND 574

The first SF team into the country was ODA 555, or Triple Nickel. It set up with Jawbreaker. Other teams soon followed in the northern part of the country. Two such teams rode, literally on horseback, with Northern Alliance forces to take Mazar-i-Sharif. ODA 555, in the Panjshir Valley with the bulk of the Northern Alliance forces, assisted in the advance across the Shomali Plain for the assault on Kabul. Under serious air attack by American forces directed by SF laser targeting and CIA money, the Taliban and Al Qaeda defenses collapsed. Kabul fell on November 14.[43]

Meanwhile, things were not going as well in the South. Where the North was dominated by Uzbeks and Tajiks, among others, the dominant ethno-linguistic group in Afghanistan, the Pashtuns, controlled the South. Pashtuns were also the base of the Taliban and were a large group in neighboring Pakistan. Far more Pashtuns were supportive of the Taliban than were the Uzbeks and Tajiks.

Finding Pashtun leaders willing and able to work with the United States proved to be difficult. CIA officers, operating out of Station Islamabad, were in touch with a Pashtun named Abdul Haq. During the war with the Soviets, he had been an effective combatant until he lost his foot to a landmine. After he recovered, he found he had also lost his drive. Now, Haq was back in the game supported by two Afghan American brothers working out of Peshawar in Pakistan. While the CIA was aware of Haq's activities, it was not controlling or directly supporting him when he decided to enter Afghanistan not too far from Jalalabad. The Taliban found him there, pursued, and surrounded him. Haq contacted the brothers pleading for American support and they contacted the Station in Islamabad by phone. The Station decided to support and diverted an armed Predator drone—the strike killed a few of the pursuing Taliban, but Haq and 20 of his men were captured and executed.[44]

Immediately after 9/11, a prominent Pashtun leader named Hamid Karzai contacted the Station in Islamabad. With broader support than Abdul Haq, Karzai seemed a better bet. However, he wanted to go into Afghanistan immediately, just as Haq did. The CIA did support him with a satellite radio-telephone, but that was all, since they had advised him to wait. Like Haq, Karzai ran into trouble but he was able to contact the Station and was extracted by helicopter, Nevertheless, he told his rescuers and his people in Afghanistan that he would return very soon.[45]

The next time Karzai infiltrated southern Afghanistan was in October. This time he had an American escort. There was a CIA team led by an officer variously called Craig[46] or Casper[47] and an SF team (ODA 574) led by CPT Jason Amerine and his team sergeant, Jefferson Davis, known as JD.[48]

Although the CIA team and the ODA were able to work together, there were evident tensions that reflected those in Washington.[49] In at least one discussion involving CIA director Tenet, SEDEF Rumsfeld, and Vice President Cheney, Rumsfeld tried to insist on clarification of who was in charge on the ground in Afghanistan. Cheney intervened and said, "Don, just let the CIA do their job."[50] That calmed the issue for a while, but it would not die. CENTCOM commander GEN Tommy Franks visited CIA headquarters and told Tenet, "I want you to subordinate your officers in Afghanistan to me." Tenet replied, "It ain't gonna happen, Tommy."[51] In country, the issue surfaced in terms of coordination between ODA 574 and the CIA team over the heliborne infiltration of Karzai with the CIA team leader changing the American personnel manifest at the last minute over the objection of CPT Amerine. It surfaced again when the CIA team took off without coordinating to find the helicopter carrying Karzai that had been forced to land a mile and a half away from the rest of the ODA, in rough country.[52] The issue of who is on charge of an operation is central to policy success or failure. The military principle of war is "Unity of Command," and the military sees it as one of a very few central concepts of warfighting. If Unity of Command does not exist, then a unity of effort must be achieved ad hoc or the risk of failure becomes extremely high.

Opening the Kabul Embassy

Kabul fell to the Northern Alliance on November 14, 2001. The American Embassy, closed for 12 years, was reopened in stages between December 11 and 22. A U.S. Marine detachment went in first, followed by the diplomats.[53] The first American diplomat in was Mary Ann Wright, who would become deputy chief of mission to Ambassador James Dobbins.[54] Dobbins, a career diplomat, was the State Department's point man on building an international coalition to assist Afghanistan in establishing a new government.

THE INTERNATIONAL SUPPORT STRUCTURE AND ACTIONS

In December, the UN convened a conference in Bonn, Germany, that brought together the various ethnic and political factions in Afghanistan with a number of donor nations to plan for the establishment of an interim government. One of the goals of the conference was to convene an Afghan "grand council," called a *Loya Jirga*, to draft a constitution and establish a permanent government. The *Loya Jirga* would be attended by Afghan tribal, ethnic, and faction leaders.[55] Attending the Bonn conference for the United States was James Dobbins, head of the Liaison Mission and soon-to-be American ambassador to Afghanistan.[56] The conference selected Hamid Karzai to head the interim government. He would later be elected president of Afghanistan.[57] Karzai was well respected by all factions, which was important because of the longtime Afghan political consensus (one of the very few that was common to the entire country) that the head of state (and/or government) must be a Pashtun.[58]

The Bush administration had developed a reasonable plan to bring Afghanistan into the family of nations. It was multilateral in the extreme. The United States took primary responsibility for the military aspects of securing the country but sought to play only a supporting role in the economic, political, social, and public safety aspects. The UN was to coordinate most of these activities through donor conferences and UN agencies. NATO would assume the lead in public safety and would play a support role in military security. Unfortunately, neither the Taliban nor Al Qaeda had been destroyed.

BIN LADEN ESCAPES

As U.S. special operators, Northern Alliance, and Pashtun militias consolidated control over populated areas of Afghanistan, the Taliban and their Al Qaeda allies were attempting to flee into neighboring Pakistan. In December, a fairly large number, reportedly including both Osama bin Laden and Taliban leader, Mullah Omar, apparently were located high in the White Mountains at around 15,000 feet in a place called Tora Bora. Working with three SF soldiers and two CIA officers, the Pakistani Army was to seal off their side of the border while Afghan tribal militias did the same on their side. The CIA-SF team coordinated air strikes on the caves where the militants were hiding. In spite of this, the border seal, on both sides, was less than hermetic, and a core of Al Qaeda and Taliban, including bin Laden and Omar, escaped to Pakistan.[59]

THE DEVELOPMENT OF ISAF AND
THE KARZAI GOVERNMENT

The UN Security Council authorized a stability operation in Afghanistan to be conducted by NATO. Initially, the military operation was a Combined (the military term for multinational) Joint Task Force, later named the Combined Forces Command (CFC). Its commander was LTG David Barno, U.S. Army.[60] Barno faced the problem that few of his U.S. officers had any concept about how to deal with the revived Taliban insurgents, who were probing the new government.[61] Barno was particularly successful in forging a strong relationship with the American ambassadors from Dobbins to Ambassador Zalmay Khalilzad, the Afghan-born Republican foreign policy specialist President Bush appointed to the position. Between them, and the UN envoy, Lakhdar Brahimi, they worked well with President Karzai in establishing an interim government, holding the *Loya Jirga*, and arranging for elections to be held.

In March 2002, NATO and Afghan militia forces launched Operation Anaconda, designed to destroy the Taliban in their last stronghold in Afghanistan, the Shah-i-Kot Valley. This time, conventional forces were involved under the overall command of MG Franklin Hagenbeck, commander of the U.S. 10th Mountain Division. The Afghan militia were advised by special operators and CIA paramilitary officers. Although the Taliban were defeated, they were still able to escape to Pakistan.

Strong support for Karzai came from President Bush, who invited him to his State of the Union address and talked regularly with him by phone. As CPT Amerine, the CIA officers who worked with him, Ambassador Khalilzad, LTG Barno, and President Bush found, Karzai was a man whose good instincts had to be stroked. When they were, Afghanistan moved toward greater freedom and democracy.

Barno was succeeded by army LTG Karl Eikenberry, whose relationship with Ambassador Khalilzad was reportedly difficult at best. Eikenberry also never really got along with Karzai. In 2003, the NATO force was renamed International Security Assistance Force (ISAF) and its writ was expanded from just the Kabul area to the whole country. In addition, ISAF command rotated among NATO countries other than the United States until 2007. After 2003, the security situation slowly deteriorated as the Taliban reentered the country as insurgents. In 2005, Karzai was elected president in a generally free and fair election. Nevertheless, the insurgency grew as the United States became preoccupied with its second war, in Iraq. By 2006, the Iraq war was clearly not going well for the U.S.-led coalition. In December, 2007, the new chairman of the Joint Chiefs of Staff, Admiral Mike Mullen, characterized both wars, saying, "In Afghanistan, we do what we can; in Iraq we do what we must."[62]

NOTES

1. Richard A. Clarke, *Against All Enemies.* New York: 2004, The Free Press. 90–91.

2. Ibid. As discussed in the Panama case, the U.S. attorneys in Tampa and Miami had indicted Noriega without the knowledge of anyone at the DOJ or anywhere else in the government. By 1993, their autonomy had been lessened but not by very much.

3. Ibid.

4. George Tenet, *At the Center of the Storm.* New York: 2007, HarperCollins. 99–100.

5. Condoleezza Rice, *No Higher Honor.* New York: 2011, Crown Publishers (Kindle Edition). Location 219.

6. Ibid. At this time, my friend and Dartmouth classmate Lou Goodman was the dean of the School of International Service at American University. Lou was on numerous working groups with Wolfowitz and indicated to me that he thought highly of him, although they were of opposite political parties.

7. Ibid., location 230.

8. Ibid., location 230–241. Holbrooke notes in his memoir that Perle played a positive role in advising the Croatians at the Dayton negotiations.

9. Ibid., location 247.

10. James Mann, *The Rise of the Vulcans.* New York: 2004, Viking. xiii.

11. Rice, location 253.

12. The term "Neo-conservative," neo-con for short, was coined by Irving Kristol to describe mainly former Democrats who were traditional Cold War liberal internationalists. They moved to the Republican side of the aisle when the Democrats began to forsake the leadership role in the world that these thinkers believed in.

13. A prime example is Michele Flournoy, who served in the Clinton administration as principal deputy assistant secretary of defense for strategy. An extraordinary talent, out-of-office Michele was on the faculty at the National Defense University, and was a scholar at the Center for Strategic and International Studies (CSIS) before starting her own think tank, the Center for a New American Security (CNAS), with Kurt Campbell. Michele returned to government in the Obama administration as undersecretary of defense for policy.

14. See Rice, Chapter 3.

15. Ibid., Chapter 2.

16. Clarke, 229.

17. The 9/11 Commission Report. Washington, DC. PDF. 73–80.

18. This discussion is largely taken from ibid., 254–260, and Tenet, Chapter 8.

19. 9/11 Commission, 259.

20. Clarke, 26.

21. That day, my wife, our nearly two-year-old daughter, and I were on the second day of our vacation on the beach in North Carolina. We had left Washington, DC, the day before and had driven down. On Sunday, we had been on a panel, chaired by my wife, dealing with insurgency in Latin America as part of the Latin American Studies Association meetings in DC. At the time, I was a professor at the National Defense University's Center for Hemispheric Defense Studies, and my office was located on the fourth floor of Headquarters of the U.S. Coast Guard, with a great view across the Potomac of the Pentagon, where I had worked in my first duty station in the army for nine years, both active and reserve (1969–1978). Over breakfast, we witnessed the two attacks on the Twin Towers on television. Later, I would learn that the attack on the Pentagon had barely missed my old office.

22. I have included the NSC in this assessment with some trepidation. Most of the principals and all of the staff were aware of this war, as were the deputies. But the NSC as an institution was not as engaged as the CSG and the intelligence community.

23. George W. Bush, *Decision Points*. New York: 2010, Crown. 126.

24. Ibid., 127.

25. This material is drawn from multiple sources, including Bush, Clarke, Tenet, the 9/11 Commission, and Bob Woodward, *Bush at War*. New York: 2002, Simon & Schuster.

26. Ibid., 17.

27. Ibid., 26–27.

28. Rice, location 1550.

29. Woodward, 66.

30. Ibid., 108.

31. Ibid., 59.

32. Ibid.

33. Ibid., 98.

34. CNN, "Bush Delivers Ultimatum." Edition.cnn.com/2001/WORLD/asiapcf/09/20/ret.afgha.bush/, September 21, 2001.

35. Woodward, 83–84.

36. Tenet, 207–208.

37. Ibid., 209. Gary C. Schroen, *First In*. New York: 2005, Presidio Press. 11–16.

38. Schroen, 16.

39. Tenet, 207.

40. Schroen, 72–83.

41. See Doug Stanton, *The Horse Soldiers*. New York: 2009, Scribner. Especially Part One, "Going to War."

42. Ibid. John Mullholland earned his master of military arts and science degree at CGSC, where I was his thesis advisor. He went on to command U.S. Army Special Operations Command (USASOC) as a lieutenant general.

43. Schroen, 371.

44. Ibid., 279–280.

45. Ibid., 288. Eric Blehm, *The Only Thing Worth Dying For*. New York: 2010, Harper Collins. Chapter 1.

46. By Schroen.

47. By SFODA 574, as reported by Blehm.

48. Blehm, Chapter 1.

49. Although Schroen does not discuss these tensions, the ODA told Blehm about some of their frustrations quite candidly.

50. Tenet, 215.

51. Ibid., 216.

52. Blehm, Chapter 1.

53. Edition.cnn.com/2001/US/12/11/ret.afghan.embassy/.

54. Ann Wright was a friend of mine. I met her when she was a U.S. Army major, on active duty at the JFK Special Warfare Center and School at Fort Bragg, North Carolina, teaching in the Civil Affairs program. From there, she went to SOUTHCOM, where she established a full-time Civil Affairs section in the J-5, later moving over to Political-Military Affairs. I was assigned to the J-5 at the same time. Ann was then promoted to lieutenant colonel and offered a regular commission, which she declined

to enter the Foreign Service. She served in numerous hot spots, including Nicaragua, before ending up in Afghanistan. She would resign in 2003 to protest the U.S. invasion of Iraq.

55. Rice, location 2092.

56. Woodward, 314.

57. Rice, location 2092.

58. There apparently was some sentiment at the conference to bring back the king, Zahir Shah, as the ceremonial head of a constitutional monarchy. The king was, of course, a Pashtun. Unconfirmed reports were that the United States refused to entertain that proposal. In any case, Karzai was the consensus to head the new government, whether it would be a monarchy or a republic.

59. Woodward, 315.

60. Dave Barno is a West Point graduate, class of 1976, along with Ray Odierno and a number of other generals, Indeed, that class rivals the class of 1915, which produced Eisenhower and Bradley and was known as the Class the Stars Fell On. The Class of 1976 was similar in the number of general officers it produced. Barno later became director of the DOD Near East/South Asia Center located at the National Defense University next door to the Center for Hemispheric Defense Studies headed by his classmate COL (RET Richard Downie.

61. Personal communication from Dr. Gabriel Marcella, professor at the Army War College, reporting on his discussion with Barno.

62. *Los Angeles Times*, December 12, 2007.

Chapter 12

Iraq: Snatching Defeat from the Jaws of Victory and Victory from the Jaws of Defeat

Operation Desert Strom began and ended in February 1991. For most of the next decade, the Clinton administration had waged a low-key air war to keep Saddam Hussein under some sort of control. By 2001, the sanctions regime was falling apart; Saddam had kicked out the UN WMD monitors, and he was constantly testing the No-Fly Zones that the UN had imposed and the United States and its allies enforced. Intelligence reports and analysis were consistent that Saddam had or was reconstituting his WMD program.[1] On October 31, 1998, President Clinton signed into law the Iraq Liberation Act, which states that it was American policy to assist the Iraqi people in removing Saddam Hussein from power. The act passed the House by a vote of 360–38 and the Senate by Unanimous Consent.

THE IRAQ TEMPTATION

On September 11, 2001, the United States was attacked.[2] On that day, after the Pentagon was struck, Secretary of Defense Donald Rumsfeld raised with his staff the possibility of going after Saddam Hussein in addition to Osama bin Laden. The next day, he raised the issue again in the NSC. Then, on September 15, at Camp David, the issue was raised again. Rumsfeld let his deputy, Paul Wolfowitz, make the case. Nobody accepted the argument. Secretary of State Colin Powell and NSA Condi Rice were the strongest voices against considering Iraq a perpetrator. White House Chief of Staff Andy Card opposed the idea. So did Vice President Dick Cheney and President Bush, himself, although for them, it may have been more a matter of timing. In the end, Rumsfeld did not support the idea, but he did not reject it either.[3] Also attending the meeting were the CJCS, GEN H. Hugh Shelton, and DCI

George Tenet, but they were advisors, not principals.[4] Similarly Wolfowitz and Deputy Secretary of State Richard Armitage attended but, except for Wolfowitz's presentation, did not participate in the formal deliberations. After the meeting, Powell, a former CJCS himself, said to Shelton, referring to Rumsfeld and Wolfowitz, "What are those guys thinking about? Can't you get those guys back in the box?" Shelton allowed that he was trying.[5] But Shelton had only two more weeks in office, after which he would be succeeded by his VCJCS, Gen Dick Myers, USAF. Myers was more deferential to the SECDEF than Shelton.[6]

THREAT PERCEPTION

In 2002, Kenneth Pollack, a former CIA analyst and NSC staffer, then working at the Brookings Institution, published a book titled *The Threatening Storm.*[7] Pollack, a Democrat, makes a strong case, based on years of intelligence analysis experience and continued contacts with members of the intelligence community, that Iraq had a well-developed and rapidly growing weapons of mass destruction (WMD) program. Not only did it have such a program but Saddam Hussein had used WMD (chemical weapons) against Iran and Iraqi Kurds. Prior to the Gulf War, his nuclear program was much farther along than anybody or any intelligence agency had believed. In 1998, Saddam had kicked out UN weapons inspectors, leaving a vacuum in the U.S. knowledge of what he was up to. Pollack's conclusion was that Saddam was on the verge of becoming an existential threat and needed to be removed. His book was an excellent unclassified summary of where the American intelligence community believed the Iraqi threat was at that time.[8]

Condoleezza Rice, the NSA, writes in her memoir:

> From the time he took office, the President had been receiving almost daily, increasingly alarming reports about Saddam's progress in reconstituting his weapons of mass destruction program. The director of the CIA, George Tenet, was at the time responsible for providing to the President the collective assessment of the intelligence agencies. . . . Even in retrospect I don't think he overstated the evidence; he drew conclusions that clearly pointed toward Saddam's progress in reconstituting his WMD.[9]

Not only did the U.S. intelligence community conclude that, but so did the intelligence agencies of U.S. allies—Britain, France, Germany, and Israel—but also Russia and many Arab states in the Middle East. However there was some variation in the degree of certainty among the agencies. Moreover, Saddam had a history of sponsoring and supporting terrorism, even if there was no evidence implicating him in the 9/11 attacks. So, despite seeing Iraq as a distraction to addressing the immediate threat posed by Al Qaeda and bin Laden, Saddam was clearly part of the larger threat picture both in terms of his potential WMD capabilities and terrorism.

EARLY PLANNING

Just 72 days after the 9/11 attacks, on November 21, Bush held one of many NSC meetings in the Situation Room at the White House. After the meeting, he pulled SECDEF Don Rumsfeld aside and asked him what kind of war plan he had for Iraq. Rumsfeld told him that he did not think the plan had been updated and the president asked him to have CENTCOM commander, GEN Tommy Franks, make sure that he had a workable plan to remove Saddam as soon as possible. Bush indicated that he did not want this planning to be widely known in the government.[10] Bush told Woodward in an interview on November 21 that he wanted to know what his options were and that, having had to scramble in planning for Afghanistan, he wanted to be ready if the United States had to take on Saddam.[11]

Unlike Afghanistan, CENTCOM did have an OPLAN on the shelf, OPLAN 1003. But CENTCOM was behind on updating its plans, which were generally scheduled for revision every two years. OPLAN 1003 was some four or five years out of date and resembled the OPLAN for Desert Storm with some offensive expansion. This did not fit with Rumsfeld's view of the need to transform the American military.[12] What he was looking for was a smaller, more agile, and technologically capable military force and he expected this to be reflected in war plans and operations. OPLAN 1003 did not reflect anything like that. Like its predecessor, it had a long, slow buildup before it could be executed. It was designed to bring to bear overwhelming force dominated by firepower. Rumsfeld, however, was an advocate of maneuver warfare relying on speed and agility to overwhelm mass.

Rumsfeld now had Franks working on a new Commander's Estimate that would become the basis for a new OPLAN 1003, one that would incorporate the SECDEF's views. Between November 2001 and February 2002, it would undergo five revisions. The new war plan would be known as the Generated Start Plan, in part because its execution of offensive operations would begin while a buildup of forces was ongoing.[13] Nevertheless, this was still all a case of contingency planning. The president had made no decision.

THE PRESIDENT'S TWO TRACKS

President Bush had decided to address the problem of Saddam Hussein with both a diplomatic and a military track. As he put it in his memoir, *Decision*

Points, he decided to focus on diplomacy first. At the same time, he had directed Rumsfeld to update the planning for war. The result was to be applied as coercive diplomacy.[14]

> Coercive diplomacy with Iraq consisted of two tracks. One was to rally a coalition of nations to make clear that Saddam's defiance of his international obligations was unacceptable. The other was to develop a credible military option that could be used if he failed to comply. The two tracks would run parallel at first. As the military option grew more viable and advanced, the tracks would converge. Our maximum leverage would come just before they intersected. This would be the moment of decision. And ultimately, it would be Saddam Hussein's decision to make.[15]

The effort to build a coalition took place through the spring and summer of 2002. In tandem, CENTCOM's military planning refined and revised the plan. A critical moment would be President Bush's scheduled speech to the UN on September 12. A key issue was what to ask for. Powell, British prime minister Tony Blair, Australian prime minister John Howard, and Spanish prime minister Jose Maria Aznar[16] all strongly recommended that the president ask for a UN Security Council Resolution.[17] Very much opposed to asking for a resolution were Rumsfeld and Cheney. In the end, the president decided to ask for one. However, when he was giving the speech, Powell, who was reading the copy, saw that the words asking for a resolution were missing. Bush noticed that as he was speaking and inserted the critical lines a sentence or two later.[18] How those lines were left out of the final draft of the speech has never been adequately explained publicly. However, if it had been done deliberately, it would not be the last time that someone, other than President Bush, overrode a decision that had already been taken.[19]

POLITICAL MOVES

President Bush was very much aware of the conflict over the use of force against Iraq during his father's administration 12 years before. Bush 41 had chosen to seek a UN authorization before going to Congress, where the vote had been much closer than anybody had wanted. This time, Vice President Cheney advised going to Congress first. Where the UN vote had helped to pass the congressional authorization in 1990, Cheney and Rice felt that a congressional authorization would be useful both domestically and at the UN. Cheney believed that since 2002 was an election year, getting all congressmen and senators on record regarding the threat posed by Saddam would be good politics and good policy by strengthening the president's hand. Rice felt that a show of congressional support would help influence the UN Security Council vote.[20]

The Joint Resolution was introduced on October 2, 2002, and passed the House 296–133. It passed the Senate by a vote of 77 to 23. The margin in both cases was overwhelming and included members of both parties, although only Democrats voted against it. President Bush signed it into law on October 15, 2002.[21]

TROOP MOVEMENTS, DIPLOMATIC EFFORTS

Throughout the fall of 2002, CENTCOM refined its war plan. GEN Tommy Franks also began moving some forces to the Middle East in anticipation of possible action. Among those forces were two armored brigades to Kuwait. Also air force elements in Saudi Arabia were strengthened, as was the Fifth Fleet in Bahrain. But most of the U.S. forces in the area were what the military calls enablers. Those are the forces that facilitate a full deployment of combat and support forces to a theater of operations.[22]

Meanwhile, at the UN, after the president's speech on September 12, the work of drafting a Security Council Resolution began. It would take some six weeks to get agreement of all the members of the Security Council, especially over the issue of the meaning of the words "serious consequences" for Saddam should he fail to comply. The United States and Britain wanted the interpretation to be that no additional UNSCR would be needed, while Russia and France felt that a new SCR should be required. In the end, the phrase was left with a degree of ambiguity in the final version of UNSCR 1441. Nevertheless, it had passed unanimously on November 7, 2002.[23] "Iraq was given one month, until December 7, 2002, to make a full and accurate declaration of the state of its weapons programs and to receive international weapons inspectors to begin the process of verifying the declaration's claims."[24]

On November 26, GEN Franks sent SECDEF Rumsfeld his draft deployment order, which called for the notification of some 300,000 troops to be prepared to deploy over the next several months. Rumsfeld reacted sharply that signing the deployment order and issuing unit notifications to both active and reserve component troops had the potential for multiple negative effects. Among these would be indicating that the die had already been cast for war and instead of strengthening diplomacy, it would cause diplomacy to fail. A more subtle and piecemeal notification and deployment schedule might well have a positive impact on the ongoing diplomatic efforts.[25] At that point, Woodward notes, Rumsfeld began to personally scrub the TPFDD, selecting units that would be notified and deployed and in what order.[26]

Again, throughout the late summer and early fall, there were NSC discussions of how the post-invasion phase of the likely conflict would be handled. Who would be responsible in the American government. "The President signaled in mid-October that the Defense Department would be the lead agency responsible for postwar planning in the immediate aftermath of the invasion, should one be necessary."[27] Thus about this time, Rumsfeld tasked his undersecretary for policy, Douglas Feith, with the planning responsibility. Not until the end of December did Feith propose a structure for postwar planning and execution. At that time he visited Deputy NSA Steve Hadley to propose a cell operating out of his policy shop that would both plan and execute post-invasion "reconstruction" operations.[28] Rumsfeld approved, as did the NSC. As CENTCOM commander GEN Tommy Franks tells it, "Then on a warm Florida afternoon, Don Rumsfeld called. 'Tom,' he said, do you know Jay Garner?"[29] Rumsfeld told Franks that he planned to name retired LTG Jay Garner to head the post-conflict cell, called Office of Reconstruction and Humanitarian Assistance (ORHA). According to Franks, Garner was to be subordinate to him as theater commander, and not work for Washington.[30]

Garner built a team that consisted of his own people, including army COL Paul Hughes.[31] Garner had the benefit of State Department's "Future of Iraq Project" as well as access to many of the experts who had done the analysis. Powell made all the analysts available to work for Garner, including the study team leader, Thomas Warrick, and a very bright sanctions specialist, Meghan O'Sullivan.[32] Garner soon received word that neither Warrick nor O'Sullivan was to be allowed to work with ORHA. Garner stated that he protested to Rumsfeld who said that this came from somewhere "above his pay grade."[33] Soon after, word came down that O'Sullivan could, in fact, work for ORHA but not Warrick.[34] This, apparently, was due to the intervention of NSA Rice. In any case, ORHA was formally established by NSPD 24, signed on January 20, 2003.

The NSPD addressed de-baathification (purging the Iraqi government of senior Baath Party members), and what to do about the Iraqi army. Franks notes that there was a need to plan for and pay the Iraqi army so that they could be immediately put to work on reconstruction.[35] Garner had given Hughes the job of dealing with the Iraqi regular army. He had made contact with senior commanders and secured their agreement to stand down in the event of invasion and send their men home with their weapons, to be recalled to provide security for the country.[36]

DEFEAT AT THE UN

The diplomatic effort shifted back to the UN. Inspectors had gone into Iraq in December finding that Saddam was still playing cat and mouse games. The interim report of January 27 was damning, however. This was followed by Secretary of State Colin Powell's presentation to the UN Security Council on February 5. Powell made a strong case against Saddam and in favor of a new SCR that would remove him from power. Still, the response broke along expected lines. Britain, Spain, and Portugal strongly supported the American position. Russia and France opposed it due, in no small part, to their investments in Iraq. French president Jacques Chirac "had let it be known that 'nothing justifies a war.'"[37] In addition, German chancellor Gerhard Schroeder, who had just won reelection with a strongly anti-American campaign, reversed his previous qualified support for action and came out against war with Iraq.[38] In the end, his reasons hinged on domestic politics and German investment in Iraq. On February 14, the final WMD inspection report was issued and was more ambiguous than the interim report. Nevertheless, a UNSCR authorizing the use of force against Saddam was introduced on February 24. It soon became apparent that France and Russia would exercise their veto and that there would not even be the required nine votes out of 15 needed to pass it if the veto were not exercised. President Bush and Prime Minister Blair withdrew the SCR, avoiding a vote. Instead, they opted for a coalition of the willing. Blair survived a vote of confidence in the House of Commons.[39]

SHOCK AND AWE: VICTORY IN SHORT ORDER

The attack was scheduled to begin on the night of March 19, 2003. On March 17, GEN Franks faxed a "letter of concern" to DEPSECDEF Paul Wolfowitz. Although Franks raised a number of issues, the main thrust of his letter was that the Washington bureaucracy needed to focus on the issues of post-hostilities Iraq. Among these was making effective use of the regular Iraqi army. Essentially, Franks was saying, *"You pay attention to the day after and I'll pay attention to the day of."*[40] Nevertheless, Garner and ORHA had deployed to Kuwait and were supposedly under the control of CENTCOM. At the same time, Garner was being pushed on any number of issues by Douglas Feith's policy shop. On March 11, just before he deployed, Garner got into an argument with Feith, where he said, "Doug, you've got two choices . . . You can shut the fuck up or you can fire me."[41] Nothing came of this immediately but in the end, Garner would be fired and the work ORHA had done to create stability through the recall of the Iraqi army was ignored.

ORHA suffered from another significant problem. That was the fact that it was neither fish nor fowl. It was a civilian agency within CENTCOM even though it had serving military members, was headed by a retired general officer, but it also had civilians from other government agencies (like Meghan O'Sullivan from State) in its ranks. ORHA fell under the general command of the Combined Forces Land Component Commander (CFLCC), army LTG David McKiernan. His other components were I MEF under marine Lt Gen

James Conway (which also had coalition elements) and V Corps (also with coalition elements) under LTG Scott Wallace. Garner's ORHA was structurally an equal component but Garner rarely could get McKiernan's or Franks's attention. As a result, ORHA had significant difficulty making its way into Iraq so that it could do its job.

The air war began with a raid designed to kill Saddam; it barely missed him. The ground war then began about eight hours before the massive air campaign. In three weeks it was over. Bagdad had fallen. Despite the Turks refusing passage to the 4th Infantry Division the northern campaign was conducted effectively by 10th Special Forces Group and other airborne assets.[42] The southern campaign was a race between I MEF to the East and V Corps to the West. In the end, V Corps tanks made what was called the "Thunder Run" through Baghdad. In general, Iraqis welcomed the fall of the regime. However, there were indications early on of trouble when irregular forces—so-called Saddam Fedayeen—in pickup trucks mounting machine guns attacked logistics convoys in the rear of the advancing troops. In the end, these attacks were more of a nuisance than a real threat to the operation.

OCCUPATION: THE CPA, MOSUL, 4TH ID

The occupation did not go well from the beginning. Feith soon was able to cast doubt on the effectiveness of the ORHA leadership. Part of that was due to Garner's inability to convince LTG McKiernan to allow ORHA into Iraq immediately after the combat troops. Another part of the problem was that nobody seemed to know who Garner worked for. Added to those issues was the incipient insurgency. In addition, there was a critical change of command that would replace both David McKiernan and Scott Wallace with LTG Ricardo Sanchez as commander of V Corps and CJTF 7 (the successor to CFLCC). Sanchez, with a staff far too small for the job, was now in charge of all allied military activity in Iraq.[43] But, it was still not clear to whom ORHA reported.

In Washington, Feith had his way. Retired ambassador L. Paul "Jerry" Bremer was asked to become the president's special envoy in charge of all post-hostilities operations except military. Bremer stated his understanding of his replacing Garner in his memoir, "And contrary to most media accounts, the White House had never intended ORHA's leader, retired U.S. Army Lieutenant General Jay Garner, to be the President's permanent envoy in Baghdad."[44] Bremer arrived in Baghdad on May 12; Garner and his team were gone soon after.

On May 9, Feith handed Bremer a draft of an order to purge all Baath Party members from government jobs down to the fourth level. He suggested that the order might be issued immediately but Bremer deferred preferring to issue it himself when he arrived.[45] This was contrary to the firm intent established for ORHA by Rumsfeld when he appointed Garner. Garner had intended to formally purge only the heads of major offices and the personnel chief, counting on natural attrition to take care of the rest. Many of the rest were simply low-level bureaucrats and teachers since anybody who wanted to work in Saddam's Iraq had to be a member of the Baath Party. The order, CPA 1, would deprive the new government of anybody who knew how to make the ministries actually work.

> Although there was no mention in the draft of the regular army, I knew that Walt Slocum,[46] the Coalition's senior adviser for Defense and Security Affairs, had been discussing the army's future with Feith now that it was clear that the force had broken ranks and disappeared.[47]

Of course, the army had not disappeared. As COL Hughes stated, the regular army's leadership had sent its men home, with their weapons, at the request of ORHA, to await recall by the Coalition to provide law and order and reconstruction support.[48] Nevertheless, Bremer issued CPA 2 disbanding the regular army at the same time as he issued CPA 1. Together, the orders would give a new legitimacy to the insurgency that had been only a few Saddam Fedayeen.

Bremer made it a point to hire as senior staff personnel he knew well. Most were former ambassadors and other senior State Department officials. That was not the case for junior staff. Many were recent master's degree graduates who were recruited through the Heritage Foundation.[49]

Another action taken on May 9, just before Bremer left for Baghdad, was his receipt of two key documents. First, was a presidential letter of appointment "as Presidential Envoy to Iraq with full authority over all U.S. government personnel, activities, and funds there."[50] This letter mirrors the letter given to all American ambassadors and was interpreted in the same way, to exclude control over major military operations. The second document was his appointment from SECDEF Rumsfeld naming him Administrator of the Coalition Provisional Authority (CPA) with full executive, legislative, and judicial power in Iraq.[51] Bremer reported to President Bush through Secretary Rumsfeld, who directed Douglas Feith to support him and be the conduit for all directives from the SECDEF. This structure left two separate and independent DOD chains of command in Iraq. The first was the chain from the president through the SECDEF and Feith to Bremer. The second was from the president through the SECDEF and CJCS (for communication) to the CENTCOM commander (Franks until July and then John Abizaid) to Ricardo Sanchez as commander of CJTF 7. Although Bremer and Sanchez lived and worked in the same former presidential palace, they rarely talked to each other. As a senior administration official told Tom Ricks, Bremer and Sanchez "really hated each other."[52] Clearly, there was a serious question of who was in charge of the American and Coalition effort in Iraq.

Even the military situation was confused. The occupation was divided geographically among military units, usually divisions. Basra, in the south, was controlled by the British. Mosul, in the north, was occupied by the 101st Airborne (Air Assault) Division under the command of MG David Petraeus, while nearby Tikrit was initially controlled by the marine Maj Gen James Mattis's 1st Marine Division and then by the army's 4th Infantry Division commanded by MG Ray Odierno. Sanchez did not exercise strong control, so each division operated largely on its own and ran the occupation its own way.

The British were welcomed by the Shi'a inhabitants of Basra as liberators, clearly happy to be out from under the oppression of Saddam. Petraeus, in Mosul, followed the lessons he had learned in his doctoral research on Vietnam and working for GEN Jack Galvin in SOUTHCOM, where he learned the lessons of counterinsurgency firsthand. In fact, Petraeus's actions in Mosul provide a textbook example both of how to conduct counterinsurgency and how to run an occupation.[53] Mattis, likewise, followed a wise occupation strategy designed to neutralize an insurgency before it began; his approach drew on the long history of the marine corps as recorded, in part, by the *Small Wars Manual* of 1940.[54]

MG Odierno's 4th Infantry Division (ID) relieved the 1st Marine Division on April 19, 2003. Unlike the marines they came in aggressively, seeing every Iraqi as a potential enemy and not as someone who had just been liberated from Saddam's yoke. Their approach was so in contrast with that of the marines that the 1st Marine Division's official history is highly critical of the actions of the 4th ID.[55] Unfortunately, the actions of the 4th ID presaged the approach that would increasingly be taken by the occupying forces through much of the country.

The one major success in the 4th ID's area of operations was the killing of Saddam's sons and the capture of Saddam. Saddam was captured on December 14 as a result of a series of interrogations of persons captured mainly by special operations personnel. The team of interrogators included army Staff Sergeant Eric Maddox, who conducted the interrogation of the detainee who ultimately gave away Saddam's hiding place. Maddox points out that at no time did he, or any of his team, use any of the "enhanced interrogation techniques" that had been approved for the War on Terror. Indeed, Maddox notes that it took him a mere 45 minutes to "break" the individual he was interrogating.[56]

The CPA suffered from a confused chain of command, a disconnect in the quality of its senior staff from the quality of its junior staff, and a real lack of support from DOD. Feith's policy office never gave the CPA the support it needed.[57] Moreover, Rumsfeld never intervened to either push Feith or adjudicate issues between the military and the CPA. It was during this year that the Abu Ghraib interrogation scandal took place, reflecting the negative results of tactics by American units like the 4th ID. Mosul, which under the 101st had been peaceful, became a hotbed of rebellion after a new unit came in. Heavy-handed troop actions became the norm over the course of the year and culminated in Abu Ghraib. Nevertheless, the CPA did establish an interim Iraqi government and turned political sovereignty over to it.

As a result of that first chaotic year of occupation, the DOD upgraded command in Iraq from the three-star CJTF 7 to a four-star command, Multi-National Force, Iraq (MNF-I). Its commander was GEN George Casey, plucked from his post as vice chief of staff of the army. At CENTCOM Casey served under Abizaid, who was an Arabic-speaking Middle East Army Foreign Area officer. Together they made a strong military team. With a new government to work with, the president appointed John Negroponte, then ambassador to the UN, as his ambassador to Iraq. Negroponte, one of the most senior career ambassadors in the State Department, who had served in many trouble spots, was a strong choice. Despite that, or because of his skills, Negroponte was always in demand and was soon picked to become the first director of National Intelligence (DNI).[58] Negroponte was replaced as ambassador to Iraq by Zalmay Khalilzad, a Republican foreign policy specialist, who had been an effective ambassador to Afghanistan and had worked well with his military counterpart. Khalilzad established a good working relationship with both Abizaid and Casey. So, by the fall of 2004, events in Iraq seemed to be moving in the right direction, after a very turbulent year.

ELECTIONS AND THE RISE OF AQI

In January 2005, Iraq finally held its first elections—for Parliament.[59] There followed a difficult period of trying to form a government. The resulting government was both unstable and strongly Shi'a dominated, leaving the Sunnis of northern and western Iraq feeling alienated. It was among those Sunnis that the resistance to the occupation had been fomented by former followers of Saddam and now was being encouraged by a new group, led by a Jordanian named Abu Musab al Zarqawi, that called itself Al Qaeda in Iraq (AQI).

In October, elections were held to approve a new Constitution that provided for some power sharing.[60] The president was to be a Kurd, the prime minister (head of government) a Shi'a, while the vice president was a Sunni. Finally, in December, elections were held for the National Assembly[61] with the same kind of squabbling over forming a government that had been experienced in June. Still, events seemed to be moving in the right direction; even the security situation appeared to have improved. Then, on Wednesday, February 22, 2006, disaster struck.

[B]ombs leveled the golden dome of the Askariya Mosque in Samarra, about 65 miles north of Baghdad, leaving it in ruins. The attack on one of the holiest Shiite shrines had been carefully planned. Shiite militias, especially those closely aligned with Moqtada al Sadr,[62] poured into the streets and in retaliation fired grenades and machine guns into at least two dozen Sunni mosques in Baghdad.[63]

These events ignited what can charitably be called a sectarian near-civil war. The sectarian conflict was layered over the insurgency that had engulfed the Sunni parts of the country. Of course, the sectarian warfare, with all its atrocities, was most active in Baghdad, where it was in full view of the international press. Clearly, this was exactly what Zarqawi had intended and was, perhaps, equally relished by al Sadr.

COMMAND AND CONTROL IN THE INSURGENCY

The year of the CPA was clearly one of learning for the U.S. government. The military command structure with LTG Sanchez as the senior officer on the ground reporting to CENTCOM—first to Franks and then to Abizaid—made little sense along with the CPA with Bremer reporting to Rumsfeld and the president. This changed in June and July of 2004, when Ambassador Negroponte was made American ambassador to the government of Iraq led by interim prime minister Ayad Allawi and when GEN George Casey was named commander of the MNF-I. This put a four-star directly into the chain and equal in rank to the ambassador, who reported through the State Department.

Casey and Abizaid seemingly had little conflict and worked well together. They were both well versed in counterinsurgency theory, and Abizaid had a strong background in the region. On matters of culture and politics, Casey tended to defer to Abizaid, while Abizaid trusted his man on the ground. When Negroponte was brought back to Washington as the first DNI, his replacement, Zalmay Khalilzad, a Middle Eastern specialist himself, fit in easily with Abizaid and Casey. He also established good rapport with the fractious Iraqi politicians. So, by December 2005, it seemed as if the Iraqi government and its international allies were beginning to get control over the insurgency. At that point, Zarqawi proved the truth of the old adage "the enemy always has a vote."

This was the moment in which American leadership in Iraq failed to distinguish between the insurgency and the new sectarian conflict. Casey and

Abizaid sought to follow a classic COIN strategy, one that empowered local forces.[64] The problem was that empowerment of national Iraqi military and police forces was simply not possible as long as Sunni and Shi'a were at war with each other and Baghdad was the primary battleground. One result was major disillusionment in the United States. That was reflected in the outcome of the midterm elections, which turned both Houses of Congress over to the Democrats. The perception in Washington was that the war in Iraq was headed toward disaster.

Nevertheless, not everything happening in Iraq in 2005 and 2006 was bad news. Efforts were under way to train, equip, and advise Iraqi military, police, and civil government, efforts that met with some success. This was recorded in a study of Security Force Assistance in Mosul, published by the Joint Center for International Security Force Assistance at Fort Leavenworth, Kansas.[65] In 2005, in Tal Afar in Western Iraq, the 3rd Armored Cavalry Regiment, commanded by COL H.R. McMaster, conducted a highly successful COIN campaign.[66] Then, in 2006, in the city of Ramadi, in al Anbar province, American forces, led by COL Sean MacFarland, partnered with the tribes to resist and defeat AQI in that city.[67] The methods of these three efforts would be incorporated into the forthcoming strategy that became known as the "Surge."

THE IRAQ STUDY GROUP, THE COUNCIL OF COLONELS, AEI, AND THE NSC

As the sectarian violence and insurgent activity in Iraq increased over the course of 2006, so, too, did American casualties. Disillusionment with the war increased among the American people, as reflected in the polls, and in Congress. Within the administration there was significant disagreement about the best course of action in Iraq. Should we follow the current strategy of trying to turn the war over to the Iraqi government and its military, or should we simply pull out and leave Iraq to its own devices? Or something else, entirely?

Congress was particularly frustrated with the lack of progress and the increasing U.S. casualties. In the spring of 2006, it created the bipartisan Iraq Study Group co-chaired by former Bush 41 secretary of state James Baker and the Democratic former chairman of the House Foreign Affairs Committee Lee Hamilton. The other Democratic members were Vernon Jordan, friend and advisor to former president Clinton; former congressman and White House chief of staff Leon Panetta; former SECDEF William J. Perry; and former governor of Virginia, former marine officer, and current senator Chuck Robb. The Republicans in the Group were former secretary of state Lawrence Eagleburger, former deputy NSA and former DCI Robert Gates (currently the president of Texas A&M), Edwin Meese III, former attorney general of the United States, former associate justice of the Supreme Court Sandra Day O'Connor, and former senator Alan Simpson.[68]

The Iraq Study Group ultimately came up with over 70 specific recommendations but focused mainly on how to withdraw American forces from Iraq. The single major exception was the recommendation for a short-term surge of forces in Baghdad, to help stabilize the sectarian conflict in the capital. If the option for a short-term surge of forces had not been included, Chuck Robb had threatened not to sign. As a result, Ed Meese, who had served as an Army Reserve military intelligence officer for 32 years, worked out compromise language with former SECDEF Bill Perry that met Robb's objections.[69] Although this recommendation was buried among the 70-plus recommendations, Robb was able to call the president's attention to it when the group briefed him.[70]

Despite the recommendation for a surge, Congress still wanted an end to American participation in the war. However, that was not the end in sight. Others had much different thoughts. CJCS marine Gen Peter Pace had convened a group of colonels—known as a Council of Colonels—to advise him and the chiefs on the best course of action to move the war forward. Leading the Council of Colonels was H.R. McMaster, who had commanded the successful operations in Tal Afar in 2005.[71] The Council of Colonels succeeded in raising major questions about the strategy being followed but not in developing any strong, effective course of action for Pace to take to the president.[72]

Over the course of the fall of 2006, Fred Kagan, of the American Enterprise Institute (AEI), a conservative Washington think tank, had been working with a team to develop a strategy for winning the war in Iraq. Kagan, the son of Yale military historian and expert on the Peloponnesian War Donald Kagan, was himself a military historian who had taught at West Point. Kagan's PhD was from Yale, and at West Point he had taught with H.R. McMaster. Kagan's team brought in a number of retired generals to consult, among them former army vice chief of staff Jack Keane. Keane served on the Defense Policy Board, was close to SECDEF Rumsfeld, and had run the army when Eric Shinseki had been ostracized by Rumsfeld for contradicting administration estimates of the manpower needed for the occupation of Iraq. Keane had been Rumsfeld's choice for army chief of staff but had chosen to retire due to his wife's health. Keane had also mentored a number of younger generals, among them David Petraeus and Ray Odierno as they were moving up the ranks. And Jack Keane was very impressed with what he saw at AEI.[73]

On December 11, 2006, NSA Steve Hadley had arranged for five outside experts to brief President Bush, Vice President Cheney, and himself. Jack Keane was among them, and he brought an abbreviated version of Kagan's briefing. Not only did it call for a surge of troops but it also called for using the additional forces in a very different way. Keane's briefing impressed his audience, and Cheney's office asked for the full AEI briefing. Again, the vice president was impressed.[74] Some word of this approach came back to the CJCS, and Gen Pace raised the AEI recommendation with the chiefs and the Council of Colonels. The ferment around what to do in Iraq was permeating the Washington atmosphere as Kagan and his team and Keane responded to the recommendations of the Iraq Study Group and the Council of Colonels reacted to them both, as well as to the generals in the field. However, none of these groups was in a position to make a decision. The only place where a specific decision could actually reach the president was through the NSC. Steve Hadley assigned the task of pulling the disparate threads together to his deputy, J.D. Crouch.

The November election had a significant impact on all these somewhat disparate events. In those midterm elections the Republicans lost control of both Houses of Congress. At that point, President Bush decided to make a major change and he accepted the resignation of Donald Rumsfeld as secretary of defense, over the objection of Vice President Cheney. Rumsfeld's replacement was Robert Gates, the president of Texas A&M, member of the Iraq Study Group, former DCI, and former deputy NSA. In his memoir, Gates notes that during his interviews for his confirmation the Democratic senators "professed to be enormously pleased and offered their support, I think mainly because they thought that I, as a member of the Iraq Study Group, would embrace their desire to begin withdrawing from Iraq."[75] Secretary Gates's confirmation set in train a number of significant changes at the DOD to include the replacement of Douglas Feith, the undersecretary for policy. It also changed the dynamics among the principals of the NSC.

Hadley's NSC strategy review under J.D. Crouch was due to brief the president after Thanksgiving. The NSC team of senior staffers from State, Defense, the intelligence community, and the NSC staff were not going to achieve consensus. Still, Hadley pointed out that among the options that had to go to the president was one for a surge of forces. This was championed by the vice president and the NSC staff. State representatives looked toward withdrawal, while DOD civilians reflected the Rumsfeld, Abizaid, and Casey strategy of leave to win. The two generals representing the Joint Staff argued, as had the Council of Colonels, that if the United States were not winning it was losing, but their recommendation was still the current strategy.[76]

BEHIND THE SCENES AT FORT LEAVENWORTH

MG David Petraeus had left command of the 101st and Mosul in 2004. After a few months in the United States he was ordered back to Iraq to take over the new organization charged with training Iraqi security forces. Turning over that command to MG Martin Dempsey,[77] Petraeus was promoted to lieutenant general and given command of the Combined Arms Center (CAC) at Fort Leavenworth, Kansas, in September 2005. The CAC commander is also the deputy commander of the Army Training and Doctrine command (TRADOC) and the commandant of the Army Command and General Staff College. TRADOC is responsible for all army training and the textbooks (field manuals). CAC is its major subordinate command, and the college is the prestigious place where staff officers and future battalion and brigade commanders are educated and trained.[78]

David Petraeus had spent much of his career studying COIN. His doctoral dissertation had addressed COIN in Vietnam. Then, while teaching at West Point, his mentor, GEN John Galvin, had brought him to U.S. Southern Command during a summer to work on COIN in El Salvador and insurgency in Nicaragua. Petraeus had applied lessons in the Balkans in 2001, in Mosul in 2003–2004, and in training Iraqi security forces. In each case, he had learned more. At Leavenworth, he undertook the project of revising and publishing the army's doctrine for COIN.[79]

Petraeus was urged by Professor Eliot Cohen of the Nitze School of Advanced International Studies to undertake a thorough rewrite of the interim COIN manual just published.[80] To head the project, Petraeus chose his West Point classmate Dr. Conrad Crane, director of the Military History Institute at the Army War College. Working closely with Crane was LTC John Nagl, with a PhD from Oxford.[81]

> With Petraeus's approval the co-authors assembled a team of experts to help draft each chapter. The manual's core propositions were developed and published in a *Military Review* article by Cohen, Crane, Nagl and others. Crediting the work of Max Manwaring, a longtime scholar on insurgency and irregular war, they identified legitimacy as the cornerstone of successful counterinsurgency.[82]

In February 2006, Petraeus, working with Sarah Sewell, former deputy assistant SECDEF for peacekeeping and now at Harvard, as his cosponsor, convened a workshop to critique the draft manual. About 100 experts met at Leavenworth to review the text.[83] A number of their suggestions were incorporated into the manual, but even more important was the buy-in from the academic and policy worlds.

THE "SURGE"

The various strands of the story finally came together at the end of November 2006. That was when Bob Gates took over as SECDEF. Now it was time to make some real changes in Baghdad and CENTCOM. The first change was to name LTG Ray Odierno as the commander of the Multi-National Corps-Iraq (MNC-I), the ground force commander. This was the same Ray Odierno who had made a mess of the occupation of Tikrit in 2003–2004. But Ray Odierno had matured as a senior officer serving as assistant to the CJCS, a position that often traveled with the secretary of state. Condi Rice, the secretary, was a skillful teacher and Ray Odierno, apparently, an apt student. One of his mentors as he was coming up the ranks of the army was Jack Keane, with whom he maintained contact while in Washington. He was a much more sophisticated leader when he returned to Iraq. He also found himself opposed to the strategy that Generals Casey and Abizaid espoused. Odierno soon became an advocate of a surge of five brigades along with the change of method articulated in the new COIN manual.[84]

The second major change was David Petraeus's promotion to four stars and his replacing of George Casey in command of MNF-I. Petraeus was the consensus candidate for the job being recommended by Jack Keane, John Galvin, and George Casey.[85] Petraeus assumed command from Casey on February 10, 2007, and Casey returned to the United States as chief of staff of the army. Soon, after, ADM William "Fox" Fallon replaced Abizaid at CENTCOM. Fallon was making a lateral move from Commander PACOM and had been recommended by Keane. Fallon's deputy would be LTG Marty Dempsey, who had succeeded Petraeus as head of the command training Iraqi security forces.

The last major change was the ambassador. Zalmay Khalilzad returned to become U.S. ambassador to the UN, another tough job for a man who had been successful in both Afghanistan and Iraq. He was succeeded by the State Department's premier Middle Eastern expert, Ambassador Ryan Crocker. Petraeus welcomed Crocker with the idea that there should never be any public daylight between them. To that end, Petraeus had arranged adjoining offices in the old presidential palace connected by a private door. From the moment Crocker arrived in Baghdad, he and Petraeus were joined at the hip. This was essential when working with Iraqi premier Nouri al Maliki. Odierno, too, was part of the inner circle of American leadership in Baghdad.

The changes of personnel in Washington and on the ground were the essential first step of the strategy change that became known as the "Surge." The second step was for the president to announce his decision. This he did in a speech on January 10, 2007.[86] The third step was for Petraeus and Odierno to implement the new strategy of protecting the population by moving off the Forward Operating Bases and living with Iraqi counterparts in the neighborhoods and villages of Baghdad and parts of Anbar province. This would be accomplished with five additional Brigade Combat Teams and extending tours of duty to 15 months. To make sure that the Iraqis went along with the new strategy, the lead fell to Ambassador Crocker, backstopped by GEN

Petraeus. Finally, the strategy would be adjusted to take advantage of the Anbar Awakening first seen in Ramadi by COL Sean MacFarland.

THE IMPACT

The first several months of the surge saw a significant increase in American casualties. By September, however, U.S. casualties started to fall and, more important, so did the deaths of Iraqi civilians due to sectarian violence. In Anbar, U.S. forces supported Sunni militias against AQI, and the Crocker–Petraeus team convinced Prime Minister Maliki to incorporate them into the Iraqi security forces under the name Sons of Iraq.

One critical issue came to light fairly early in the Surge. It was the question of who was in charge of how American forces operated in Iraq. It was not the usual issue between the military commander and the ambassador but rather between the military commanders, ADM Fallon at CENTCOM and GEN Petraeus at MNF-I. Under the Goldwater-Nichols Act, Fallon was the nominal superior but Petraeus was on the ground fighting the war. Conflict between four stars is like date of rank among second lieutenants.[87] The issue is really who should be supporting whom. MNF-I was, in fact, a theater command that needed to be supported by the combatant commander but Fallon thought that Petraeus should meet CENTCOM's requirements. The issue was resolved after Jack Keane brought it up in Washington and Fallon was relieved, ostensibly over a different issue. This left LTG Marty Dempsey as CENTCOM's acting commander. He would remain so until replaced by Petraeus. There was no question that the three-star supported the four-star.

In April, Senate Majority Leader, Harry Reid (D-NV), said, "this war is lost and . . . the surge is not accomplishing anything. . ."[88] On September 10, Petraeus and Crocker testified before Congress that the surge was, in fact, working and that a Marine Expeditionary Unit (MEU), deployed as part of the surge, would be returning home that month.[89] Later, Prime Minister Maliki decided to take on the firebrand Shiite cleric Moqtada al Sadr and launched a major attack on his Mahdi Army. Coalition forces assisted and made sure the Iraqi military succeeded. That marked a major reduction in sectarian violence.

IRAQ ON JANUARY 20, 2009

Before 2008 was out, the Bush administration had negotiated a status of forces agreement (SOFA) with Iraq. The agreement was to last until the end of 2011 with every expectation that a new SOFA, very similar in form, would be negotiated to replace it. On January 20, 2009, the new president of the United States, Barack Obama, inherited an Iraq that was nearly at peace. Sectarian violence had dissipated to the point of being almost nonexistent. AQI had been defeated and very nearly destroyed, only remnants remained and the Sunni parts of the country appeared to have made their peace with the Shi'a and the Kurds.

Afterward

Ray Odierno replaced Petraeus as commander MNF-I and Petraeus took command of CENTCOM. Odierno was made chief of staff of the army two years later, replacing George Casey. Ryan Crocker retired from the Foreign Service only to be called back to be ambassador to Afghanistan. He was replaced by Chris Hill, a career Foreign Service officer, with no experience in the Middle East and no command of Arabic. He was also reported to have had conflicts with GEN Ray Odierno, commanding MNF-I. Hill failed to negotiate a new SOFA. As a result, all U.S. forces left Iraq at the end of 2011. The incorporation of the Sons of Iraq into the security forces stalled and ended. Iran became the principal supporter of Iraq. AQI was resurrected and reincarnated as the Islamic State in Iraq and Syria (ISIS, also known as ISIL, the Islamic State, or Daesh). In 2014, ISIS took control of Mosul, Fallujah, Ramadi, and about a third of Iraq. American forces have been reintroduced to Iraq, albeit on a relatively small scale but one that appears to be increasing incrementally.

CONCLUSION: LESSONS FROM THE IRAQ WAR

The Iraq War can be considered in three major phases plus the aftermath. Different lessons emerge from each phase, although a few are, in fact, quite similar. Phase I involves the decision to go to war. Although President Bush's team was made up of highly experienced national security leaders, or perhaps because of that fact, it acted as if it could accomplish all of the president's goals as well as the sometimes conflicting goals of the principals. The Bush team also forgot that intelligence is an art and that analysis must be reconsidered at regular intervals. The intelligence was not relooked carefully enough when new facts came into view.

Related to the idea that intelligence is an art is the notion that "the enemy always has a vote." Nobody took account of the possibility that Saddam, for his own reasons, wanted both his adversaries and his own military to believe that he had an extensive supply of chemical weapons that he was ready to use and that he was well on his way to reconstituting his nuclear program. The United States and its allies never saw that Saddam's behavior did not fit the world's definition of rationality. We had forgotten this recurring pattern from before the Gulf War.[90]

We also forgot the importance of the post-fighting period, whether that is a liberation or an occupation. Planning for that period needs to be undertaken by the warfighter, in this case CENTCOM. It cannot be passed off to elements within the DOD, the State Department, or any other agency. The warfighting commander must take ownership or the post-fight efforts tend to degenerate into more fighting. All of this happened in Iraq.

The second phase of the war is the period of initial occupation through the command tenures of John Abizaid at CENTCOM and George Casey in Iraq. The constant changes in civilian leadership in Iraq from Jay Garner to Paul Bremer to John Negroponte to Zalmay Khalilzad meant for a highly unstable relationship with the Iraqi politicians who were trying to learn to govern. The military command structure dictated by the Goldwater-Nichols reforms proved inadequate until a four-star general, George Casey, was given command of coalition forces in Iraq. Although a kind of political-military stability was achieved by these changes of players, it fell apart because the United States forgot that "the enemy always has a vote." This time the enemy vote came from Abu Musab al Zarqawi and his AQI.

The AQI attack on the Golden Mosque changed the nature of the war from an insurgency to a sectarian conflict. Unfortunately, the American military leadership in Iraq, at CENTCOM, as well as the DOD leadership failed to understand that the nature of the war had changed.

This change introduced the third phase, which we know as "The Surge." Although it took him too long, President Bush finally realized that to achieve his goals for Iraq, he needed to make changes. He also needed to listen to different people. He did both. His new leaders changed the strategy, tactics, and organization of the war and the diplomacy with the Iraqis. By the end of the Bush presidency, the Iraq war had been largely a success.

The sad part of the story is that the new president either did not learn the lessons of his predecessor's successes and mistakes, or he learned the wrong lessons. Where President Bush's belated decision to change his military and civilian leadership in the Pentagon, CENTCOM, and the American embassy in Iraq facilitated a new and successful strategy, President Obama's personnel changes from 2009 until June 2011 contributed to the abandonment of victory in Iraq. It also required the return of some American combat troops to Iraq to combat a renewed AQI under the new name, the Islamic State.

NOTES

1. While there was some variation in the certainty of the analysis, that is, some analysts dissented, there was a general consensus on the "key findings" among the intelligence agencies around the world. Intelligence analysis is an art, not a science, and the U.S. intelligence community has a provision when a member agency disagrees to footnote the analysis with its objection.

2. See Chapter 11.

3. Bob Woodward, *Plan of Attack*. New York: 2004, Simon & Schuster. 24–25.

4. Ibid., 25–26.

5. Bob Woodward, *Bush at War*. New York: 2002, Simon & Schuster. 61.

6. The CJCS is the principal military advisor to the president and the secretary of defense under the Goldwater-Nichols Act. Under that same legislation, he is also in the chain of communication with the combatant commanders but not in the chain of command and clearly subordinate to the SECDEF in that role. However, he is not subordinate in his advisor role and has a direct channel to the president. Shelton balanced this tension much better than Myers did.

7. Kenneth Pollack, *The Threatening Storm*. New York: 2002, Random House.

8. After a career of over 20 years as an army intelligence officer both active and reserve, I was teaching a course on American foreign policy at George Washington University's Eliot School as an adjunct professor. I used Pollack's book to show how good intelligence analysis can inform policy. Today, I would modify that lesson to note that even good analysis can sometimes be wrong.

9. Condoleezza Rice, *No Higher Honor*. New York: 2011, Crown (Kindle Edition). Location 3134–3140.

10. Woodward, 2004, 1.

11. Ibid., 30.

12. During Rumsfeld's tenure, I served as National Defense University's representative to the DOD working group on training transformation and for a year was the cochair of one of the education subgroups.

13. Woodward, 96.

14. George W. Bush, *Decision Points*. New York: 2010, Crown. 230.

15. Ibid.

16. Aznar's office is often rendered as president, a translation of the Spanish president of the Council of Ministers. But Spain is a constitutional monarchy with a parliamentary system; therefore, the best representation of the office is prime minister.

17. Woodward, 183.

18. Ibid., 183–184.

19. Although the evidence is circumstantial, I see it as having been done deliberately, especially when combined with the decisions on occupation discussed later. The alternative hypothesis is that it was simply the result of bureaucratic error.

20. Ibid., 168.

21. www.govtrac.us/congress/vote/107–2002/s237.

22. Woodward, 232.

23. Rice, location 3428.

24. Ibid.

25. Woodward, 232.

26. Ibid.

27. Rice, location 3552.

28. Woodward, 281–282. Reconstruction covered far more; this was the organization that was to run the occupation and stand up a new Iraqi government.

29. Tommy Franks, *American Soldier*. New York: 2004, HarperCollins. 422.

30. Ibid., 422–423.

31. Much of the discussion in this section is based on a series of conversations with Paul Hughes in 2004 when we were colleagues at the National Defense University.

32. Woodward, 283.

33. Statements made by LTG Jay Garner at a conference at Fort Leavenworth. Garner did not know who actually made the decision, but the subsequent action suggests that it was not the president. My speculation is that the decision maker was really Rumsfeld, who, after talking with his old friend, Vice President Cheney, sought to deflect the decision upward.

34. Woodward, 284.

35. Franks, 441.

36. Hughes pointed out that the regular army had a long tradition dating back to British colonial times with a tradition of service to Iraq and not to Saddam or the Baath regime. See also Rice, location 3609–3615.

37. Rice, location 3730–3742.

38. Ibid.

39. Ibid., location 3742–3766.

40. Franks, 440–441. Italics in the original.

41. Thomas E. Ricks, *Fiasco*. New York: 2006, Penguin. 105.

42. 10th SFG was commanded by then COL Charlie Cleveland, who would later command USASOC as a three-star. Charlie was a veteran of 7th SFG, who, as a captain in Bolivia, showed me around his counterdrug operation in the Chapare.

43. Ricks, 172–175.

44. L. Paul Bremer III, *My Year in Iraq*. New York: 2006, Simon & Schuster. 7.

45. Ibid., 39.

46. Slocum had been Under SECDEF for Policy in the Clinton administration.

47. Bremer, 39.

48. I heard this myth stated many times by various senior people, including Dr. Wm J. Olson, a former deputy assistant secretary of state who was recruited to a senior position in the CPA. What had actually been done with the army was told to me by Paul Hughes and is, at least partially, corroborated by Franks in his memoir.

49. One of those was one of my master's students in the School of International Service at American University who had taken my course, *Combating Terrorism*.

50. Bremer, 12.

51. Ibid., 13.

52. Ricks, 324. Wm. Olson was kinder when he told me that their relationship was "correct."

53. Multiple sources. My time in SOUTHCOM overlapped with Petraeus's. His mentor, GEN Galvin, was one of the most knowledgeable officers on insurgency ever produced by the U.S. Army.

54. See Ricks, 313–315.

55. Ricks, 142–143.

56. See Eric Maddox, *Mission: Black List #1*. New York: 2008, Harper Collins. Eric Maddox told me the story of that last interrogation, pointing out that he had only 45 minutes because he had to catch a plane out of Iraq.

57. Personal communication from Dr. Wm. J. Olson, a senior staff member of the CPA.

58. From there, the new secretary of state, Condi Rice, would ask him to become her deputy SECSTATE.

59. Ricks, 413.

60. Ibid.

61. Ibid.

62. Moqtada al Sadr, a firebrand Shiite cleric, son of a beloved Shiite imam murdered by Saddam, was and remains close to the Iranian leadership and violently opposed to the United States, Iraqi Sunnis, and the Kurds.

63. Bob Woodward, *State of Denial*. New York: 2006, Simon & Schuster. 444.

64. See John T. Fishel and Max G. Manwaring, *Uncomfortable Wars Revisited*. Norman: 2006, University of Oklahoma Press.

65. Robert Thornton, John T. Fishel, and Marc Tyrrell, *SFA-Mosul: Case Study*. Fort Leavenworth, KS: 2008, Joint Center for International Security Force Assistance (JCIFSFA). Also published by *Small Wars Journal* (online).

66. Linda Robinson, *Tell Me How This Ends*. New York: 2008, Public Affairs. 98.

67. Thomas E. Ricks, *The Gamble*. London/New York: 2009, The Penguin Press. 57–58.

68. Bob Woodward, *The War Within*. New York: 2008, Simon & Schuster. xv, 42.

69. Woodward, 252.

70. Ibid., 262.

71. A Council of Colonels is a relatively common practice designed to achieve some consensus on a tough problem from senior operators. McMaster, who was a student at Leavenworth when I was on the faculty, received his PhD in history from Duke with his dissertation on the failure of the JCS during the Vietnam War. It was later published as *Dereliction of Duty*.

72. Woodward, 240–244.

73. Ibid., 277.

74. Ibid., 279–282.

75. Robert M. Gates, *Duty*. New York: 2014, Alfred A. Knopf (Kindle Edition). Location 25–255.

76. Woodward, 232–239.

77. Later deputy commander of CENTCOM, acting commander of CENTCOM and CJCS.

78. Robinson, chapter 3.

79. Ibid.

80. Cohen is a well-respected academic and policy advisor to the DOD and later serving as counselor to the State Department from 2007 to 2009.

81. Robinson, 76–77. Crane and I served on a panel together discussing COIN. Nagl interviewed me for his dissertation, later published as *Learning to Eat Soup with a Knife*. Still later, I had John come to OU for our annual international affairs symposium.

82. Ibid., 78. Manwaring and I have published numerous books and articles together on COIN and related topics. Many of those were written with Ambassador Edwin Corr, and others including GEN John Galvin, ADM William J. Crowe, and former secretary of state Lawrence Eagleburger.

83. Ibid. Among the experts was Dr. Tom Marks of the DOD's College of International Security Affairs at the National Defense University. Tom told me about the meeting. I had also worked on a project during the Clinton administration for Sewell and her boss, Michele Flournoy, then principal deputy assistant SECDEF for strategy, on peace operations.

84. See Ricks, 107–119.

85. Robinson, 86. Also ibid.

86. Woodward, 312–314.

87. The date that a second lieutenant is commissioned is his date of rank. He is senior to any commissioned after him and junior to any commissioned even a day earlier. However, all second lieutenants are so low in the military pecking order that seniority as measured by date of rank is meaningless.

88. Woodward, 345.

89. Ibid., 386.

90. David Jablonsky addresses this well in his *Rationality Is Not Enough*. Carlisle, PA: 1991, Strategic Studies Institute.

Chapter 13

The Afghanistan Surge: Obama's Finest Hour?

THE WAR OBAMA INHERITED

According to President Obama, during his campaign for the presidency, Iraq was the "bad" war while Afghanistan was the "good" war. It certainly was not that simple, but the proposition reflected the view of many, if not most, Americans. However, when Obama came into office, the "good" war was not going well. As CJCS Mike Mullen had said, "In Iraq we do what we must. In Afghanistan, we do what we can."[1] Part of the argument was that the Bush administration had allowed itself to become distracted by the Iraq War. Bigger reasons, however, were the inadequate original analysis of the problem, a strategy that failed to address the real issues, the difficulties of coordinating a coalition built around the NATO alliance, and a command and control system that violated the principles of war. This was what SECDEF Bob Gates found when he took office in early 2007.

Prior to 2007, the NATO-led International Security Assistance Force (ISAF) had been commanded by non-U.S. NATO officers. In February 2007, U.S. GEN Dan McNeill replaced British general Richards as ISAF commander. This was the first time an American had commanded ISAF. Prior to that time, the commander of American forces in Afghanistan—then LTG Karl Eikenberry—reported to the commander, USCENTCOM, while GEN Richards had reported to the Supreme Allied Commander, Europe (SACEUR). At that time, SACEUR was GEN Bantz J. Craddock, U.S. Army.[2]

McNeill commanded only about half of some 8,000 to 10,000 U.S. and other coalition soldiers assigned to Afghanistan, who, under the rubric of Operation Enduring Freedom (OEF), reported to a separate U.S. three-star general (Eikenberry), who in turn reported to the four-star commander of Central Command in

Tampa. A significant percentage of the Special Forces operating in Afghanistan reported to yet another commander (of USSOCOM), also in Tampa.

This jerry-rigged arrangement violated every principle of unity of command. And to make matters worse, Craddock and McNeill did not get along with each other.[3]

Gates also points out that civilian coordination of governance and development activities was confused at best. And then, there was the problem of Afghan president, Hamid Karzai, a difficult ally. Many Americans who had to deal with Karzai over the course of both the Bush and Obama administrations were inclined to see him as paranoid, unreliable, and corrupt—a hindrance to success. After Khalilzad left, even the American ambassadors tended to ignore Karzai, as did the military commanders. Gates, however, listened, as did President Bush, realizing that while Karzai was often over the top, he also was not entirely wrong and did have the best interests of his nation in mind.

In June 2008, McNeill was replaced by GEN David McKiernan. McKiernan saw the Taliban gaining strength and began to point out the need for more forces. His appointment as commander of ISAF did solve one problem in that he wore a second hat as commander of all U.S. forces in Afghanistan. This created unity of command in-country since McKiernan commanded all NATO forces and all U.S. forces, including most of the Special Forces. Unfortunately, it did not solve the problem of dual command of the commander. As commander of ISAF, McKiernan reported to SACEUR but as U.S. commander he reported to commander, USCENTCOM. McKiernan's greatest problem was that he was a very conventionally oriented officer in a war that was very unconventional. He was correct on the need for more troops but had no real idea of how to employ them effectively to prosecute the war he faced. He also tempered his request for increased forces to what the staff officers in the Pentagon told him were available.

STAFFING THE NEW NATIONAL SECURITY TEAM

The presidential election of 2008 gave the United States a new president from the opposition party. Barack Obama had been a first-term senator from Illinois who took office on January 3, 2005. His three years in the Senate were punctuated by large gaps spent running for president. Obama sought to compensate for his lack of experience in defense and foreign policy with his choices for subordinates. His vice president, Joe Biden, had been chairman of the Senate Foreign Relations Committee. In one of his wisest decisions, he asked Bob Gates to stay on as SECDEF. For SECSTATE he chose his former rival for the nomination, Senator Hillary Clinton, also the former First Lady.

President Obama then chose as secretary of homeland security Arizona governor Janet Napolitano. As his NSA he selected retired marine corps commandant and former SACEUR Gen Jim Jones. For Jones's deputy he brought in Tom Donilon, a longtime Democratic Party foreign policy official,[4] and for key NSC Staff, Denis McDonough and Ben Rhodes. As DNI, President Obama appointed retired ADM Dennis Blair, former commander of U.S. Pacific Command. He also named former White House chief of staff under Bill Clinton Leon Panetta as his director of CIA and elevated him to principal status on the NSC. White House chief of staff was Rahm Emanuel, and longtime CIA officer John Brennan became his counterterrorism guru. LTG Doug Lute was retained on the NSC staff to manage the Afghanistan/Pakistan portfolio. In an unusual twist, President Obama made Deputy SECSTATE James Steinberg a full member of the Principals Committee and the NSC as well as the Deputies Committee. This was Steinberg's condition for taking the job, but unlike the normal two seats of the DOD (which usually coordinated positions between the SECDEF and CJCS) Steinberg often disagreed with Secretary Clinton.[5]

In general, the NSC—Principals, Deputies, and Staff—broke down along the lines of foreign policy and security professionals in contrast to the political specialists. However, that was not a hard dividing line as some of the policy professionals sided with the political types on some issues; likewise some of the political specialists lined up with the policy folk on key issues.

NEW AMERICAN LEADERSHIP IN-COUNTRY

During the first half of 2009, the administration made key changes to its representation in Afghanistan. In April, President Obama named newly retired LTG Karl Eikenberry to be ambassador to Afghanistan. He presented his credentials in May. Eikenberry had previously commanded U.S. forces in Afghanistan and had formed a very negative view of President Karzai. In May, SECDEF Gates, with the advice of CJCS Admiral Mike Mullen, decided to replace David McKiernan as commander ISAF and U.S. Forces in Afghanistan. The new commander, GEN Stanley McChrystal, had commanded the Joint Special Operations Command (JSOC) developing a strong interagency team that had worked closely with both Iraqi and Afghan special operations forces. Following that assignment, McChrystal had served as assistant to the CJCS, where he had developed the reputation as a consummate problem solver.

One other key appointment during this period was that of Richard Holbrooke as special envoy to Afghanistan and Pakistan. Holbrooke was the choice of SECSTATE Clinton but he never really jelled with President

Obama and his brash manner did not work well with either Karzai or President Zardari of Pakistan.

FORCE-LEVEL REQUESTS

In January 2009, pending on the DOD plate was GEN McKiernan's request for 30,000 more troops.[6] The Bush administration had not acted on this, seeing it as the prerogative of the new president.

> When President Obama came into office . . . he found [that request] for thousands of additional troops to block the Taliban's expected summer offensive and provide security for the upcoming Presidential elections. We discussed the proposal in one of our first National Security Council meetings after the inauguration. Despite our campaign pledges to put more resources into the war in Afghanistan, it was reasonable to ask whether it made sense to deploy more troops before we had time to decide on a new strategy. But the military logistics necessary to deploy those forces by the summer necessitated a quick decision.[7]

President Obama had commissioned his campaign foreign policy advisor, Bruce Riedel, to conduct a 60-day review of the Afghan war. However, as Gates made clear in the previous quote, logistics drove an early decision. When the president asked Riedel if he should approve the deployment before the review was finished, Riedel said to go ahead.[8] "The President approved the deployment of seventeen thousand troops on February 17."[9]

STRATEGIC REVIEW (RIEDEL)

Bruce Riedel was a longtime CIA analyst specializing on South Asia. He had become an advisor to candidate Obama, and the new president felt comfortable with him and had a great deal of confidence in his judgment. Riedel had just finished a book on the threats from and in Afghanistan and Pakistan when Obama asked him to conduct a strategic review over a period of 60 days. Riedel came on board on February 2 to conduct the review under the ostensible leadership of Under Secretary of Defense for Policy (USDP) Michele Flournoy and special envoy for Afghanistan and Pakistan (AF-PAK), Richard Holbrooke. He was to be supported by LTG Doug Lute, who had that portfolio on the NSC Staff and members of his team. The day Riedel reported to the NSC for work, February 2, he made clear to Lute that he would not need much help. Lute concluded that Riedel was going to essentially extract his book.[10]

Riedel's report was delivered in March and emphasized that Afghanistan and Pakistan were a single challenge with the focus on training host nation forces. It also recommended a "fully resourced counterinsurgency" using all the instruments of national power, not just military. In fact, Riedel argued that civilian assets were at least as important as military ones.[11]

President Obama announced his new strategy for Afghanistan on March 27. His defined objective was "To disrupt, dismantle, and defeat al Qaeda in Pakistan and Afghanistan and to prevent their return to either country in the future."[12]

While these discussions were taking place both before and after the inauguration, vice president-elect, Joe Biden, had met with Karzai on at least two occasions in 2008 and January of 2009. The meetings did not go well. During the 2008 meeting, Biden stormed out of the dinner and the one in January was almost as tempestuous.[13] "One of Biden's messages to Karzai . . . was that Obama would not engage with . . . [him] nearly so much as had Bush."[14] Biden's obvious disdain for Karzai and the message he delivered foreshadowed a real weakening of American influence with the Afghan president, especially when coupled with similar disdain from AF-PAK special envoy Holbrooke and the new U.S. ambassador, LTG (Ret.) Karl Eikenberry.

MCCHRYSTAL'S RECOMMENDATIONS

In May, Secretary Gates informed GEN McKiernan that he was being replaced and recommended that LTG Stan McChrystal be his replacement. President Obama nominated McChrystal for his fourth star and for the position of commander ISAF and U.S. Forces in Afghanistan. Over the course of May, the Joint Staff and the DOD civilians in the Office of the Secretary of Defense (OSD) discussed future force requirements for Afghanistan. One number being mentioned was an additional 21,000. This would double the number that Obama had approved in February and March. On June 2, at his confirmation hearing, McChrystal used that number.[15]

NSA Jim Jones called Gates and Mullen in to his office to discuss the issue of creeping force levels. After all, they had just gone through the Riedel strategic review and the president had sent a total of 21,000 more troops—two-thirds of the full request made by GEN McKiernan the year before. Now the military was talking about doubling the forces again without any apparent reason. Jones suggested that McChrystal conduct a review of his needs for 60 days after he took command.[16]

On June 8, Gates met with McChrystal, LTG David "Rod" Rodriguez, McChrystal's newly named deputy, Admiral Mullen, VCJCS James "Hoss" Cartwright, and USDP Michele Flournoy to discuss the new command structure and to advise McChrystal that he would be expected to conduct a 60-day review of how to implement his strategy and the forces he would need to do so.[17] The next day, at a meeting with the president, vice president, Chief of Staff Rahm Emanuel, and other staffers, Gates briefed Obama on what had been discussed at the Pentagon. From the president on down, all the White House people expressed opposition to asking for more forces, according to Gates, pretty aggressively.[18] Biden and Emanuel were especially strong in their opposition. "I was aware of Biden's conviction—and probably that of others in the room—that this request and the McChrystal assessment were part of an orchestrated squeeze play by the military to get the president to approve a lot more troops."[19] Gates, however, was himself skeptical about a large troop increase and expressed his reservations. He was disappointed in the political turn the discussion had taken.[20]

Nevertheless, GEN McChrystal was confirmed and headed to Afghanistan to take charge and begin his own strategic assessment. What he found when he arrived was a rapidly deteriorating military situation. Taliban and other insurgent attacks were on the rise and, for one week in May, had reached some 400.[21]

That summer, the new national security team began to come apart. It became apparent that Biden and his staff, some of the NSC Staff, all of the White House political folks, saw Afghanistan quite differently than did Gates, Mullen, Clinton, and Blair.[22] Jones appeared to view the issue similarly to Gates and his allies, likewise Panetta at CIA.[23] Jones's deputy, Tom Donilon, seemed to line up with the Biden group, as did Doug Lute.

Again, the political White House personnel were saying that the military were trying to box the president in—"jam" him—giving him no options but higher and higher force levels.[24] These complaints would continue throughout the process, especially when the recommendations were couched in terms of three options, one too small to be effective, one so big that it stood no chance of getting through Congress due to its costs, and one that was "just right."[25]

By late June, GEN McChrystal was indicating that the situation in Afghanistan was much worse than he had thought. The Taliban and other insurgents were on the rise; the Afghan security forces were far fewer than appeared on paper and much less well trained. Governance was weak outside of Kabul and a few cities, while corruption was rampant. Too many civilians were being killed by ISAF forces, and there was no real partnership between the Afghan security forces and the foreign troops. By August, McChrystal was arguing for a large increase in troops but, more important, a much different focus for the international effort. This would involve protecting the population, partnering with the Afghans, and changing the rules of engagement to a more restrictive use of air power and artillery. In short, he planned to conduct a classic counterinsurgency (COIN) operation. But to do so, he would need significantly greater resources.

As McChrystal was conducting his assessment, AF-PAK special envoy Richard Holbrooke and Ambassador Karl Eikenberry were becoming warier than ever of Karzai, who, in turn, was thoroughly distrustful of them. The issue was the presidential election scheduled for August 20 and whether there would be a run-off if no candidate got over 50% of the vote as the Afghan Constitution required. Karzai was resisting and Eikenberry took a hard line with him, telling him he had recommended that President Obama not take his phone calls on this matter.[26] "Meanwhile, Holbrooke was doing his best to bring about the defeat of Karzai in the August 20 elections."[27] McChrystal quickly concluded that the success of his mission depended on a strong, positive relationship with the Afghan government and this translated into a close working relationship with Karzai. Given Karzai's volatility and his undeniable patriotism, the general consulted with him regularly and directly and sought to accommodate his concerns wherever he could.[28] This stance clearly brought McChrystal into conflict with both Eikenberry and Holbrooke.

GEN McChrystal submitted his assessment on August 31, as planned. Copies went to Gates, Mullen, Petraeus at CENTCOM, and to Admiral Jim Stavridis, the new SACEUR. Those were the only people to receive it at first. The next day, Petraeus endorsed the assessment. Soon after, Gates shared it with Michele Flournoy, his USDP, who discussed it with Deputy NSA Tom Donilon. They agreed that the assessment would be distributed to the relevant NSC staff immediately after Labor Day. Then "it would be discussed at limited attendance meetings of both the deputies and the principals."[29]

The resource piece of the strategy included a robust civilian development component but nearly all the public focus would be on troop strength. McChrystal was requesting a truly significant increase of forces—a full-fledged surge—of 40,000 more troops. Although the exact numbers would not become public immediately, the notion that the commander was asking for more troops did. At Mullen's confirmation hearing for a second term as CJCS, he publicly stated that "McChrystal's strategy of a properly resourced counterinsurgency *'probably means more forces.'*"[30] Although his statement had been sent to the White House as a heads-up and the NSC chief of staff, Denis McDonough, had cleared it, the president, Emanuel, and Donilon, among others, took it as more evidence that the military were ganging up to force Obama into approving this escalation of the war.[31]

DELIBERATIONS AT THE NSC

The NSC began formal meetings to review McChrystal's strategic assessment and force-level request in late September. On September 30 the NSC met on this for the second time. On October 9 it met for the fifth time.[32] Three issues dominated the NSC discussions. First were the confounding relationships in the Afghanistan–Pakistan border area between the Taliban and al Qaeda, as well as other Islamist extremist groups. There was disagreement as to whether the Taliban had to be defeated to eliminate the threat of al Qaeda or whether there might be some role for them in a future Afghan political order. Second was the issue of the kind of strategy the United States and its allies ought to follow. Should it be the fully resourced COIN approved by President Obama in March and expanded on by GEN McChrystal in his assessment or should it be the Counterterrorism-Plus (CT-Plus) favored by Vice President Biden?[33] Gates states, "In the case of CT-Plus, could it work if the United States lacked the resources on the ground to protect the population and without adequate intelligence to be effective?"[34]

The third issue was the resources needed to make either strategy work. Could CT-Plus be successful with a lower force level than McChrystal requested? Did COIN need the full 40,000 troops requested? And what were the costs? How would the costs impact the president's domestic program?

NSC-LEVEL PERSONNEL ISSUES

By October, the principals in the NSC had lined up in two fairly solid groups. The first group consisted mainly of Secretaries Gates and Clinton, CJCS Mullen, with DCIA Panetta mostly in support. They all advocated the approach of Generals McChrystal and Petraeus for a fully resourced COIN strategy with the force levels proposed by McChrystal. This strategy conformed to the earlier Riedel review and the one that President Obama had announced in March.

Opposing that approach was the political group led by Vice President Biden and White House Chief of Staff Emanuel. It also included VCJCS GEN Cartwright, retired LTG Doug Lute, NSC Chief of Staff Denis McDonough, and his assistant Ben Rhodes. A critical member of this group was the American ambassador in Afghanistan, retired LTG Eikenberry. Eikenberry had sent two cables to the NSC without coordinating them with McChrystal or through the State Department, flogging the behavior of Afghan president Karzai and supporting the CT-Plus strategy. According to Gates:

> Even Secretary Clinton would speak of Eikenbery's insubordination, that he would not do what she directed. Though both Clinton and I wanted Eikenberry replaced—because his relationship with Karzai was beyond repair and his relationships with both Defense and State were so poor—and repeatedly told Jones so, the ambassador was protected by the White House.[35]

Although NSA Jones sought to be an honest broker, he appeared to lean toward the CT-Plus strategy.[36] Deputy NSA Donilon, however, would ultimately support the COIN strategy. Afghanistan-Pakistan (AF-PAK) special envoy Richard Holbrooke was also a skeptic regarding the COIN strategy.[37]

MORE DELIBERATIONS

Soon after the October 9 NSC meeting, the president asked Gates for his analysis in private. Gates wrote a memo that they discussed in a one-on-one meeting in the White House on October 13. In the secretary's view, the scope of the mission needed to be narrowed but in any case, there was a requirement for force levels at, or near, what McChrystal proposed. Gates suggested that 30,000 American troops would likely be enough if the allies could be persuaded to offer from 5,000 to 10,000 more. He urged the president not to be precise on the number of troops because different configurations required different numbers. He also suggested that the strategy be reassessed in about a year and, if it was not working, that it should be changed.[38]

Two weeks later, on October 26, the president invited Clinton and Gates to meet at the White House. They were the only outsiders. The entire team of skeptics, including Biden, Emanuel, Jones, Donilon, and John Brennan, were present. At this point, Donilon had not yet come around to supporting the COIN strategy. The discussion became quite heated but the president kept his own counsel.[39]

In early November the deliberations had narrowed the focus to three options. Option 1, CT-Plus, had been increased from 10,000–11,000 to 20,000 troops, half to train Afghan forces and half for CT. Option 2 was McChrystal's proposal of 40,000 for the fully resourced COIN strategy. Option 3 (Gates calls it Option 2A) was the SECDEF's proposal for 30,000 U.S. troops with an additional 5,000 to 7,000 from the allies.[40]

Later deliberations focused on how quickly the additional troops could be flowed into Afghanistan and how long they would stay. The military planners had been looking at a year or more but the president wanted it done quicker. He wondered aloud how this could be called a "surge" if it took that long. Six months soon became the target. The other question, how long the surge troops would stay before beginning to come out, was resolved in favor of 18 months, until July 2011. This was to put some pressure on Karzai and his government to make the changes necessary to have a chance to take over and win the war themselves. Gates understood that the July 2011 date was the beginning of a process rather than an abrupt pullout of the additional forces. In his view, President Obama agreed to a pace of withdrawal based on conditions on the ground.[41]

THE PRESIDENT DECIDES

After nine full NSC meetings and a number of smaller group meetings with the White House national security team, the president came to a decision in the last week of November. As part of that decision he personally dictated a "terms sheet"— five single-spaced pages.[42] The key points of the document were that President Obama approved a surge of 30,000 troops with a possible 10% increase on a case-by-case basis for enablers, to degrade the Taliban and give the Afghan government time to demonstrate it could both govern and assume responsibility for its own security. It would make clear that al Qaeda and the Taliban could no longer maintain safe havens in Pakistan. It set December 2010 as the time to review the strategy to determine the degree to which it was being successful, and it set a firm date, July 2011, to begin withdrawing the surge forces. The pace of the withdrawal would be determined by conditions on the ground.[43]

The "terms sheet' was a presidential order, and the president went over it in detail at a meeting late in the afternoon of Sunday, November 29. Present for the meeting were Biden, Gates, Mullen, Cartwright, Petraeus, Jones, and Emanuel. Obama gave them all time to read the document and then asked each one if he could and would support the decision. Although Biden and Emanuel were clearly less than pleased, they all agreed to fully support the president's decision. He then went through the same process by video teleconference with GEN McChrystal and Ambassador Eikenberry. Both affirmed their support.[44]

THE WEST POINT SPEECH

Two days later, the president flew to West Point to announce his decision in an address to the Corps of Cadets and the nation. Flying with him, on Air Force One, were Clinton, Gates, Mullen, and Jones. The speech had been written by Ben Rhodes, the former aspiring novelist, who had become Denis McDonough's assistant on the NSC for strategic communications. Obama announced that he was sending 30,000 more troops to Afghanistan and that they would begin to come out 18 months later, in July 2011. As Woodward points out, "the headline in the next day's *New York Times* was 'Obama Adds Troops, but Maps Exit Plan.' "[45] One other aspect of the announcement was the American combat role in Afghanistan would end in December 2014.

ASSURANCES TO THE SECDEF AS
THE DEBATE CONTINUED

In the discussions of the trajectory of the Afghan surge, Gates had sought and received assurances from President Obama that the pace of the drawdown that would begin in July 2011 would be dictated by conditions on the ground.

In the immediate aftermath of the West Point speech, Gates and Clinton testified before Congress and made that point. Vice President Biden and several of the NSC staff, however, were asserting at the same time that the drawdown of forces would be steep and rapid. That debate never ended during Gates's tenure as SECDEF.[46]

THE MCCHRYSTAL DEBACLE AND THE PETRAEUS SOLUTION

Although the public debate over the Afghan strategy had died down over the spring of 2010, it remained very much alive within the government. The tension between the political White House—the President's political staff and their allies on the NSC staff—and the departments of Defense and State continued unabated. In Afghanistan, it was symbolized by the essentially nonexistent relationship between GEN McChrystal and Ambassador Eikenberry who were explicitly divided in their views of how to treat Karzai. As a partial solution, McChrystal had elevated the senior NATO civilian, British diplomat Mark Sedwill to be his senior civilian point of contact with the Afghan government. McChrystal did this wearing his hat as ISAF commander with the full concurrence of SACEUR (ADM James Stavridis), COMCENT (GEN David Petraeus), and the DOD (both Gates and Mullen). The SECSTATE made no objection. Eikenberry, however, remained a favorite of the vice president and his allies.

In April, GEN Stan McChrystal had agreed to allow a reporter for *Rolling Stone* to embed with him and his staff. Unfortunately, they failed to make any of the discussions the reporter listened to "off the record." The magazine published the article "The Runaway General" on June 22.[47] The night before, Gates received word of the article and called NSA Jim Jones to inform him. The article "contained some disparaging and mocking comments from McChrystal and his senior staff about administration officials. One unnamed McChrystal aide called Jones a 'clown' . . . The article also quoted . . . aides who took shots at Biden, Holbrooke, and Eikenberry."[48] The furor was intense. Taking full blame, McChrystal offered his resignation. President Obama ordered him home, met with him, and accepted his resignation.

Obama's immediate problem was to decide who would replace McChrystal. The solution was obvious: Dave Petraeus was commanding CENTCOM. The only problem was that sending Petraeus to Afghanistan would technically subordinate him to his peers at SHAPE/EUCOM and CENTCOM. Petraeus, however, had a good relationship with Stavridis (SACEUR) and he would have input on his successor at CENTCOM. He recommended marine Gen James Mattis. Moreover, the reality was that both commanders would be supporting him, not the other way around. Luck played a big role; if Petraeus had not been available then Obama would have had a much more difficult problem.

MICROMANAGING THE WAR FROM THE WHITE HOUSE

Throughout the run-up to the surge and, indeed, during all of Gates's tenure and that of his successor, Leon Panetta, the NSC staff at the White House attempted to micromanage actions in the Afghan war. At one point, Secretary Gates asked Jim Jones how many people Doug Lute had working for him. Jones said that it was around 25.[49]

> "When you have that big an operation at the NSS," I told him, you're doing the wrong things and looking for ways to stay busy." The National Security Staff had, in effect, become an operational body with its own policy agenda, as opposed to a coordination mechanism. And this, in turn, led to microman-agement far beyond what was appropriate. Indeed, on one visit to Afghanistan, I spotted a direct phone line to Lute in the special operations command center at Bagram Air Base. I ordered it removed. On another occasion, I told General Jim Mattis at Central Command that if Lute ever called him again to question anything, Mattis was to tell him to go to hell.[50]

The issue never was resolved. In fact, the NSC staff continued to grow throughout the Obama administration, reaching an estimated 400 in 2015, with its attendant push to micromanage.[51]

KILLING BIN LADEN

On May 1, 2011, the manhunt that officially began on September 11, 2001, ended. Two days before, President Obama approved a raid by SEAL Team 6 (also known as the Development Group, or DEVGRU) into Pakistan to kill or capture Osama bin Laden. The raid, while conducted by the military, specifically the Joint Special Operations Command (JSOC) under ADM William McRaven, was based on intelligence developed mainly by the CIA. In fact, JSOC was operating under the control of CIA with direct communication between the director, Leon Panetta, and ADM McRaven. The story of the raid, officially codenamed Operation Neptune Spear, has been told many times. Suffice it to say that it was well planned and executed in spite of some unexpected difficulties. Bin Laden was killed; his corpse was identified and buried at sea. A treasure trove of intelligence was collected from his compound in Abbottabad. In Afghanistan, conditions on the ground had apparently changed.[52]

TRANSITION AT DEFENSE

Before President Obama even took office in January 2009, he had prevailed on Bob Gates to stay as secretary of defense. They had agreed on a year. The year had stretched to two and Obama had asked for more. They had settled on six months, until the end of June 2011. That spring, Gates had recommended that he be replaced by Panetta, then director of the CIA. Panetta and the president had discussed the move, and the director accepted the offer. Obama announced the appointment on April 28, 2011. He also announced other changes that included Petraeus moving to the CIA to replace Panetta and marine Gen John Allen to replace Petraeus in Afghanistan.[53]

WHATEVER HAPPENED TO THOSE ASSURANCES?

The killing of bin Laden seemed to the White House a game changer. Conditions on the ground were clearly different; al Qaeda was on the run (as the president would claim all through the election campaign of 2012). The threat of attacks on the United States from Afghanistan—the reason the United States had gone to war there in 2001—seemed to have diminished greatly. The president turned his attention to his domestic agenda and decided that the DOD would be the bill payer. Because the game in Afghanistan had changed dramatically, President Obama accelerated the rate of withdrawal of surge forces, largely without regard for the tactical conditions on the ground. The assurances he had given to Gates with regard to both the pace of the drawdown and the defense budget became a dead letter. No matter how effective a SECDEF Leon Panetta was, he did not have the defense stature of Gates. Neither he nor Clinton could make much headway in the face of the greatly expanded NSC staff.

THE EVER-CHANGING ENDGAME

In July 2011 the drawdown of U.S. forces in Afghanistan began at an accelerated pace—one that almost approximated Vice President Joe Biden's prediction. After the U.S. election in 2012, President Obama could begin to say that he had ended the war in Iraq and was ending the war in Afghanistan—as promised. Even though Taliban attacks began to rise, U.S. and ISAF forces stayed on track to end combat operations at the end of 2014.

But as 2014 drew to a close, there were reports and claims of responsibility for terrorist attacks made by al Qaeda and by a new adversary, ISIS. The Islamist Jihadist movement was metastasizing. ISIS, born in Iraq and Syria, was now in Afghanistan. When ISAF combat operations ended in December 2014, the training mission continued. There were about 10,000 American troops in country to conduct it. The force level was to be reduced to half in 2015, and to zero by the end of 2016. It would not happen. The Taliban and its competitors increased their attacks and control of territory. Further drawdowns were delayed. Force levels were to fall to just over 5,000 by the end of 2016. In the summer, however, the drawdown stopped at just under 9,000. It would sink no farther during Obama's term in office.

NOTES

1. See Chapter 11.
2. Robert M. Gates, *Duty*. New York: 2014, Alfred A. Knopf (Kindle Edition). Location 3722.
3. Ibid., location 3729.
4. See Chapter 10.
5. Gates, location 5231.
6. Bob Woodward, *Obama's Wars*. New York: 2010, Simon & Schuster. 70.
7. Gates, location 2328–2334.
8. Woodward, 97.
9. Hillary Rodham Clinton, *Hard Choices*. New York: 2014, Simon & Schuster (Kindle Edition). Location 2333.
10. Woodward, 89–90.
11. Clinton, location 2336.
12. Quoted in ibid., location 2342.
13. Gates, location 6088.
14. Ibid., location 6093.
15. Woodward, 123.
16. Ibid., 123–125.
17. Gates, location 6307.
18. Ibid., location 6318.
19. Ibid., location 6323.
20. Ibid.
21. Woodward, 126.
22. Gates, location 6334.
23. Woodward, 126–128. Also Leon Panetta, *Worthy Fights*. New York: 2014, Penguin Press. 250–253.
24. Gates, location 6340.
25. Panetta, 253.
26. Woodward, 146–148.
27. Gates, location 6486.
28. Mujib Mashal, "McChrystal-Karzai Relationship Steels the News in Afghanistan." *New York Times*, June 28, 2010. Atwar.blogs.nytimes/2016.06/28.

29. Gates, location 6540–6546.

30. Woodward, 172.

31. Ibid., 173.

32. Ibid., 186, and Gates, location 6751.

33. Gates, location 6729–6735.

34. Ibid.

35. Ibid., location 6724–6729. It should be noted here, once again, that the SECSTATE is not in the chain of command of the ambassador, who is appointed by and serves the president. The SECSTATE is in the chain of communication to the ambassador and has greater influence over a career diplomat who must return to the Foreign Service than over a political appointee.

36. Clinton, location 2442.

37. Ibid.

38. Gates, location 6768–6812.

39. Ibid., location 6812–6867.

40. Ibid., location 6867–6873.

41. Ibid., location 5496.

42. See the document reprinted in Woodward, 385–390. The document was classified SECRET/NOFORN, dated November 29, 2009, titled MEMORANDUM FOR THE PRINCIPALS, From: National Security Adviser, AFGHANISTAN-PAKISTAN STRATEGY.

43. Ibid.

44. Woodward, 325–330.

45. Ibid., 335.

46. Gates, location 8632.

47. Michael Hastings, "The Runaway General," Rolling Stone. www.rollingstone.com/politics/news/the-runaway-genera-20100622.

48. Woodward, 371–372.

49. Gates, location 8765. See also Panetta, 335–336, 375–376.

50. Gates, location 8765–8771. During President Obama's first term, he had merged the NSC and the Homeland Security Council (HSC) and their staffs, renaming the staff the National Security Staff (NSS). In the second term, the name was changed back to the NSC Staff. I have generally used that term throughout this book.

51. *Washington Post*, "White House Tries for a Leaner NSC Staff." https://www.washingtonpost.com/world/national-security/white-house-tries-for-a-leaner-national-security-council/2015/06/22/22ef7e52-1909-11e5-93b7-5eddc056ad8a_story.html.

52. This version of the killing of bin Laden is drawn mainly from Panetta, 320–331.

53. Panetta, 317.

Part IV

SOME CONCLUSIONS

Chapter 14

How National Security Policy Is Really Made: Lessons from the Cases

American national security policy is shaped by many factors. First, it is shaped by how we understand the world we live in. This is defined for the practitioner largely in terms of international relations (IR) theory. Second, policy is shaped by the legal authorities of the U.S. Constitution and federal laws passed by Congress. Third, it is shaped by the capabilities of the organizations and institutions of the U.S. government. Fourth, national security policy is shaped by the processes and procedures of the government. Finally, although not explicitly stated, it is shaped by how individual play the hands they are dealt.[1]

The cases considered in the book modify this initial analysis. They add features not considered in the early chapters, or not considered in enough depth. The function of this chapter is to review the overall approach and modify it according to the lessons recorded in the case chapters.

HOW WE UNDERSTAND THE WORLD SHAPES WHAT WE DO

The initial chapter asserts that American national security policy makers see the world through two lenses: realism and liberalism. They tend to analyze the world around them in terms of realism seeing states as the primary actors, acting rationally in their own interest. They also tend to develop policy based on goals that are informed by the liberal tradition in America. This pattern is generally common throughout the cases.

Consider first the Panama case. Here the perception of a threat developed gradually over time. SOUTHCOM, the embassy, and the NSC all analyzed it similarly. It was complex and there was disagreement over the degree to which GEN Noriega was working with the United States or against the United States. But there was no disagreement that he was a destabilizing factor. When it came time that a decision had to be made, President George Bush gave four reasons for the invasion: (1) Protect American lives and property; (2) Maintain the security and neutrality of the Panama Canal; (3) Restore Panamanian democracy; and (4) Bring Noriega to justice. The first two reasons are pure realism; number three is pure liberalism, while number four is a mix.

Desert Shield/Storm illustrates the dominance of realism. Saddam's invasion of Kuwait challenged the entire post–World War II order. It was in the interest of the United States and the other Great Powers to reverse his aggression. Liberal idealism was reflected in using the UN to orchestrate the response, but it was the realist mechanism of the Security Council that provided the method.

Somalia represents the liberalism dimension but tempered by realism, at least during the Bush administration. President Bush made the decision to go into Somalia based on the humanitarian crisis that was being shown on the nightly TV news. The purpose of the mission was humanitarian, although the mission itself was crafted very narrowly in accordance with a realist view of the world. Neither President Bush nor any of his team sought to right all the wrongs in Somalia. As a result, the mission was to create a safe and secure environment for the delivery of humanitarian relief. In contrast, the Clinton administration adopted the expansive view of Secretary-General Boutros Boutros-Ghali that the UN should achieve a stable and reasonably well-governed state in Somalia. With the Battle of Mogadishu, President Clinton decided, on a realist basis, that the American interest in that country was not great enough to risk any more military lives.

Perhaps, the administration most driven by liberalism was that of George W. Bush. This is somewhat ironic because it came into office explicitly rejecting the "nation building" of the Clinton administration. Yet, following the 9/11 attacks, President Bush clearly articulated and supported what he called the "Freedom Agenda" in both Afghanistan and Iraq. The goal in both cases was to establish functioning democracies and to do so on a multinational basis. In Afghanistan, the base of the coalition was NATO, while in Iraq, it was a "coalition of the willing." The theoretical basis of the "Freedom Agenda" was an explicit, empirical variant of liberalism called Democratic Peace Theory.[2] This follows from the fact that democracies rarely go to war with each other to the hypothesis that it is because democracies provide real alternatives to violence to settle disputes. Therefore, the cause of peace in both countries and their region would be served by helping them become fully functioning democracies.

NOT ONLY DOMESTIC AUTHORITIES CONSTRAIN US—THE UNITED STATES IS NOT ALONE IN THE WORLD

While it is clear that the Constitution and federal legislation determine what can be lawfully done in the national security arena, who does it, and how (in very general terms), we do not usually consider how international authorities both enable and constrain us. In the Panama case, the international legal and treaty authorities had a mostly general effect. This was a bilateral conflict and was constrained in only the most general way by the UN and OAS charter, and specifically by the international laws of warfare and the two Panama–U.S. treaties. On the other hand, Desert Shield and Desert Storm were enabled by the UN Charter and the resolutions of the UN Security Council.

In a similar way, Somalia, Haiti, and the Balkan peace operations were enabled by UN Security Council Resolutions. However, just because there is legal authority from a UNSCR does not mean the operation will achieve success. Somalia is the best example of this. To pass an SCR requires nine of 15 votes on the Security Council with no negative votes (vetoes) from the five permanent members. This always requires a negotiation. Once the SCR passes, then the undersecretary-general for peacekeeping looks for countries willing to contribute forces. Once force contributors are identified, then what they agree to do must be negotiated as well as what they expect from the UN in return. The results of these negotiations are recorded in a document called a Terms of Reference (TOR) that, while based on the SCR, are much more detailed. In the Somalia case, the TORs were negotiated with the force contributors to implement UNSCR 814. But then, only a little over a month into the operation, the Security Council passed SCR 837, which changed the nature of the mission on the ground. Several force contributors, most notably Italy, stated clearly that this change of mission was not in accordance with their TOR. Clearly, international authorities are not the same as domestic ones.

WE CAN ONLY DO WHAT OUR ORGANIZATIONS ARE CAPABLE OF—OFTEN THAT IS QUITE A LOT

Every single case illustrates the roles played by the various organizations involved—and not just those of the U.S. government. Considering organizations begins with federal departments and agencies. Not surprisingly, the greatest number of capabilities is found in the Department of Defense, which has more resources than any other agency or department and has capabilities that overlap with those of many other agencies. For example, the DOD was able to develop and execute plans for the relief and reconstruction of

Panama without the assistance of the State Department or USAID. Although both agencies were brought in, they followed where DOD—SOUTHCOM in particular—had led. This was true to a greater or lesser extent in all the cases.

Sometimes, however, the very mass of capabilities of the DOD makes the department slow to move. It is like a huge aircraft carrier with tremendous capacity but slow to turn. Its lack of agility, in general, is its major weakness. This was most evident in the response to 9/11 when we needed to move quickly into Afghanistan. The CIA had the agility to move almost immediately, but even the DOD's most agile forces, 5 SFG (Airborne), took more than a month to be inserted.

A second example comes from Operation Desert Shield. The DOD showed a capability to move quickly with air force assets and the Ready Brigade of the 82nd Airborne Division. Navy and marine assets were slower because they were located at sea. The real problem, however, was what if we had needed an offensive capability early on. The only solution was Col. John Warden's CHECKMATE shop in the basement of the Pentagon. Although it was innovative, it never was a full-fledged offensive air campaign and therefore was not implemented in that form.

The Balkans show how a State Department–led team could orchestrate an effective end to a nasty conflict. The first thing to note about the team was that it was interagency and made up of State, Defense, and NSC players. Second, it had departmental support and support from the NSC Staff. Third, the DOD supplied most of the resources along with some key players. Fourth, NATO, an international actor, played a key role and provided critical resources.

Where the Balkans were highly successful in bringing organizational resources together, the planning for Haiti shows the weakness of the interagency system. The Haiti planning was extraordinarily innovative in attempting to produce an interagency plan. This was driven by the planners at USACOM and supported by the NSC, particularly the IWG. Unfortunately, the IWG was not staffed by the departments, other than State and Defense, with the same players each time it met. This became clear at a meeting where the Department of Justice representative said that the DOJ simply did not have the capability to carry out its previously agreed part in the planning. This was because the DOJ representative had never heard of the commitment made by his predecessor on the IWG. As a result, ACOM (DOD) planners produced the plan, demonstrating again the redundant capabilities within the department.

The invasion of Iraq demonstrates what can happen when the resources of several departments are not integrated. The fact that President George W. Bush made the DOD the lead agency for the post-fighting period raised no alarms in any of the other departments. This was particularly true of State, which, under the leadership of Secretary Colin Powell, had produced a detailed study called "The Future of Iraq." Powell made the director of the study and all of its members available to serve in Jay Garner's ORHA, which was to plan for and carry out the post-conflict reconstruction. Because Garner was prohibited from using key study members, especially the leader, the capabilities that State brought to the operation were seriously diluted.

The interagency problems of ORHA were compounded when (1) CENTCOM's Land Component Command failed to recognize it as a key DOD subordinate element and (2) when it was disbanded and replaced by the CPA, an even more hybrid and ad hoc organization. The CPA was a DOD entity, directly subordinate to the SECDEF (operating through the USDP), staffed at the top mainly by former senior people from State but at the junior level by entry-level personnel recruited by the Heritage Foundation. In other words, the major capabilities of both DOD and State for occupation and reconstruction were ignored and replaced by a much weaker ad hoc hybrid.

PROCEDURES AND PROCESSES

It was essentially the Scowcroft reform that established the NSC in its modern form with the PC and DC, and with a set of subordinate committees whose names change with each succeeding administration. How this actually works and how well depends, however, on how the current president wants to use the system. Scowcroft was particularly successful in getting State, DOD, and the Intelligence Community on the same sheet of music. However, other departments and agencies were not as effectively integrated.

Even before the reforms, as shown by Panama, the Department of Justice was operating outside the NSC structure. In February 1988, during the Reagan administration, General Manuel Noriega of Panama was indicted by two grand juries, one in Miami and one in Tampa, that nobody else in the federal government knew had been called. Although this particular failing has since been remedied, during the second Clinton presidency and the first part of George W. Bush's term, the FBI (part of both DOJ and the Intelligence Community) did not share information even within the bureau about the men who would become the 9/11 hijackers. In the Haiti case, as well, we saw how the DOJ was not well integrated into the NSC system. Although it was a member of the Haiti IWG (lowest tier of the Clinton NSC system), Justice could not achieve continuity of membership on the IWG, leading the DOD (USACOM) to pick up its task.

To generalize, the lowest tier of the NSC system tends to suffer from less stability of members and changes in how it is organized. Scowcroft envisioned it as a series of permanent committees; Clinton structured it ad hoc. Both Bushes and Clinton had regional committees chaired by State's regional assistant secretaries and functional committees by NSC Staff. The Obama team, however, made all third-tier committees chaired by NSC staff, thereby centralizing policy in the White House even more than it had been before.

Large bureaucracies tend to be slow to respond. As noted, it is hard to turn a large ship, However, one method for achieving responsiveness in a large organization is to have effective planning systems and exercise them often. The DOD does this with its defense planning systems, most effectively with the JOPES. To a significant extent this applied to its predecessor, JOPS. The several cases all show that JOPES planning achieved a great deal of responsiveness. But they also show that where planning and execution procedures were ignored, responsiveness went out the window.

In Panama, the moment GEN Woerner heard that Noriega had been indicted, he directed his Plans Division to begin planning for a situation in which the Panama Defense Forces (PDF) would be the enemy. Although the situation was new, the planners did have plans on the shelf that could be modified to fit the changed circumstances. This is exactly what was done and, when JCS directed, it was done under Crisis Action Planning. When the crisis became a chronic ailment, the planning effort was less effective since the orders created did not fall under the standard operating procedures for revision of plans. Moreover, because JOPS did not specify execution, that phase developed somewhat ad hoc. This included Operation Ma Bell, which resulted in the surrender of most PDF units without fighting. It will be addressed in more detail in the section on individuals.

The classic example of JOPES working exactly as intended is Operation Desert Shield. Because CENTCOM had OPLAN 1002–90 fully updated and because it had been evaluated in Exercise Internal Look earlier that summer (1990), the command was prepared to execute it as an Operations Order. It was almost as simple as changing the title from OPLAN to OPORD and adding a date. However, because the planning at that time was carried out under the previous JOPS system, there were no details on how combat operations would be conducted.

To address the issue of combat operations, GEN Schwarzkopf requested the assistance of a group of planners from the army's School of Advanced Military Studies at Fort Leavenworth. This second year of Command and General Staff College for 55 select officers had been developed during the 1980s. The Gulf War was the first time the program was tested and clearly proved its worth. Operation Desert Storm was as well conducted as it is possible to do in what Clausewitz called "the fog of war."

Somalia provides several different lessons. First, Operation Restore Hope, conducted by the U.S.-led UNITAF under UN mandate, shows how having planning and organizing procedures facilitates mission success. The Bush administration crafted UNSCR 794 very carefully to make certain that the mission was doable. The DOD was tasked to execute and delegated it to

CENTCOM. The commander, Marine GEN Joseph Hoar, established a Joint Task Force under one of the two types of combat headquarters with the capacity to command and control the operation. In this case, he used I MEF, a Marine three-star headquarters with a marine division and air wing, augmented by an army division, navy and air force elements and incorporating allied forces.

The new Clinton administration did not quite comprehend the reasoning behind the Bush team's insistence on the narrow focus of UNSCR 794. As a result, they backed the more expansive position built into UNSCR 814. Nevertheless, the United States insisted on a command and control structure for UNOSOM II that was American in all but name, a decision reached in the NSC system. Unfortunately, that decision failed to proliferate through all the DOD procedures, especially those that drove UNITAF. The UNITAF command team wanted to hand over the operation to UNOSOM II as soon as possible and became fixated on the planning date of May 4, 1993, for the handoff, regardless of conditions on the ground. Clearly, CENTCOM, the higher headquarters, supported the UNITAF position. Then, as the UNOSOM II force was taking over, GEN Hoar chose to establish a non-doctrinal command structure for American forces in country. Instead of the normal procedure that the commander, U.S. Forces-Somalia (dual-hatted as deputy UN Force commander) would have operational control (OPCON) of *all* American forces, he withheld OPCON of the Quick Reaction Force, granting the lesser Tactical Control only for training and bona fide emergencies. This would strongly contribute to the fiasco that became known as "Black Hawk Down" after the introduction of Task Force Ranger, also not under the OPCON of the commander of U.S. Forces-Somalia. The procedural failures were major contributors to the final failure of the mission.

From Somalia and Haiti, the Clinton administration learned valuable lessons that it applied to the next crisis in the Balkans. In that case, particularly the ending of the war in Bosnia, the NSC, the State Department, and the DOD worked well to forge a negotiated settlement backed by real military capability. NSC principals played their proper role of setting policy and then protecting the interagency team, led by Richard Holbrooke, in executing it in a way that responded to the conditions in the field. Neither the NSC, nor State, nor Defense seriously attempted to micromanage the negotiating team.

The George W. Bush administration took office with a great deal of national security experience. NSA Condoleezza Rice wanted to restore the third tier of the NSC system to the more structured format of the Bush 41 system. She and the president hoped to have policy issues rise from the field to the PCCs, to the DC, PC, and finally to the NSC and president. Policy output would go to the executing departments, and the PCCs would oversee and coordinate. This was the process being implemented with the counterterrorism NSPD that was ready for PC discussion on September 10, 2001. The attacks the next day voided the carefully constructed system. Much policy during this presidency would emanate from the NSC/PC (often meeting as one with select members and called the War Cabinet).

Both the invasions of Afghanistan and of Iraq were largely driven from the NSC/PC and executed by the CIA and the DOD (CENTCOM and SOCOM) in the case of the former and the DOD in the case of the latter. For Afghanistan, CENTCOM had to use the Crisis Action Planning of JOPES from scratch in the complete absence of a war plan. For Iraq, an OPLAN existed, 1003, but it was out of date. SECDEF Rumsfeld directly supervised its revision, to the point of micromanagement. That decision, along with his decision to assign post-fighting reconstruction to the USDP, removing it from CENTCOM, had major consequences. The subsequent decision to replace ORHA with the CPA vitiated ORHA's planning and resulted in an ad hoc occupation and a major resistance insurgency.

The subsequent "Surge" was the result of lessons actually learned on the ground and a serious rethinking of doctrine. The planning took account of both factors and adequately resourced the operation. Getting to that point, however, took the Bush administration far outside of the DOD, in fact, outside the Executive Branch. Congress created the Iraq Study Group, most of whose 70-odd recommendations were either ignored or only seen as being of secondary importance. However, it provided a catalyst for addressing the issues within the Executive. The CJCS convened a Council of Colonels (a common approach to intractable problems) to help the chiefs focus their advice to the Chairman, SECDEF, and the president.

The "Surge" also brought to light a procedural issue that stems from the Goldwater-Nichols Act. Under that legislation, the chain of command runs from the president to the SECDEF to the combatant command commander and thence to the subordinate commander. Conceptually, under the law, the subordinate commander commands a Joint Task Force, a service component, or a sub-unified command. In each case, that is envisaged as a three-star billet. In Iraq, however, the subordinate command, MNF-I, was made a four-star command when GEN George Casey came on board. Between Casey and his nominal superior at CENTCOM, GEN John Abizaid, there were no real issues. Casey deferred to Abizaid for his knowledge of the region and Abizaid deferred to Casey for what was going on in Iraq. Moreover, they both viewed CENTCOM's role as supporting MNF-I. The combatant command in support of the actual war fighting command is exactly what the situation requires when the war fighting command is under someone equal in rank to the GCC. That is the reason that MNF-I was established in the first place, replacing CJTF 7.

When GEN David Petraeus replaced Casey and ADM William "Fox" Fallon replaced Abizaid, the situation changed. Fallon assumed that, as the GCC, he was in command and that Petraeus worked for him. In contrast, Petraeus clearly believed that Fallon should be in support of him, as if he were a supported GCC. The issue was resolved when Fallon was forced to retire, ostensibly for unrelated reasons, and his deputy, LTG Martin Dempsey, became the acting commander at CENTCOM, a position he held until Petraeus was named as the new GCC. Nevertheless, the underlying issue was not resolved. Although it has not risen again, that appears to be due to good interpersonal relations between the commanders in the field and the relevant GCC.

A similar conflict existed in Afghanistan between GEN Dan McNeil and SACEUR GEN Bantz Craddock, but McNeil was replaced and soon after so was Craddock. No real issues of direct command relationships surfaced again in Afghanistan between SACEUR and the ISAF commander or between CENTCOM and the U.S. forces commander—the same general wearing two distinct hats. But that was due to the close coordination among the three generals, who all saw the commander in Afghanistan as the one being supported. In any case, the issue needs to be addressed, probably by regulation.

A related issue is the relationship between the American ambassador and the commander of U.S. forces in a country where full diplomatic relations exist along with a major ongoing military operation. The ambassador's appointment letter makes it clear that the ambassador is in charge of all U.S. government activity in a country, including military activity and personnel, *except* when a major military operation is under way. In that circumstance, there is real ambiguity as to who is in charge. How that is resolved depends on the arrangements made between the individuals involved. Although any president could designate the official in charge in such a circumstance, no president has ever done so.

THE ENEMY ALWAYS HAS A VOTE

In every case discussed in this book, the United States and its allies were not alone. There were always other parties, sometimes enemies and sometimes just not friends, who have their own agendas. These agendas sometimes coincide with that of the United States and are sometimes in conflict. In Panama, the vast majority of Panamanians supported the invasion. Indeed, Noriega's opposition regularly called for American action. When the invasion came, however, significant elements of the PDF fought and some fought bravely. Still, as an institution, it generally lost its loyalty to Noriega and surrendered quickly when contacted by an officer who had fought bravely. In terms of the trigger for the invasion, Noriega had done his best to push to the brink of conflict but never quite cross the line. In the end, he lost control of his troops who killed an American officer and sexually molested the wife of another. Rather than step back from the brink, Noriega doubled down and gave President Bush the justifications he needed to order the invasion.

In both the Gulf War and the subsequent Iraq War, Saddam Hussein, like Noriega, tempted fate and would not step away. Also like Noriega, he had alienated most of his people and a good percentage of his army. Unlike Noriega, he had retained the loyalty of the large elite forces and Iraq, unlike Panama, was a country divided on sectarian and ethnic lines. Saddam loyalists were able to exploit these and take advantage of the chaotically planned occupation to launch a guerrilla resistance followed by a sectarian insurgency.

It was the rise of the sectarian Sunni resistance to both the Shiite government and the allied occupation that was largely taken over by the Jihadist al Qaeda in Iraq (AQI) that changed the nature of the war. What Generals Abizaid and Casey and Ambassador Khalilzad had been facing was a guerrilla resistance/insurgency. They chose to fight it according to a standard COIN approach that tried to minimize external involvement. AQI changed the nature of the conflict that the American leadership on the ground failed to understand. With the change of leadership and the change of strategy focused on protecting the people from the sectarian fighting and the incorporation of the fighters of the Anbar/Sunni Awakening (themselves former resistance fighters) against AQI, the government and its American and Western allies began to gain the upper hand.

The failure to understand the religious component of enemies in Somalia, Iraq, and Afghanistan hampered the effort in the several conflicts. Although neither Somalia nor Iraq began with a significant religious component to the conflict—the Somali warlords-led secular clan-based militias and the resistance in Iraq was originally Saddamist and Baathist—Islam became an important organizing principle and rallying cry. In Afghanistan, the Taliban, like their al Qaeda allies, were radical Islamists from the beginning. In spite of this, the Westerners acted as if the people they were supporting were secularists and even that the insurgents could eventually separate politics from religion. The point is that religion can be, and often is, a strong motivation for fighters. An unwillingness to recognize this results in conducting a war without comprehending the enemy and why he is fighting. As the Chinese military sage Sun Tzu said 2,000 years ago, "If you know the enemy, and know yourself, you need not fear the result of a hundred battles." He also said that the reverse was true; these conflicts proved him right again.

POLITICS—BUREAUCRATIC AND PARTISAN—IS A CRITICAL DRIVER[3]

Many of the events of the several cases are either explained or informed, in whole or part, by politics, both bureaucratic and partisan. The replacement of GEN Woerner in the summer of 1989 was a political decision by the Bush administration to break with the perception that Woerner, and, by extension, the Reagan administration were not tough enough on Noriega. The decision to take on the Somalia crisis was an effort to redeem President Bush and his team from their humiliating electoral defeat. President Clinton's decision to withdraw from Somalia was partly due to his fear of electoral consequences of more losses of American servicemen for a mission that few understood. The "intervasion" of Haiti was partly a response to the Democratic governor of Florida and his problems with the large number of Haitian refugees arriving on the beaches of his state. It was also a response to the concerns of the Congressional Black Caucus and other activists.

The Iraq War during the George W. Bush administration illustrates any number of political issues. Well before the decision to invade Iraq, during the NSC debate over Afghanistan, the DOD advanced the idea of taking down Saddam, The idea was resisted by the State Department and the NSA. Later, the decision to get congressional authorization for the use of military force was requested both to bring the Democrats on board before the midterm election and as a lever to pressure the UN Security Council.

The Obama administration shows significant conflict between the departments and agencies on one side and the NSC and White House political staff on the other. This was clearly manifest during the debate over the Afghan Surge. An ongoing political struggle was over the power of the NSC Staff to demand information from the DOD, from both deployed troops and various headquarters. Secretaries Gates, Panetta, and Hegel complained bitterly about micromanagement from the White House.

In short, the importance of political issues cannot be denied. Politics must be taken into account whenever one is addressing the making of national security policy.

INDIVIDUALS MATTER MOST

In the nineteenth century, the British historian Thomas Carlyle put forth the Great Man Theory of history. The British philosopher and sociologist Herbert Spencer debunked the theory, arguing that events are determined by underlying structures and forces. Clearly, this argument has never been wholly settled. This book began looking at the impersonal, the ideas, legislation, structures, and procedures that underlay the making of national security policy. As important as these things are, the cases show that it is individual actors that make the real difference.

It was Brent Scowcroft who established the NSC in its modern form, a form that has lasted almost a quarter of a century. It was George H. W. Bush who said, "This will not stand—this aggression against Kuwait," committing the United States to drive the Iraqi army out of Kuwait. President Bush also built the coalition of forces that achieved his desired outcome. It was Gen Joseph Hoar who decided to ignore American military doctrine for command relationships in Somalia, a decision that contributed to the debacle in Mogadishu. And it was President Bill Clinton who blinked first when confronted by the mutual bloodletting in that war-torn city.

At a lower level, it was MG Marc Cisneros, commanding U.S. Army-South in Panama, who launched Operation Ma Bell on his own authority. The operation ended the fighting during the invasion and secured the surrender of all PDF garrisons outside Panama City and Colon without firing a shot. In the Balkans, special envoy Richard Holbrooke coordinated the support from State, Defense, and the NSC in Washington with the on-the-ground diplomacy in the region and then at the Dayton conference. It was his determination and initiatives, his persistence, that brought the conflict to a successful close.

Almost entirely outside the government, former president Jimmy Carter was able to negotiate a permissive entry into Haiti by American forces and the process by which the legitimately elected president was restored to office. Although the initiative originally came from the Haitian junta leader, Carter made it happen, ably supported by retired GEN Colin Powell, Senator Sam Nunn, and Bob Pastor who had served as Senior NSC Director for Latin America during Carter's presidency. The other critical initiative external to the government was the work of Dr. Fred Kagan of AEI and retired GEN Jack Keane, who provided the Bush 43 administration with the outline of what became the "Surge."

In many ways the "Surge" is a story of individuals. There was Senator Chuck Robb of the Iraq Study Group who refused to sign the report if it did not include a recommendation for a troop surge to stabilize Baghdad. There was COL H. R. McMaster who led the Council of Colonels and had proven the worth of good COIN doctrine at Tal Afar, where he had commanded U.S. forces. David Petraeus at Leavenworth had put together a new COIN doctrine manual, which he would be called on to implement in Iraq, and, in Iraq, he was joined by his civilian counterpart, Ambassador Ryan Crocker, who understood fully the need that there never be daylight between them.

Most of all, the character and determination of President George W. Bush comes through. He showed, even if too slowly, that he could recognize that he had made a mistake and make decisions needed to rectify it. Bush was not willing to lose Iraq; he was not willing to let what he saw as the liberation of the Iraqi people be lost to sectarian warfare. So, he chose a hard course, changed the leaders, gave them the authority to do what they believed needed to be done, and backed them up. Without George W. Bush, Iraq would have been a lost cause in 2006. Instead when Bush turned the presidency over to Barack Obama on January 20, 2009, he gave him a relatively stable Iraq.

The Afghan surge came early in the Obama presidency. It reveals a great deal about his style of decision making and how his learning curve developed. Where Bush made decisions quickly and stuck with them—sometimes until almost too late—Obama deliberated. At times he appeared to second-guess himself. At other times, he dug in and kept doing the same thing. In the Afghan surge deliberations he was new to the job. As a result, he gave a lot of weight to key principals. In particular, he valued his SECDEF, Bob Gates, very highly. Gates worked closely with SECSTATE Hillary Clinton, CJCS Mike Mullen, and CIA director Leon Panetta. Of course, they were supporting the position of the commander in the field, GEN Stan McChrystal and CENTCOM GCC GEN David Petraeus. Obama found it hard to resist the argument of these professionals. Still, he looked for a solution that gave something to both sides of the argument and Gates gave him such a solution. Then, as Gates pointed out, Obama appeared to have no confidence in the strategy he approved and as soon as (1) bin Laden had been killed and (2) Gates had left, Obama began to look for ways to accelerate America's extrication from Afghanistan.

In short, individual human beings make all the difference.

CONCLUDING THOUGHTS

Social scientists often speak of multivariate analysis. This is a view that any specific outcome has multiple causes. We most often describe these causes as independent variables. They explain the dependent variable, the outcome to be explained. This book posits that among the independent variables are basic IR theory—the way that practitioners see the world, the constitutional and legislative authorities under which they operate, the organizational capabilities they have to employ, the processes and procedures they must use, and the individual characteristics that leaders have as human beings.

Although the book began with the understanding that each one of these independent variables was important to the outcomes of the cases examined, it made no effort to determine which among them were more important than the others. Yet, as each case developed, each one seems to have turned on who the key leaders were and how they addressed the problems they faced. In the end, the cases seem to show that while all of these variables are important, the personalities of the individual decision makers are the most critical. It clearly makes a difference whether George W. Bush was president or Barack Obama. It made a difference that MG Marc Cisneros was in the right place at the right time. It made a difference that Richard Holbrooke had the confidence of both Secretary of State Warren Christopher and President Bill Clinton. It also made a difference that Saddam Hussein was the dictator of Iraq rather than a more sophisticated and more rational actor.

In many ways, the historians of the nineteenth century were right. One cannot understand the substance of national security policy and how that policy is made without focusing on the individuals who occupy the positions where critical decisions are made. In the end, people make policy. Some are brilliant. Some are pedestrian. Some are not entirely rational either with respect to their goals or how they seek to achieve those goals. All are flawed human beings. Most of the time, those flaws have been overcome. They tend to be overcome because of a combination of worldview, legal and procedural constraints and enablers, organizational capabilities, and, most important, the capabilities of individuals in key positions to influence the decisions made.

NOTES

1. See Graham T. Allison and Philip Zelikow, *Essence of Decision.* New York: 1999, Longman.

2. See Bruce Russett, *Grasping the Democratic Peace.* Princeton, NJ: 1993, Princeton University Press.

3. For the purpose of this discussion, politics is defined very narrowly. It is the quest for power by an individual within the bureaucracy or the body politic or by a group within the body politic of a state.

Bibliography

Abrams, Elliot. Interview. June 15, 2015.

Allison, Graham T. "Conceptual Models and the Cuban Missile Crisis," *American Political Science Review*, Volume 63, Issue 3 (September 1969), 689–718.

Armed Forces Staff College. *Joint Staff Officers Guide.* 1997.

Avant, Deborah. *The Market for Force: The Consequences of Privatising Security.* New York and London: 2005, Cambridge University Press.

Baker, James A., III. *The Politics of Diplomacy.* New York: 1995, G.P. Putnam's Sons.

Ballard, John R. *Upholding Democracy.* Westport, CT: 1998, Praeger.

Ballasy, Nicholas. "Brzezinski. Scowcroft: Obama Should Shrink 300-Plus National Security Staff." November 2014.

Bennett, William C. "Just Cause and the Principles of War." *Military Review.* March 1991.

Best, Richard A. *The National Security Council: An Organizational Assessment.* Washington, DC: 2010, Congressional Research Service.

Blehm, Eric. *The Only Thing Worth Dying For.* New York: 2010, HarperCollins.

Brake, Jeffrey D. "Quadrennial Defense Review (QDR) Background, Process, and Issues." Library of Congress Congressional Research Service. June 21, 2001.

Bremer, L. Paul., III. *My Year in Iraq.* New York: 2006, Simon & Schuster.

Bush, George and Brent Scowcroft. *A World Transformed.* New York: 2011, Vintage Books (Kindle Edition).

Bush, George W. *Decision Points.* New York: 2010, Crown.

Bush, George W. "Suspension of Allied Offensive Combat Operations." Television address. February 27, 1991. In *Military Review.* September 1991.

Cisneros, Marc. Interview. April 15, 1991.

Clarke, Richard A. *Against All Enemies.* New York: 2004, The Free Press.

Clinton, Hillary Rodham. *Hard Choices.* New York: 2014, Simon & Schuster (Kindle Edition).

Couch, Dick. *Always Faithful, Always Forward.* New York: 2014, Berkley.

Daalder, Ivo H. and I. M. Destler. "The Clinton Administration National Security Council." In *The National Security Council Project: Oral History Roundtables.* Washington, DC: December 8, 1998, Brookings.

Daalder, Ivo H. and I. M. Destler. "The Nixon Administration National Security Council." In *The National Security Council Project: Oral History Roundtables.* Washington, DC: December 8, 1998, Brookings.

David, Bill. Interview. Panama. 1995.

Daze, Thomas. Interview. 1997.

"Description of the Joint Strategic Planning System (JSPS)." U.S. Army War College, PowerPoint presentation. Dde.carlisle,army.mil/LLL/DSC/L13_JSPS.pdf. July 2009.

DOD. *Glossary of Defense Acquisition Acronyms and Terms.* December 2012.

Drew, S. Nelson (ed.). *NSC-68: Forging the Strategy of Containment* (analyses by Paul H. Nitze). Washington, DC: 1994, National Defense University Press.

Dziedzic, J. and Eliot M. Goldberg (eds.). *Policing the New World Disorder.* Washington, DC: 1998, National Defense University Press.

"50 USC Sections 1541–1548."

Fishel, John T. *Civil Military Operations in the New World.* Westport, CT: 1997, Praeger.

Fishel, John T. *The Fog of Peace.* Carlisle, PA: 1992, Strategic Studies Institute.

Fishel, John T. "The Interagency Arena at the Operational Level: The Cases Now Known as Stability Operations," Chapter 10 in *Affairs of State: The Interagency and National Security.* Edited by Gabriel A. Marcella. Carlisle, PA, Strategic Studies Institute, 2014. 409–446.

Fishel, John T. "The Interagency in Panama 1986–1990." In *U.S. Army and the Interagency Process.* Edited by K. D. Goff. Fort Leavenworth, KS: 2008, Combat Studies Institute Press.

Fishel, John T. *Liberation, Occupation, and Rescue: War Termination and Desert Storm.* Carlisle Barracks, PA: 1992, Strategic Studies Institute.

Fishel, John T. and Max G. Manwaring. *Uncomfortable Wars Revisited.* Norman: 2006, University of Oklahoma Press.

Foreign Intelligence Surveillance Act (FISA).

Foreign Policy. "The Ivory Tower," www.foreignpolicy.com/articles/2012/01/03/the_ivory_tower.

Franks, Tommy. *American Soldier.* New York: 2004, HarperCollins.

Galvin, John R. *Fighting the Cold War: A Soldier's Memoir.* Lexington: 2015, University of Kentucky Press.

Gates, Robert M. *Duty.* New York: 2014, Alfred A. Knopf (Kindle Edition).

Gilpin, Robert M. *War and Change in International Politics.* New York: 1981, Cambridge University Press.

GlobalSecurity.org. www.globalsecurity.org/military/agency/end-strength.htm. July 2010. Accessed July 22, 2013.

Goldberg, Jeffrey. Interview in *The Atlantic.* November 12, 2014.

Hartman, Frederick H. *The Relations of Nations* (Sixth Edition). New York: 1983, Macmillan.

Hartz, Louis. *The Liberal Tradition in America.* New York: 1991, Harvest/HBJ.

Hayden, Michael. "The State of the Craft: Is Intelligence Reform Working?" *World Affairs Journal.* September/October 2010. http.//www.worldaffairsjournal.org/article/state-craft-intelligence-reform-working.

Holbrooke, Richard. *To End a War.* New York: 1998, The Modern Library (Kindle Edition).

Homeland Security Act, 2002.

https://www.aclu.org/national-security/aclu-report-documents-fbi-abuse-911 (accessed September 17, 2013).

Jones, Joseph M. *The Fifteen Weeks.* New York: 1955, Harcourt Brace Jovanovich.

Kegley, Jr., Charles W. and Shannon L. Blanton. *World Politics: Trend and Transformation* (12th Edition). Boston: 2010, Wadsworth.

Kretchik, Walter E. "Haiti's Quest for Democracy." In *Capacity Building for Peacekeeping: The Case of Haiti.* Edited by John T. Fishel and Andres Sainz. Dulles, VA: 2006, Potomac Books.

Kretchik, Walter E., Robert F. Baumann, and John T. Fishel. *Invasion, Intervention, "Intervasion": A Concise History of the U.S. Army in Operation Uphold Democracy.* Fort Leavenworth, KS: 1998, U.S. Army Command and General Staff College Press.

Locher, James R., III. *Victory on the Potomac.* College Station: 2002, Texas A&M Press.

Lyons, Terrence and Ahmed Samatar. *Somalia: State Collapse, Multilateral Intervention, and Strategies for Political Reconstruction.* Washington, DC: 1995, Brookings Institute.

MacInnis, John A. "Piecemeal Peacekeeping: The United Nations Protection Force in Former Yugoslavia." In *"The Savage Wars of Peace:" Toward a New Paradigm of Peace Operations.* Edited by John T. Fishel. Boulder, CO: 1998, Westview Press.

Maddox, Eric. *Mission: Black List #1.* New York: 2008, HarperCollins.

Mann, James. *Rise of the Vulcans.* New York: 2004, Penguin.

Mansfield, Jr., Harvey C. *Taming the Prince: The Ambivalence of Modern Executive Power.* Baltimore: 1993, Johns Hopkins University Press.

Mashal, Mujib. "McChrystal-Karzai Relationship Steals the News in Afghanistan." *New York Times*, June 28, 2010. Atwar.blogs.nytimes/2016.06/28.

McDaniel, Mike. "Joint Individual Training Challenges: Training for Integrated Operations." Joint Deployment Training Center, Briefing for the Worldwide Joint Training & Scheduling Conference. March 29, 2010. #6.

Mead, Walter Russell. *Special Providence: American Foreign Policy and How It Changed the World.* New York: 2001, Knopf.

Morgenthau, Hans J. *Politics among Nations: The Struggle for Power and Peace* (Sixth Edition). Revised by Kenneth W. Thompson. New York: 1985, McGraw-Hill.

Mr. X (George Kennan). "The Sources of Soviet Conduct." *Foreign Affairs*, July 1947.

National Security Act, 1947.

The 9/11 Commission Report. Washington, DC.

Nye, Joseph S. *Soft Power.* Cambridge, MA: 2004, Public Affairs.

Oakley, Robert B. "An Envoy's Perspective." *Joint Force Quarterly*, Autumn 1993.

Panetta, Leon. *Worthy Fights.* New York: 2014, Penguin Press.

Polt, Michael. Interview. April 3, 1991.

Pollack, Kenneth. *The Threatening Storm.* New York: 2002, Random House.

Rice, Condoleezza. *No Higher Honor: A Memoir of My Years in Washington.* New York: 2011, Crown.

Ricks, Thomas E. *Fiasco.* New York: 2006, Penguin.

Ricks, Thomas E. *The Gamble.* London/New York: 2009, Penguin.

Robinson, Linda. *Tell Me How This Ends.* New York: 2008, Public Affairs.

Rodrigues, Robert S. Interview (telephone), May 8, 1991.

Rothkopf, David. *Running the World.* New York: 2005, Public Affairs (Kindle Edition).

Russett, Bruce. *Grasping the Democratic Peace.* Princeton, NJ: 1993, Princeton University Press.

Schroen, Gary C. *First In.* New York: 2005, Presidio Press.

Schultz, George P. *Turmoil and Triumph: My Years as Secretary of State.* New York: 1993, Charles Scribner's Sons.

Shenon, Philip. "Ex-Official Says Bush Urged End to Iran Arms Shipments." *New York Times*, January 23, 1989.

Stanton, Doug. *The Horse Soldiers.* New York: 2009, Scribner.

Stewart, Richard W. "The United States Army in Somalia: 1992–1994." In *United States Forces in Somalia: After Action Report.* Washington, DC: 2003, Center for Military History.

Tenet, George. *At the Center of the Storm.* New York: 2007, HarperCollins.

Thomas, Lynn and Steve Spataro. "Peacekeeping and Policing in Somalia." In *Policing the New World Disorder.* Edited by Robert B. Oakley, Michael J. Dziedzic, and Eliot M. Goldberg. Honolulu, HA: 1998, University Press of the Pacific.

Thornton, Robert, John T. Fishel, and Marc Tyrrell. *SFA-Mosul: Case Study.* Fort Leavenworth, KS: 2008, Joint Center for International Security Force Assistance (JCIFSFA).

Touval, Saadia. "Lessons of Preventive Diplomacy in Yugoslavia." In *Managing Global Chaos.* Edited by Chester A. Crocker, Fen Ostler Hampson, and Pamela Aall. Washington, DC: 1996, U.S. Institute of Peace.

Tuchman, Barbara. *The Guns of August.* New York: 1963, Dell.

United States Senate. "Summary of Intelligence Reform and Terror Prevention Act." Washington, DC: December 6, 2004. http:///www.fas.org/irp/congress/2004_rpt/s2845-summ.pdf.

USA PATRIOT Act.

Waltz, Kenneth N. *Man, the State, and War.* New York: 1981, Columbia University Press.

"War Powers." Library of Congress, Law Library. www.loc.gov.org/wiki/Library_of_Congress

"White House Seeks a Stronger Hand at Pentagon to Manage Crises." *Washington Post*, November 25, 2014.

"White House Tries for a Leaner NSC Staff." *Washington Post.* June 20, 2015

Whittacker, Alan G. et al. *The National Security Policy Process: The National Security Council and Interagency System.* (Research Report, August 15, 2011, Annual Update). Washington, DC: Industrial College of the Armed Forces, National Defense University, U.S. Department of Defense.

Woerner, Fred F. Interview. Boston, MA, May 6, 1991.

Woodward, Bob. *Bush at War.* New York: 2002, Simon & Schuster.

Woodward, Bob. *The Commanders.* New York: 1991, Simon & Schuster.

Woodward, Bob. *Obama's Wars.* New York: 2010, Simon & Schuster.

Woodward, Bob. *Plan of Attack.* New York: 2004, Simon & Schuster.

Woodward, Bob. *State of Denial.* New York: 2006, Simon & Schuster.

www.fbi.gov/about-us/investigate/What (accessed September 17, 2013).

Yarger, Harry R. "How Do Students Learn Strategy? Thoughts on the U.S. Army War College Pedagogy of Strategy." In *Teaching Strategy: Challenge and Response.* Edited by Gabriel Marcella. Carlisle, PA: SSI, 179–202. 2010

Yates, Lawrence A. *The U.S. Military Intervention in Panama.* Washington, DC: 2008, Center for Military History.

Zegaart, Amy B. *Flawed by Design: The Evolution of the CIA, JCS, and NSC.* Stanford, CA: 1999, Stanford University Press.

Index

About the Author

John T. Fishel is on the faculty of the College of International Studies at the University of Oklahoma. He is Professor Emeritus of Strategic Studies at the National Defense University in Washington, DC. He has also taught at the School of International Service of American University, the Eliot School at George Washington University, and the U.S. Army Command and General Staff College. He was a military intelligence officer serving in the Pentagon as a strategic intelligence analyst, in several reserve intelligence units, and in U.S. Southern Command, where he ran the Civil Affairs section of the Directorate of Strategy, Policy, and Plans, the Policy and Strategy Branch, and was the principal planner for Operation Promote Liberty in Panama (post-conflict operations). During his time in Southern Command he also planned and conducted an assessment of the El Salvador armed forces in conjunction with the Salvadoran Joint Staff. He ended his military career as a research analyst at the Strategic Studies Institute of the U.S. Army War College and as the psychological operations officer and acting J-5 of Special Operations Command-South. He retired from the army as a lieutenant colonel. Dr. Fishel is the author or editor of several books on international relations and civil-military affairs. He lives in Blanchard, Oklahoma, with his wife, daughter, and assorted dogs, cats, and horses.